The Porcupine Wilderness Journals

Christopher J. Julian-Fralish
Stacey L. Julian-Fralish
James S. Fralish

Published by
The Stacis Group, Ltd.

The Porcupine Wilderness Journals

~First Edition~

Copyright © 2001 by The Stacis Group, Ltd.

Published by The Stacis Group, Ltd.
P.O. Box 37
Carbondale, IL 62903-0037

Porcupine Mountains Wilderness State Park
412 South Boundary Road
Ontonagon, MI 49953

Printed in the United States of America.
Allen Press, Inc.
810 East Tenth
Lawrence, KS 66044

Cover Art
Mirror Lake 4-Bunk Cabin
Watercolor by Hyosun Park

Back Cover
Porcupine Mountains Wilderness State Park Area Map
The Upper Peninsula Traveler
http://www.exploringthenorth.com/mich/mich.html

Acknowledgements

First and foremost, we would like to thank everyone who scribed their thoughts, ideas, creations, and visions into the many log books that we researched. Your contributions and the insight they provide are immeasurable.

We are indebted to Park Manager Dan Plescher, Park Interpretor Robert Sprague, and former Park Manager Ron Welton for access to the log books and their support during the making of this compilation.

We would also like to express our appreciation to Michael Rafferty and Robert Sprague whose book, The Porcupine Mountains Companion, formed a basis for the history described in the introduction.

Sharon Kindall, Steve Fair, and Guy Dresser of Allen Press were instrumental in helping us print this book and process it for publication.

William H. Meadows, the President of the National Wilderness Society, deserves our gratitude for generously writing the foreward to this book.

Our final thanks go to Chuck Smith, who helped us research the many volumes of text, and Hyosun Park, who provided us with the wonderful cover art of Mirror Lake 4-Bunk Cabin.

We dedicate this book to all
lovers of wilderness, whose passion
for the wild places was
the inspiration for this anthology.

Foreword

In a desperately poor area of Brooklyn, New York, a remarkable event unfolded recently. The Mayor of New York decided to sell off the neighborhood's few remaining open spaces; open spaces that people in the neighborhood had turned into community gardens. Instead of concrete, garbage, and decay there was an oasis of vegetables, trees, and flowers. Sadly, the Mayor saw no value in these natural elements and only recognized the price the property itself might fetch on the open market.

But the people understood the true value. They created such a tremendous uproar that the Mayor had no choice but to back down. Was the outcry about growing tomatoes, green beans, or snapdragons? No, it had more to do with the community land. Neighbors shared a nurturing place to gather, a place they proudly called their own, a place where children had the opportunity to stick their hands deep into the soil.

Around the same time, hundreds of people gathered in Seattle for a highly unusual event—a candlelight vigil to pray for the recovery of the salmon. Sponsored by the Partnership for Religion and the Environment, the vigil brought together a notable diversity of people representing a broad array of faiths and traditions including Native Americans, Christians, Jews, Buddhists, and Muslims. The common purpose was captured in the closing prayer: "We join together as many and diverse expressions of one loving mystery, for the healing of the Earth and the renewal of all life." Again, the people spoke of their connections to salmon and their sense of community with each other and the natural world.

For over fifty years in Michigan's Porcupine Mountains Wilderness State Park, thousands of individuals have recorded their personal wilderness experiences in journals placed in cabins scattered throughout the interior. Drawing from these cabin journals, the Fralish family has created a remarkable wilderness story. A story of a community that developed over fifty years, a community connected to the Porcupine Mountains.

In reading the journals, one understands this deep, profound connection to place that gives rise to the commitment and courage demonstrated time and again by conservation activists from Maine to Alaska, Florida to California, Texas to Michigan. Each of us is working to protect a special place, one that we grew up with as children or perhaps grew to love as adults. To each of us, in our own way, these are sacred places that grace our lives with beauty and wonder, offering us a way to experience solitude and connection simultaneously. These wild places help make our lives whole.

It is in the Porcupine Mountain Wilderness where many people have found such solitude, connections, and wholeness. The journals speak of mystery, memories, and awareness. We read of self-reliance, recovery, and romance. People record their stories in poetry and through art. We read tall tales about black flies, outhouses, and "grizzly" mice. We learn about lake monsters, escaped prisoners, and bears—many bears.

People reflect on the universe, speaking of sunsets, meteor showers, and the Northern Lights. There is rain, snow, storms, and floods. We read of skunks, beavers, porcupines, osprey, warblers, wrens, geese, woodpeckers, foxes, eagles, trout, and even a mermaid.

But throughout the journals there are admonishments to listen to the quiet, to recognize the Porcupine Mountains Wilderness State Park as a place where one comes to "heal my soul, nurture my spirit."

The Fralishes have given wilderness voices to thousands of people who love the Porcupine Mountains. It is not surprising that they found such remarkable stories. We want to write about places that are special to us. We want to capture the experience for ourselves, to make it unique to us individually. In this book we see how universal these experiences can be. Through these wilderness experiences we recognize our common histories and how we as a people remain connected to the land.

The Wilderness Society has a tradition of storytelling at our annual staff retreat. We ask the staff to bring an object—a rock, a leaf, a feather—something that reminds them of a place important in their lives. At the beginning of this sacred object session, we set aside thirty minutes for staff to speak. The thirty minutes stretched into two hours, then three, with over forty staff members speaking about their sacred objects and their own sacred places. Their stories were personal, spoken from their hearts. There were stories of childhood and children, of families, of mothers, of fathers.

Whether working a community garden, praying for salmon, writing in a cabin journal, or telling wilderness stories, people reveal their deepest personal beliefs. In doing so, we document the importance of places, people, and families. We begin to understand our connections to each other, a true community.

The Fralishes have provided us with extraordinary stories about a fascinating place. Whether we have been to the Porcupine Mountains or not, we see the powerful attraction that this special place has had for thousands and thousands of people over five decades. I hope it encourages others to write and speak about the wilderness areas they love.

William H. Meadows, President
The Wilderness Society

Contents

IntRoduction

The Porcupine Wilderness Journals constitutes the most unique wilderness book ever written. Arrogant words coming from those who fashioned it. However, the names of the authors do not appear on the front cover. But rather, those names entwine themselves within the entire text of this compilation. This book is a product of thousands of pages and thousands of entries, written by thousands of people who have chosen to spend a short part of their lives in the Porcupine Mountain Wilderness Area. It is a product of the past half century of entries from various journals located in each of the sixteen back country cabins located within the borders of the park. So in fact, this book was written by many authors, a little bit at a time, over the past fifty years. These authors are special, as they share a remarkable kinship even though they have never met, and probably never will.

The Porcupine Mountains, located on the shore of Lake Superior in the Upper Peninsula of Michigan, were dedicated a state park by the State Legislature in 1944, when a purchase of forty-six thousand acres was made. The foundation of this wilderness as a state park was partly due to the efforts of P.J. Hoffmaster and Raymond Dick, creators of the Save the Porcupine Mountains Association. The first cabin to be rented was Mirror Lake 8-Bunk in 1946. Some of the cabins have been purchased from private owners, such as Speaker's Cabin. Also, many face-lifts and changes have been made to the cabins over time. Some of these changes are due to normal wear and tear while others are due to the forces of nature such as fire, flood, and erosion. But the cabins have survived these natural elements, the threat of logging and other corporate entities, as well as a drive by political forces to phase the cabins out of the wilderness setting in the 1970's. Now encompassing approximately sixty thousand acres, this wilderness and the cabins within have survived all attempts, natural and man-made alike, to be reduced to only memories.

This is not a book about the cabins themselves, but a look into the psyche of the people who visited them. The inspiration for this book came from the memories provided by the logs. My parents visited the park and stayed in Buckshot Cabin during the late summer of 1995. While there, they perused the log book as many before them had, hoping to catch a glimpse of the insight provided by so many on the pages. What they discovered was profound. It was a story of three brothers, now grown, who had come to the Porkies (as they are affectionately called) to renew their bonds and unearth the relationships they had with each other as adults. It was a story of change, mutual respect, admiration, and closeness brought on by the wilderness setting and a tiny cabin in the woods.

My mother and father, deeply touched by this honest and emotional revelation, saw an opportunity to explore their love of wilderness through the eyes of others. They began reading more logs, and their appreciation for the everyday people who visited the park and told their tales grew. They perceived great potential for the personal and collective history contained within the cabin logs and wanted to share that with others. My wife and I became involved as researchers and editors for we, although our names are on the cover, are truly not the authors of this book. And though we have visited the park frequently, we are not as intimately knowledgeable of the Porkies as some are. However, reading the many logs and experiencing the emotions and descriptions inspired by the natural setting, we benefited from the knowledge and experiences that the authors shared with each other. We wished to share that knowledge and those experiences with the world. From our experience in the Porkies, from our experience in wilderness, and from our research of the log entries, we found a passion for the park through the eyes, emotions, and voices of the authors. We couldn't help but be touched by what we read.

Being inspired by the writings and artwork was the easy part. Choosing the entries to fill this anthology was much more difficult. Out of approximately one hundred and forty log books and about forty thousand pages of text, there was only room for so many entries. Making the choices was difficult and the research time consuming. In this book, it was imperative to let as many voices as possible be heard, and to let our opinions as editors be inconspicuous. To be historically accurate, all the logs would have to be published as complete volumes. However, it is our belief that we have accurately represented a majority of the authors' viewpoints within the text. Most of the entries were positive, descriptive, inspirational, thought-provoking, creative, funny, and emotional. The few entries whose views we chose not to represent seemed more intent on selfish and inconsiderate use of the resources. So in essence, the book became an insight into the importance of wilderness in our society, and what it means to the everyday person whose views dominate the journals. Admittedly, we let some bias enter the editing. But more to the point, what is in this text represents most of the views of the people who visited the cabins over the past fifty years.

As for the entries within this volume, we tried to change as little as possible from the original text. Unfortunately, a typed and formatted book such as this loses some of the original essence that a log book with the hard to read pencil writing, original artwork, scratched out lines, wax on crumbling, yellow pages, and the dead, smashed flies flattened by the years has to offer. Some of the writing was difficult to read, reminding me of translation in foreign language class. Some spelling has been corrected, some entries are only partial in nature, and some of the artwork has been cleaned up, all necessary evils for publication in a book such as this. But I believe a glimpse into the collective and individual minds overrides the loss of authenticity by focusing in on what each person has to say.

What the process of creating this book has provided for us, "the fashioners," is immeasurable. We found a deeper appreciation for all wilderness that we come in contact with. We realized the importance of experiencing the simple, yet important labors necessary to satisfy our basic needs. We identified ourselves as a part of a natural ecosystem, found it imperative to reflect upon life within the bosom of life itself, and learned to live in nature on nature's terms. We saw ourselves in the written word of others contained within this volume, as well as the many entries that were not included. We hope that all who read this compilation look for themselves within these pages. Not only will you discover humanity's place within the natural wilderness, but you may find your own place as well.*

THE CABINS:
Speaker's Cabin
Little Carp Cabin
Lake Superior Cabin
Big Carp 6-Bunk Cabin
Big Carp 4-Bunk Cabin
Buckshot Cabin
Section 17 Cabin
Greenstone Falls Cabin
Lily Pond Cabin
Mirror Lake 2-Bunk Cabin
Mirror Lake 4-Bunk Cabin
Mirror Lake 8-Bunk Cabin
Lake of the Clouds Cabin
Whitetail Cabin
Union River Cabin
Gitchee Gumee Cabin

* Historical information included in the introduction referenced from the following :
Rafferty, Michael and Robert Sprague. *Porcupine Mountains Companion: Inside Michigan's Largest State Park*, 3rd ed. White Pine, MI: Nequaket Natural History Associates, 1996.

I am glad I shall never be young
without wild country to be young
in. Of what avail are forty
freedoms without a blank spot on
the map?

Aldo Leopold
A Sand County Almanac

Perspectives

November 8, 1990
Lily Pond Cabin
We're here. Today I found that my life consists of much more than the constant routine of familiarity. I've discovered that without our being in my usual world, I may exist in an unusual way. In spite of constancy of change, people live as those who lived before them. I find myself fighting for the feeling of warmth, and the freshness of clear spring water.
Nature has granted us the opportunity of becoming one with our maker-
Nature has granted us the opportunity of becoming one with another-
Nature has granted us the opportunity of becoming one with ourselves.

Paul & Jeff

May 1994
Mirror Lake 8-Bunk
Stuff the universe in your eyes!

Beth

August 30, 1986
Big Carp 6-Bunk Cabin
I was looking for a break from work. I was becoming beaten down by the stress on the job (the place I work at has all the subtlety of a kindergarten recess), and so we came here. We drove fourteen hours...and then hiked for a few hours with sacks full of rocks on our backs. Then we chopped firewood, started a fire, killed flies, set up beds, and generally, worked. But the thing is, and for those of you who have gone to the lobby for refreshments, I will wait a moment—stupid phrase, "the thing of it is...." Could be talking about anything from bear poop to didactic materialism—is that it is a good type of work. Instead of having to decide whether or not to tell some jerk on the phone that he is a jerk, or to simply pretend that we have a bad connection and hang up on him, decisions up here are of a purer and more satisfying nature: what is the best way to cross this river, or which angle should I take up the side of this hill.

All of this suggests to me that humans can reach a point of having satisfied their lower needs (I used to think that a Maslovian hierarchy was a wrestling hold), such as food, clothing, and shelter...and at that point, they attempt to satisfy higher needs, such as intellectual stimulation, need for self-worth, art, beauty, and probably certain forms of sex. And one of these attempts is, perhaps, an atavistic desire to re-experience the beauty, strength, and danger of nature. We have insulated ourselves from the majesty and depth of our world, and also from the life-and-death struggles for survival that have characterized the greatest portion of our existence.

And so we travel to secluded (or so we thought) spots such as this for many reasons. To test ourselves, to experience life without rush (other than setting up a camp before dark). But consider the difference: the day, without a watch, is measured and marked by the sun's path across the sky, there is no second hand, and the other is measured by a device so (seemingly) accurate that you can know within a one one-thousandth of a second how late you are for a meeting to be chewed out by your boss. To feel the silence of a glade where the sound of no motor trespasses. Today, I listened to the bubbling of a minute rill as it bubbled and danced down a slope, finally to disappear into a hole with a musical, twinkling sound.

Ricardo

June 18, 1981
Buckshot Cabin

I've loved my stay here at Buckshot and in the park as a whole. In reading these logs, I sense an eerie, yet uniquely pleasant camaraderie of the ages-a linking of mankind and his spirit-seldom seen elsewhere. From the first person to come here, to us, so much has happened, so many have experienced so much. There is a sadness I have felt here every evening around sunset, that in no small way must come from my spirit (soul), reaching out to all the others who have been here over the years experiencing much the same things that I have. Where are all those people now? Part of each is here, you can feel the presence, but the greater parts of them are at work, at school, etc.—have they retained the peace they've gained here, have they kept the lessons they've learned when confronting nature on fairly equal grounds? I'd love to meet each one—from the man who was killed by the bear in '78, to the Scouts who hiked over twenty miles to earn their merit badges, to the athletic group who snowshoed in here, to the slobs who really didn't appreciate the place. Still, I feel I have met them; but funny, after reading a specific entry that I really relate to, I want to say, "Hey, I agree, let's talk," and, sadly, it is impossible!

Steve

July 15-19, 1972
Section 17 Cabin

It seemed like coming home to get back to Section 17 after an absence of four years. It is in such beautiful shape, we almost felt we were expected. In fact, we've talked a lot about that these days. Evidently, these cabins have been in the Porkies for almost thirty years. Yet there's almost no graffiti on the tables, walls, anywhere. The furniture and furnishings show only the effects of use, but careful use. And as you read these pages, almost everyone has fixed something, added something, worked out a problem, left advice and felt a real pride in leaving the cabin in good shape for the next people, who are

9

total strangers! It restores your faith in people as the woods restores your perspective and smooths out your insides.

We have been coming to the Porkies for some fifteen years, and have hiked nearly every trail and stayed in all of the cabins but two. Several times, we found no wood, but only once was the cabin so filthy we had to clean it before we could move in. Where else can you find such a batting average? Is it that most campers care, or that camping makes people care?

Jo & Taffy

May 22, 1990
Lake Superior Cabin
If you enter this cabin in the spirit of love and wonderment, then you have everything you need to have the best of times.

Robert & Susan C.

September 24, 1991
Whitetail Cabin
We are here from the farm on which we live and work and play. It's not our livelihood yet, but we are aspiring to be successful organic farmers. The Fall harvest is in, save the pumpkins and squashes (that's for next week). Our freezer is full of our harvest this year: tomatoes, peppers, corn, beans, carrots, cucumbers, beets, and various soups we've made from our produce. We consider ourselves very lucky to be able to grow our own food. The work is hard as well.

This cabin will create its own history and now we are a part of this wonderful living diary. To all who stay here, stay well, to better know yourself.

The feeling I get from looking out the window as the waves pound the shoreline, lap up over the big rock at the doorstep, and the trees undulate to the rhythm of the wind is calm. To be so insignificant a person, a being, smaller than the lake and younger than the trees. I feel small.

The wind on my face, the nip of cold on my nose, warm socks in high-top boots leave me printing the earth with my size, only to be washed away by the snows. We all are but a speck of time in the history of geology. The rocks we held in our hands tonight are older than we are. Sedimentary sandstone remembers the waves, as we will remember the waves, one hundred years from now. Imagine yourself as a rock. I am a rock. Think your body in the mud, only your face at ground level. Look up. Imagine your world from only this peripheral vision. This is your life. A tennis shoe appears; white with green treads. Steps on you. Leaves it's mark until Spring. A fawn at the edge of your vision barely comes into view. She's got white spots. Her mother jumps over your face and lands safely on the other side. Kisses her child.

They turn and walk away. The lake remembers last night's storm billowing wildly over your head and crashing at your feet (which are in the mud). Cold September Superior envelops you. You are as we write tonight. "Only a pathway?" you ask. Ask again.

Rick & Sherril

May 29, 1959
Big Carp 4-Bunk Cabin
Camp very clean. Fishing good Saturday. Sunday, rain and fog, no fishing. Caught one mermaid Saturday. Let it go back in the lake. Not enough woman to love and not enough fish to eat.

Bud B.

December 26, 1995
Union River Cabin
I've come up here to think. I just graduated from UW-Madison on December 22 with a double major in botany and conservation. Now I am exhausted and the real work is just beginning. For just awhile I want to forget all the science and let the magic come back. I had a delightful dream at Whitetail in which I discovered my "magic" colors. I had no idea that I was searching for magic colors or what I shall do with this new found insight. But I do know that one of the colors is a popular appliance color, and that may come in handy.

I am reading a lovely book by Zora Neale Thurston, *Their Eyes Were Watching God*. Here is an excerpt of a young girl coming into womanhood:

She was stretched on her back beneath the pear tree soaking in the alto chant of the visiting bees, the gold of the sun and the panting breath of the breeze when the inaudible voice of it all came to her. She saw a dust-bearing bee sink into the sanctum of a bloom; the thousand sister-calyxes arch to meet the love embrace and the ecstatic shiver of the tree from root to tiniest branch creaming in every blossom and frothing with delight.

Nicely botanical, yet magical. All together satisfying. Can there be a marriage of science and magic? Where do we fit in with all of our consumptive, selfish ways? I have plenty of thinking to do so I'll leave off here.

Unknown Author

August 26, 1978
Buckshot Cabin
A personal note to Dave Balboa, Park Manager, and his staff. It's not possible, given the constraints of language, to adequately express appreciation

for not only the park, its facilities and services, but for the human response and concern exhibited on a couple of occasions when crises arose. As a family, we express our deepest, heartfelt gratitude to you all.

A note of gratitude, also, to the many authors whose prose, poetry, and history are recorded in these pages; it is reassuring and hope-inspiring to be reminded again and again that we really are brothers and sisters of the family of man. Commonly held, fundamental yearnings and hopes find expression in so many different forms throughout these writings. The opposites which seem to astound serve only to keep us from getting bored with each other; whether it is feminism vs. male supremacy, conservative vs. liberal politics, the critically disapproving caution of years vs. the confident cockiness of youth, fatigue vs. energy, the philosophical vs. the pragmatic, and so on. It is like a delightful stew of contrasting flavors and aromas. One can only revel in this 'whole' we call the human existence.

The Alan S. Y. Family

Unknown Date
Lily Pond Cabin

Unknown Artist

12

August 25, 1977
Little Carp Cabin
 All that can be written about the beauty of this place I'm sure has all been said in the preceding pages—but what about people's efforts to keep it this way? Not only this park, but the metro parks or parks that are close to where people live. To spend a day, a week, or a month here and act like an "outdoorsman" or get "back to nature" is stupid if the same thoughts and feelings don't carry over to your everyday life. This doesn't mean to pretend like you're on a retreat or something, but use this experience out here to teach yourself about life, how precious life is, and to teach you about yourself.

Joe I.

May 31, 1985
Mirror Lake 8-Bunk Cabin

I puhpoweed* much as a mushroom would
From a darkness not understandable
I felt her, my first conscious memory
Her flesh composed of soft and sensuous curves
She adored the sun, yet accepted rain
As she cared enough to sustain my life
Through growth did I become indifferent
With artificial thoughts I used her so
Until one day I saw the waste so near
That Northern Lights suppressed within my soul
Let forth a brilliant glow I had not known
She gives all yet I just use and abuse
How can I take part in this brutal rape
For she is the darkness, my wife and earth.

* Puhpoweed: Ojibway word meaning to appear suddenly from an unseen
  source

Jim R.

June 24, 1986
Greenstone Falls Cabin
 The sound of the river is so soothing compared to the constant "city sounds." The bird songs help me to remember a different aspect of my nature, more so than the computer printer at work. I love being here. The clean air is something I'm particularly aware of…. The contrasts in perception are what brought us up here….
 Chop wood. Carry water. Basic. Simplicity is difficult to achieve in our society of VCR's, computer screens, and all the objects we're supposed to

need. Here, simplicity is easy. There is a clarity in that, a peace. Beauty surrounds us.

Aruna

July 7, 1982
Lily Pond Cabin
Things of great value are, in the end, also mysterious. Things outside of humankind's influence retain the greatest mystery and hence, the greatest value. That we can experience these mysteries transcends great cultural barriers of time and technology and puts us back in contact with our ancestors. Although their lives were not as comfy as ours, they valued what we often ignore. We came here to be in contact with a great celestial rhythm and the corresponding rhythm of earth, water, and sky. These for them were the lives of their spirits. Our goal is to carry this spirit out with us....

How old do you think that red pine (the big one by the path) is? We guess about two hundred years. About as old as our country.

Perry & Soo

September 3, 1990
Big Carp 6-Bunk Cabin

Remember, treat the earth well.
It was not given to you by your parents.
It was loaned to you by your children!

"Dad"

August 30, 1988
Big Carp 4-Bunk Cabin

We arrived a little late and tired.
Made a fire with wood that had been left by people before.
Ate a fine meal
And read the log by candlelight until night
Called us to sleep.
I thought
Eloquence must answer this—
This magic place
And all these good people who have come before us.
I owe no less.
It is three days later as I write this,
And late upon the eve before departure.
Words are but meager things
And even a wordsmith may fail in their use.
Are not some things by nature ineffable?

This has not been a major 'adventure.'
"The Bear," as if there were only one,
Has not come to visit us as yet.
Indeed, we saw more extraordinary wildlife
Before we came in; bear, eagle, peregrine.
But there is something about the place.
I'd noticed it before when I'd taken day hikes in to fish,
But living here really slams it home.

Watch the Mergansers run atop the water.
Reach up with your eyes to the height of a virgin pine.
Find a Brook Trout in a pool upstream and see just how
—fast—
A fish really is when you get too close.
Listen to the red squirrels and kingfishers chatter at you
As if you had no business in the forest.

You who come in immediately after us will be here
As the stream runs thick with trout and salmon.
Each morning I've seen them cruising the lake shore
And the turning to rush up the shallow run
That is this season's river mouth.
As you flail the water, whether for trophy or for meat,
Stop and consider the trout,
Blessed with beauty, grace, guile, speed, strength, and
Delicacy.
Nature has seen fit to balance the gifts of this finest
Of fresh-water fish
By making it swim to its own end.
Crawling on its belly across the rocks,
Starving yet unable to eat,
Ripping itself down to nothing
Because a whisper from the stream
Has called it to do so.
The gifts of the trout are extraordinary,
Its death, ignoble.
There is a balance in this world,
Once outside the efforts of man.

To those of you whose feet are not yet on the path;
Keep your eyes, ears, and mind open

>And this place will leave you better
>Than when you found it.
>
> Frank & Heidi

June 18-21, 1970
Lily Pond Cabin

We have camped before in many lovely and interesting places, only to have the experience soured by inconsiderate campers nearby. This first experience at backpack camping is delightfully different! It's amazing that the state of Michigan should be the provider of such a highly specialized experience. I wonder who talked the authorities into it?! Clearly we need more, not less, of this wilderness camping, and all of the considerate people who make it possible....

We were expecting to find that the packing done here in the Porcupines would compare with that practiced in the western mountains, but quite the opposite! Found mounds of glass bottles and tin cans, plus other outlandish debris in the garbage pit! We would like to see some kind of "pack-in, pack-out" policy tried here, with several predicted benefits: 1) lighter weight pack loads, 2) fewer unsightly garbage dumps, 3) less danger from bears who become over-tame by feeding at dumps.

The T. Family

May 18, 1997
Section 17 Cabin

The extent of snow cover was totally unexpected. There's probably a good foot of the lovely white frosting still present, though melting fast. This is probably my twentieth trip to this paradise, but my first with snow on the ground. Why, I don't know? Sloth? This area may seem vast to us clothed apes, but in reality, it is not. The big critters need much more. I cannot over-emphasize the need to educate humanity about the need for big wilderness. Big critters range over large areas. Bring back the timber wolf, the elk, the mountain lion. They can only make our spiritual existence that much richer. Your soul will thank you. We need to inform our family, friends, and especially our politicians about the need for big wilderness. Unfortunately, the power lies in their hands. It is absolutely essential! Some may cringe their noses at these musings. It's merely politics. They are dead wrong. Wilderness is not about politics. It is about life itself. It is about the continuation of evolution. The beautiful dance of plant life. It's myriad of patterns, processes, and interactions that together form this splendid existence on Mother Earth. Treat her with reverence, for she is to be revered. Work for the Earth, with our hands and our wallets. Pay your rent as they say. There are plenty of groups up north that do wonderful work for the north woods.... These groups need our support. They provide baseline education, lobbying activities, and research projects all in support of this great land. OK, I'm done.

Immerse yourself in this resplendent landscape. Teach yourself and let Mother Earth teach you. She has much to inform you of. The answer to life's problems lie within these woods. This may seem like a grandiose statement, but in reality, it's not. I know. I've experienced it first hand.

Revere every critter, every plant. They would not be here if they did not have a purpose. The Great Spirit knows.

Don't take life too seriously. Treat each other well. Don't take anything for granted. For in an instant, whether they are friends, family, or some other species, they may be gone. I wish you peace.

FOR THE WILD!

Ed

May 25, 1993
Big Carp 6-Bunk Cabin
If two roads were ever diverged, I'd take the one closest to the river and wouldn't forget my fishing pole.

Unknown Author

May 31, 1996
Whitetail Cabin
I can't believe we actually survived! Six female, high school seniors, on our own, no electricity, no running water, no nothing. If it wasn't for Sarah, "the Fire Starter," we would have froze.

This was a very special night for us. It was our last sleep over before we graduate. The big day is tomorrow, so I hope today goes by really fast.

I really enjoyed staying here. If it wasn't for the fact that graduation is tomorrow, I would never leave. It is so peaceful, so calm, so beautiful. The lake was so calm, it was nice to wake up and be able to just walk down to it.

Well, before we are all packed and ready to go, I would like to say what this trip was all about. It was about friends. Friends having one last get together before they leave each other for a final time as children. We are about to enter into the adult world, frightful and anxious, but not entirely alone. We will always have memories of times like these when life was simple and calm. Wherever we end up, we will never forget each other or our school days together. Wow, I wish I was this inspired when I wrote my speech. Anyway, I must start helping the others get ready to leave.

Take care of this place. It deserves the effort.

Roni H.

June 21, 1992
Mirror Lake 2-Bunk Cabin

I first came to the Porkies twelve years ago, and regularly since then. This time I had a family with me. Youngest kid is eight months.

At first, I was disappointed—so many people. Trash, overused trails. The woods didn't seem special anymore, the lake not significantly more beautiful than other North Country lakes. And of course, the kids need attention and take some of the focus away from where you are. So why am I here?

Well, the spirit of this place is still alive. Look and feel past the trees and the lake and find the spirit. It was real hard to find this time for me. But it is here. The Porkies are one of the special places on earth where there is strength in just being here.

But I think, at the same time, the spirit is a fragile thing. Why are the white pine dying along Mirror Lake? They were alive 4 years ago? Old age? Encroachment? Who knows? Err on the side of caution here. Keep a low profile, walk softly, and hear and speak with your heart.

Frank

June 8, 1989
Greenstone Falls Cabin
...a poor, obsessed student who just finished a giant term paper on Existentialism for an equally giant university deep in the depths of the metropolis known universally as Chicago...

Our minds have grown too active, too complex and demanding to be satisfied in a place like this for a long period of time. We have been conditioned for industry, consumption, technology, for things that do not last. We live in a state of mind of relativity, of adaptation and change...perhaps this is why we become so bored so quickly here...Advice: Turn this dissatisfaction inward and find the essence of yourself that does not adapt, change with the environment...In a sense, find the part of you that remains as stable and unmoving as the hills and ravines around this cabin. Only then can you return to the outward self and accept the transitory nature of life.

Brenda K.

October 1-3, 1992
Lily Pond Cabin

High praise to the DNR and the park staff for all that is furnished here, so we can share it with others who fall in love with it too.... We noticed some laments about people taking things from cabins, or leaving only a mess. It made us remember the old saying, "The world is full of 'givers' and 'takers.'

The 'takers' eat better. The 'givers' sleep better. I like feeling that I have something to leave, to give. It makes me feel rich and full....

I hate to leave. I've never backpacked in anywhere before. My daughter asked us to come with her. I love it! It's so good to know places like this are here, and still relatively safe from civilization's ravages.

The M. Family

September 2, 1969
Lily Pond Cabin
Hiked back from Section 17. I guess we haven't reached the point yet where our muscles get stronger and backpacking gets easier. Our muscles are just getting more tired. We had another perfect day. The weather was warm, without being hot. There was hardly a leaf stirring around the pond. You felt that somehow you were part of a picture postcard. I kept getting the feeling that I'm Alice in Wonderland and this isn't all real.

Dick & Linda T.

February 11, 1989
Little Carp Cabin
Beautiful weather snowshoeing in on Pinkerton Creek Trail. Sighted whitetails in abundance, both at the deer yard near Presque Isle and along our route in. They appear both healthy and relatively bold in regard to we primates.

I imagine the winter scenery here is rather different than that described by the warm weather visitors. The woods, of course, are beautiful, deep, and peaceful, but I am most struck by the awesome sight of Gitchi Gumee spreading before us to the horizon.

We did some traversing of the shore ice this afternoon. Of course, it's thrust up and buckled by the force of the underlying waters. Great, jagged chunks of flow ice extend out to open water. My first impulse is to describe it as looking like another world (Phobos, a moon of Mars, perhaps?), but it is this world in one of its many moods. How little we know of our own home, or the vast powers that dwell here.

Robert Aitken said, "I would not want to live in a place that had no natives." I am continually struck by our own alienation from this, our only and always home. It is a challenge to come back to a simple, humble, and visceral experience of "the native." That's why I come to the Porkies again and again. Beyond their beauty and the challenges, they have a lesson to teach....

This log book offers a definite insight into the minds of we visitors. It seems that few of us are unaffected by these surroundings. We are only here for the evening and yet the influence of the woods is felt.

Recall coming in on the Government Peak Trail a season or two ago. The beauty of the Upper Carp River and its waterfalls in the autumn weather was such that I honestly expected to find a Zen monastery or Taoist hermitage around the next bend. There is a way in which a place like the Porkies becomes a landscape of the mind. Like the cloud-shrouded, ink paintings of ancient China, it is ultimately real and yet mysterious, even as you walk through it. Anything may happen in the country of the mind.

Unknown Author

May 3, 1996
Big Carp 6-Bunk Cabin

Each night as we sleep, unawares, the army of millions of icebergs beat a retreat out to "sea." At daybreak, no lone sentries remain save a few taller, wilder strips very close to shore. As the day wears on, the troops once again advance toward shore until, at nightfall, they resume their places at their old posts. This event repeats itself each day. It's nice to be here long enough to begin to see the patterns and to witness one of the most magnificent displays of a late, hard winter struggling against an inevitable spring, as I've yet to witness as a lifelong resident of Michigan.

An earlier entry makes mention that time goes too quickly out here, and while I share the sentiment of having to leave this piece of Heaven on Earth, I find it to be the contrary. Time expands so that I actually feel as if I've gotten a real, full day's work of life in each day. Amazing how quickly life zooms by at the work-a-day world pace. And although I fancy myself a pretty good hand at enjoying each day as best I can, for it might be my last, there's something otherworldly about being in this much nature, undisturbed by modern conveniences. Only other times I notice this sort of thing is in the villages in Alaska. When friends say "What do you do there?," the only reply that comes is, "Well…nothing…and everything…." You take each day as it presents itself and fit yourself neatly into the greater sleeve of things, usually not knowing very well what is going to take place. Go with the flow. Don't push the river. Although "trite-sounding" phrases attempt to capture a means of defining the process, I'm darned if I've been able to adequately explain it.

In any case, this feels good. Life. Peace and storm, quiet and strife. It's all a part of the big picture. I'm not so philosophical when it's the storm and strife times, but I know they're a part of things, too…

Each night there has been an incredible sunset. I think the legions of icebergs just heighten the experience.

Star-gazed until I got myself spooked last night. (So when is it that the bears begin to emerge from this especially rugged winter, hungry and ornery?) Saw three shooting stars and seventy-nine satellites (man, we have an awful lot of that kind of traffic up there! I wondered if any of those satellites was looking at me!). And both evenings at sunset we've seen an eagle in flight along the shoreline of Lake Superior, but high up. Graceful and strong.

Found a disappointing amount of unnecessary liter. Not accidental "drops" from someone's pocket, but obvious laziness, I guess. My Mom and Dad instilled such a powerful sense of not trashing up the environment, that we'd think it a sin to do so. There are times when it would be a lot more convenient in the short run to just "toss" something, but I can never justify it…and when you see how all of those "just this one thing/one time" add up (just look at the trails and around the cabins, campsites, and fire pits) it just doesn't make any sense. This has been the only bummer, really. Styrofoam cups, unopened apple sauce (fermented, with two animal teeth punctures), old bait in styrofoam containers, pop cans, water jug plastics, bread wrappers, plastic tubs, a gajillion cigarette butts jettisoned into the river, candy wrappers—this in just three days! Wow! What a mess!

Thanks to the rangers and park personnel for what has obviously been a big series of clean-ups.

Thanks to the folks (most of the bunch, thankfully) who not only have packed out their stuff, but help by grabbing others' things left behind.

Thanks to everyone who has helped their fellow hiker/camper/fisher/hunter/explorer to better enjoy nature and her beauty.

And thank God, gods, Allah, the Spirits, Buddha, etc., etc., etc., for the gift of a place like this.

To Raymond Dick, Ed Johnson, Ben East, and PJ Hoffmaster, et al…you folks may have thought you knew what you were doing when you set into motion the preservation of the Porcupine Mountains, but there's no way you could have imagined the truly amazing contribution you have made to all of us, many of whom weren't even born yet, when the idea for saving this place was born.

Hat's off. Grateful. Thanks. You did good.

B., J., J., & G.

Memorial Day Weekend, 1967
Mirror Lake 8-Bunk Cabin

A most pleasant weekend. Four days of fishing, sleeping, eating, and more fishing. About twenty trout in all, mostly splake. Weather was beautiful—no rain, much sun.

A great way to spend the weekend before my marriage. Maybe I could talk my future wife into spending our honeymoon here. I am sure she would love it, except for the bugs.

She should see me now, with my nose and ears burned a bright red, plus my week's growth of beard. To top it all off, I smell to high heaven. Come to think of it, if she did see me now, there night not be a wedding next weekend.

A note to those who follow: this is your land, this is my land. It belongs to us all. Please respect it and care for it because this is our backyard. It is simply thrilling to be a part of this virgin wilderness and virgin timber. And yet it is rather sickening to walk through this virgin land only to discover empty beer cans along the way.

There will be more people to follow us tomorrow and the day after tomorrow and for many years to come. Let's not spoil it for them after we have enjoyed it so much.

Dick H.

June 8-9, 1995
Speaker's Cabin
It's very interesting how your priorities and values so quickly change in the wilderness. Building a fire on a cold night seems to absorb one totally in the moment, as important as anything we do in our normal lives. How silly it seems to get all stressed out over our petty problems. Staying here, even for a short while, makes one take a much larger (and more realistic) view of life. With the wilderness being destroyed more every year, one wonders how much longer we will have the opportunity, as a race, to gain that kind of perspective.

Larry

May 5, 1978
Buckshot Cabin
I've taken this trip every year now. This is about my fifth time up here to the Porkies, and every time it seems more remote and removed from society. I mean, that a person can completely let go-he doesn't have to conform to the rules of society. Up here in the woods, he is himself, what the individual wants to be. We didn't bring a watch because we didn't want to be governed by time. Instead, we are trying to live by instinct-eat when we want, sleep when we want, etc.—anyway, the calmness of this place (no matter what the weather is like) is just amazing. In fact, we are just sitting here. Neither one of us is talking. I think the last words uttered were five minutes ago. We are just taking in the silence of a fly buzzing around the room, with neither of us even contemplating killing the damned thing.

Scott M.

May 16-18, 1997
Lake Superior Cabin
A moment of reflection, an eternity of anticipation, watching sunrise carry away the pastels of yesterdays gone by...magical inspirations come with a subtle warning. "Are you truly prepared to face your destiny?" You'll know the answer when you face this question.

When you face your crossroads, which you'll do one day, remember to listen to your inner voice, your higher self, your extreme intuition. Look for the coming insights in your life, and you'll know the way for you.

Kathy

May 11-12, 1978
Lily Pond Cabin
See the stump in front of the cabin? Last year it was a nice, large tree, very old and beautiful. Except that in front some idiot started hacking away at it. Either for fun or for firewood, either reason was worthless and stupid. So because of this, the rangers cut it down. I guess, before it fell on somebody or the cabin. I hope no one else does this to any trees around here, or anywhere for that matter. Look what a waste it is, and there's plenty of other wood around without this one. Well, enough philosophizing. It seems most everybody in this log does that at one time or another. I guess the beauty and calm of the outdoors gets people thinking about other things in life than just "me, myself, and I," and wondering what life really means.

Lynn

Unknown Date
Speaker's Cabin

Steve

January 6-8, 1993
Union River Cabin

It is beautiful up here.
And quiet.
And cold.
I wanted to come up and slow down
and think, I guess.
Think and get space.
Space from commitment and confusion and from
the anger that's been buzzing around my head
for—
well, probably for a long time-
but it comes and goes.
Comes and goes.
Sometimes I wish it would just go.

Go and stop smarting
like a fresh wound, barely scabbed over.

I was raised to think it is something I do-
I'm keeping, holding this anger
prideful in its resentment
like I've got a big fucking chip on my shoulder.

And sometimes I guess I do.

That part I don't like—
that chip, or resentment, or whatever you
want to call it, I have a hard time with.
Even though I work on accepting its pain
in hopes that I'll grow through it.
It's just that
sometimes that chip
drives a wedge between
me and people I care
about.
Sometimes.

And that smarts. Hurts like a son-of-a –bitch and it
doesn't always feel like I can manage
my rage.

But, of course,
it's not just something
I do.

I'm not the only one trying to love,
struggling to understand, longing to
be taken seriously,
and frequently,
(after watching clouds move on a windless day)
taking herself
too seriously.

Nope.
It ain't just me messing up the kitchen counter.

So that makes it harder sometimes.
What shit is mine, and what is
somebody elses?
And what do we share?

Well, I think we share a lot. And you know, that's
been a helpful way to look at it.
For me, anyway.

My anger isn't just my problem,
anymore than your neediness
or your guilt
is yours.

Sure, some of it might be.

But some of it might not.

LaVendee

September 1, 1991
Buckshot Cabin
I enjoy the forest. It touched something primeval in me. I felt at home, protected, and at ease. But my favorite place is the shore. I can hear the waves crashing on the rock. It's gentle power is comforting to me. I watched the sun end its life-giving performance for today. To the applause of the waves, it sank below the horizon, the pink sky a fervent promise that it will rise again.

25

Later, alone with the water, I sat on a boulder and saw the galaxy misted across the sky, as the pale green Northern Lights danced on the horizon.

I realized then that I truly wasn't important. That the universe will continue, with or without me. I am not alarmed or dismayed by the fact. Rather, I'm reassured, as if I have abdicated the responsibility of trying to make my mark upon this insane world. Of course, I shall endeavor to do my best in what I do, but that is for me. I enjoy the fruits of my labors. By the same token, I must not infringe upon the rights of others. I must not ridicule or belittle them when their beliefs do not coincide with mine. What would the world be like if everyone took care of their own business, cleaned up after themselves, and generally lived by the Golden Rule: "Do unto others as you would have them do unto you?"

How eloquent is that concept? How amazingly simple, but so very complete. Why can't we live by that? Why don't we? Are we too tolerant of our fellow man? Or too afraid?

Matt B.

July 4, 1976
Section 17 Cabin

You just can't help wondering how it must have been two hundred years ago on this date. In this cabin, one can take himself back in time to a period when things were simpler, but still very harsh. It's one thing to spend a few days here, but quite another to live here the year round. But peace of mind is one thing many of us come here for and I suppose we share that ideal with those pioneers two hundred years ago.

I think we're all still pioneers of a sort, all looking for something new and something very personal. Our frontiers are very different, but they are still, nevertheless, frontiers.

And so, from a not-really-so patriotic camper, it's been a good Fourth, and I'm sure your stay here will be good too.

Unknown Author

January 12, 1994
Union River Cabin

In stillness one travels farthest.

Unknown Author

October 2, 1981
Lily Pond Cabin

Hiking is great! That's what my mind and soul are saying; my physical body is rebelling. As this is my first trip, no second (who could forget yesterday at Buckshot?) time hiking, I have discovered beauty of the unspoiled wilderness and several sore muscles I never knew existed! My advice: LISTEN! Listen to the quiet, it is deafening. Let it clear your mind. Since we all have to face "civilization" again all too soon, this is our only salvation. Soak in the beauty of Mother Nature, but do not mar it. I hope I pass this way again soon. Good-bye, Lily Pond.

Becky C.

September 20-21, 1978
Mirror Lake 8-Bunk Cabin

I'm contemplating the inevitability of my return to civilization. Why did I have to go five hundred miles for peace, beauty, and serenity? Why must I return to my daily rigors which I can so easily despise? Why are our daily lives deprived of the enjoyment that I have experienced the past several days?

One might argue that the environment of the Porkies is not conducive to our daily work, but then again, there are many of us who do not desire our daily work. What keeps us chained to the factories, warehouses, schools, etc.?

There is a specter haunting our society...one that proclaims the end of servitude to our bosses, not the end of work, but the freedom to choose our destiny. Will it be one of peace, land, and bread or war, decadence, and slavery?

P.B. & M.R.

September 20, 1980
Lily Pond Cabin

Lost myself in the woods one day. And I'll come back to find him some other day.

T.C.R.

July 23, 1968
Little Carp Cabin

To maintain one's balance and values, one must see more than concrete and television.

Bob S.

September 25, 1993
Lake Superior Cabin

We are two sisters, a brother, the brother's wife, and a sister's husband—an extended family in an extended childhood eating, sleeping, and playing twenty-four hours a day. We packed here from the Mirror Lake cabin yesterday. That was the right direction because it's mostly downhill. We followed the wise advice of those who came before us and hung our packs from the rafters of the cabin to keep them away from the mice. Last night the place looked like a pinata factory. We watched the sunset and applauded when the sun vanished over Gitchee Gumee. A voyager in a loaded canoe approached from the west and paddled into the Big Carp River to tie up along side the 6-bunk cabin. At night, the stars are even brighter above this cabin then they are over Lake Superior. A special treat is to star gaze from the bridge where you have a bench and can lean back comfortably. We saw two shooting stars and a satellite.

A true camper is one who sleeps comfortably on a hard bed; one who will hold the skillet steady even when smoke gets in their eyes; one who eats the eggs even after the dog licks the batter; one who uses their coffee cup after tossing out the mouse turds; and one who stays in the outhouse long enough to zip up.

Meryl Lee N.

June 8-10, 1984
Mirror Lake 8-Bunk Cabin
"Reflections from the Mirror Lake Cabin"

I feel a sense of awe as I look around at the massive, old timbers in this cabin. What stories they must have to tell! They carry on the strength and grace that their grandfathers before them had. In those days, before the white man came, there were whole forests of tall, strong pine and hemlock. The bears and deer were abundant, the Indian respected that which was a gift from the earth. The only danger the trees would have were natural ones like fire, lightning, or disease. The white man came, and like everything else he has touched, he was not happy until he could control and destroy nature. Finally realizing that mass lumbering of the whole area was not beneficial to nature, or himself, men set aside parks like this one to preserve the beauty for all generations of people and nature.

The trees in this cabin were felled and hand-worked to reveal their grains and knots. They are here as a reminder that at one time, there were hundreds of thousands of their kind standing tall and majestic.

Run your hands over them and feel their warmth. There have been thousands of hands touching them since they were laid here. Some have been caring and considerate. Others have not. Like the generations of men before them, there are still people who gain satisfaction from destroying and carving something which is so beautiful. Those same people are the ones that leave litter and noise pollution.

Leave your happiness and laughter for these logs to remember, not your initials scratched into their surface.

Karen P.

June 23, 1974
Section 17 Cabin

"The fallout is really heavy today."

E.M.P.

October 8, 1996
Buckshot Cabin
Thoughts and Observations Section:
1) This is Buckshot Cabin!
2) The sun also rises

Summary of Thoughts and Observations Section:
In the first part of the thoughts and observations section, it was noted, rather emphatically suggested by use of an exclamation mark, that the cabin in which you are now reading this journal is indeed named Buckshot. And, to hasten identification and lessen the conclusion of those who might mistake this cabin with Buckshot Lodge in northern Ontario, the word "cabin" was

affixed to the sign posted above the cabin door. In retrospect, this was deemed unnecessary because anyone intelligent enough to gain the lawful use of this cabin through the issuance of the proper permit would not have mistaken this cabin for Buckshot Lodge or any place in Ontario.

In regard to the second statement, "the sun also rises," the author fails to make it clear to what end he/she draws this comparison. Is it that bread rises? The tide?

In summary, you are in Buckshot Cabin in the Porcupine Mountains, not in Ontario, and the sun also rises like other objects, animated or real, yet unnamed.

Dustin

June 16, 1995
Greenstone Falls Cabin
At Carp River I read a quote:
"Time is not measured in minutes but moments."
And I would add that moments make memories. These memories will age well and become more precious as time goes by. Aching feet and sore necks will be soon be forgotten, but our memories will forever grow in importance in our hearts and minds.

Chris A.

August 12, 1972
Lily Pond Cabin
Man must understand that he is a part of nature, and not apart from his environment. It is this lack of understanding that has dominated our natural resources and will continue to do so until trees are zoo species....

The value of this park lies in its ability to teach us that we are only a part of an overall system of nature. Places like this exist to provide man with proper perspective. It is not money, big cars, social standing, race, color, or religion that count. It is our ability to recognize ourselves as individual parts of an overall system. By returning to nature, we gain the ability to see the self.

Fritz & Colleen D.
Nadia & David L.

September 29, 1995
Whitetail Cabin
I'm leaning into this journal, getting ready to fill it with thought provoking vinettes, and wondering if the flame from the candle will jump the ten to twelve inches of space onto my gel and spray saturated hair. What a gorgeous drive my friend Mark and I had from Detroit via Cheboygan. The leaves were proudly displaying their colors! What a symphony of colors: red, tan, and

orange. As if anyone can really doubt that a Supreme Being exists! My second time here and I brought my good friend, Mark (I say good friend because he's reading this as I write) to see this idyllic park. On my first visit, I was astounded by the beauty and while standing above Lake of the Clouds, I wondered why, because I was solo, at times things seemed more beautiful when you share the experience with someone? I really haven't answered that conundrum yet—maybe you can?

Daniel N.

July 25, 1993
Union River Cabin

People are like phases of the weather,
Stormy, cloudy, hazy, or in between.
Or maybe even sunny or clear
But I have yet to see
More than two or three
People who can find the
Eye of the storm

Cyanna M.

May 5-6, 1997
Mirror Lake 4-Bunk Cabin
The earth provides enough to satisfy every man's needs, but not every man's greed.

Unknown Author

May 4, 1977
Section 17 Cabin
Why do I feel like I am writing to an old friend? Because I am writing to myself. We are all one. Including this cabin and log.

Bob

1974
Lily Pond Cabin
I have been smoking pot for about two years now, and can truthfully say that I have stopped and don't really want to start again. I was searching for something, maybe an answer to it all, and at times I really thought I was getting somewhere, but never did I reach where I thought I might go. This may not make sense to some, but that may be because you have never experienced this before. I was on an endless wheel of thought going around and around, thinking I was getting closer to that one moment when I would suddenly have a realization of my own being.... After two years of trying to reach my goal, I

decided to try a different way to reach total peace of mind and true content-ment. This may sound ironic, but all the time I was smoking pot, trying to find happiness, I was actually getting farther away from it, all the time wishing to be happy, and at the same time not being happy. I believe a person can achieve peace only through himself, not from external sources.

Unknown Author

October 29, 1986
Big Carp 6-Bunk Cabin
   The experience that is the Porcupines. What does one say about it? This time, it is the continual washing of the waves. I can almost hear each rock knocking against the other rocks, the splash of each drop of water-quiet as each is individually-on the rocks and driftwood, even on itself. Mixed with this is the fall of the water of the Big Carp River. This is very like the wind in the leaves of the forest. Soothing in a way. Frightening in another. Shockingly loud! Multidimensional. Something like static on a radio or the sound of the TV after the last program is finished. We turn that off. But this???
   I heard the other day that the ear repeats each sound. The brain gets a sec-ond chance at recognition. Some ears make sounds even when there is noth-ing to repeat-the so-called roof noise of the yogic student? I've been here four nights. I'm barely an initiate of these sounds. You can bet the Indians studied them, know them. We won't even mention them in poem or song-except maybe romantically. But romance, that's a caricature of reality! Does any modern person study these sounds? Since my own eight day hike and tenting trip to Door County this summer, I yearn for the sound of the leaves. The all night thunderstorm on Rock Island with wind in the trees, waves beating a sand beach, rain pelting the tent rain fly, was nourishment to me. Normally, I'm frightened of such storms, scared to death of possible tornadoes and sim-ple windstorms. Is it the house that could crumble that scares me most?

Mary F.

May 2, 1975
Buckshot Cabin
   Please, everyone take care of this cabin. It has an aura of permanence. All over this park, one feels the unchangeable mist that hangs over an area unru-ined by man. In the city, all neighborhoods...last only a few years before they are torn down and renewed. Here, the environment tears down and builds up constantly, so it never changes. Only the seasons change, proclaiming an infi-nite number of possibilities.
   This evening, I read this entire log and could feel the vibrations left behind by all these conscientious people and hope this cabin, too, will adjust to the changes constantly occurring in the material universe. If you can under-

stand this, perhaps in simpler terms, we can both help this environment to prevail.

Paul M., Betty H., & Molly Dog

October 20, 1985
Speaker's Cabin

 The lake has its quiet face on this A.M. Today we have the sadness of leaving this magical place to go "back." Every time we are here, I am struck with how complicated it is to live simply. It seems like a paradox. I am thankful for this time to get away from the clank of the world and find the joy of time, quiet, and relaxed conversation. It is hard to find time to know the people you care about when you are "back."

 Thanks again to this subtle place, where I always feel like the intruder, but always feel welcomed. My mind and soul are soothed and more at peace.

Jill

April, 1977
Mirror Lake 8-Bunk Cabin

 A time will come when all of this will pass. All the love in the world for the "wild places" will do no good without the willingness to sacrifice. To sacrifice the "luxuries" of modern day civilization. Things and objects of use and misuse which will eventually lead, indirectly, to the destruction of those "wild places" we cherish. One must be willing, for the sake of the future, our children's children, to begin fighting for the preservation of that which must ultimately fall before the advance of the automobile and the four-lane highway.

 To be aware of this splendor is the first step to becoming "at-one-with." And after this stage is reached, one can begin to understand the desperate need for the sacred lands of solitude.

 So when do we all start listening?

 When do we get so sick of all the wasted plastic that is strewn/thrown all over planet Earth?

Strider

June 21, 1981
Buckshot Cabin

 In the city, there is always a pressure to show others that you are doing something. Keeping busy. I mean, some of us feel compelled to fill our calendars, every day, with more and more activities, so that we can say we are productive, we are adequate, we are in demand. If we lay back for one minute with a blank mind and no plans, some of us, most of us, wonder why and try to think of something to fill that moment....

33

I guess the point of what I've been rambling about lies somewhere in the fact that whenever I've gotten that compulsive apprehension about sitting idly in this little spot, I can look around me and hear the sounds of clean life and worry leaves me. I can melt into the woodwork. Kind of doing that now, as a matter of fact.

Jeffrey D.

June 17, 1993
Greenstone Falls Cabin

> To observe nature in it's disorder
> brings order.
> To experience human institutions
> brings confusion.
> Ideals are offered by leaders
> but often without truth.
> Institutions structure us further
> from nature.
> Hope lies not in these structures.
> Each person needs to touch
> nature and renew their soul.
> They are the dynamic.
> They are the peace.
> They are the order in the
> disorder.
> There is a future.

W.G.M.

July 14-18, 1987
Lily Pond Cabin

I'm up here alone. This is my first time going it alone. All of my friends and family were concerned because I'm a woman. B.S. and big deal. It's probably safer here than where I live!...

Now I know why women got married in the past; they needed each other to share the chores just to be able to exist. Now I knew that before, intellectually, but I now know it physically, too....

Spent all afternoon writing about how difficult it is to be a woman in today's world. There is no clear-cut definition, like past women had to work with, to define themselves. Today, it appears that being female has a lot to do with how your body looks. I'm not complaining. I've got a nice body, but it took time to realize and accept that you can be beautiful even if you're not tall and skinny. This whole note really is the result of a lovely California niece who (sixteen years old) is an anorexic/bulimic. She'll binge on food and then stick her finger down her throat to force herself to vomit. Why? So she'll get slim and stay slim. Anyway, being up here alone gave me time to think how I've been "duped." I was smart enough to realize beauty is defined more than from a physical perspective. I wrote her a letter with a story about a woman who spent her life trying to look beautiful and was missing how beautiful she really was. That men liked her because of who she was, not because of how she necessarily looked. Anyway, I wrote all afternoon.

I wonder how many men worry, to the point of doing things that are having a negative impact on their lives, about how they physically look? Do they realize how a lot of women get caught up in trying to look a particular way instead of accepting what their genetic code has given them and make that the best it can be?

Jackie

September 4, 1978
Mirror Lake 4-Bunk Cabin

What is frail?
green leaves and youth
What is deep?
the ocean and truth
What is heavy?
sea, sand, and sorrow
What is brief?
today and tomorrow

Sue, Sharon, Karen, Marie, & Nanette

August 13, 1972
Little Carp Cabin

Preserving the beauty of this area is going to require everybody's cooperation. I wonder if America is capable of doing it? If so, we all are going to have to stop being "rugged individuals," and start thinking about each other and the beauty of our country as a whole.

William N.

March 3, 1992
Union River Cabin

I have found this cabin and these surrounding woods to be bringers of peace and serenity. The warm (and I do mean warm) fire and glowing candles all remind me of the more simple things in life that we all seem to forget. These things may be different for each person that makes this cabin their home for a short time, but are remembered more clearly with each passing hour here. For me, these simple things are open communication and the love

35

of good friends. How easily we forget, pursuing our busy schedules of every-day life, how important these simple things are. All of them, for everyone. I hope each of you that come to stay here are able to remember the simple things and keep them in your hearts.

K.P.

August 2, 1974
Speaker's Cabin
THE OUTHOUSE: It is not a question of whether you want to, it's a question of whether you have to.

Unknown Author

October 16, 1965
Buckshot Cabin

Dietmar K.

April 6, 1985
Buckshot Cabin

Have you considered the ramifications of Haley's Comet? That's right. Oh no! Haley's Comet!

H.C., as it is affectionately known in the scientific community, is a mass emitting enormous amounts of radiant energy, hv.

This entity, as our resident expert has put it, "a big mother," and when traveling as near to the earth as it will be, the physical relationships and possible permutations become astounding.

We have all been subjected to the "full moon" theory of human behavior. Briefly, it supposes that deviant behavior is increased during these periods. Again associated here is the physical phenomenon of tides, a gravitational or magnetic effect, associated with the lunar cycle.

If you will, then, H.C. will exhibit the same relationships. But, because of the duration of exposure, the magnitude of this behavior will be much greater. That is to say, those people exhibiting deviant behavior under normal conditions will, under the exposure of the comet, exhibit even more deviant (behavior).

This concept could possibly hold to form if it is viewed from a thermodynamic sense.

We are all made of the same substance, i.e., for those who will, "dust to dust." Knowing that matter cannot be created or destroyed and that the interrelationships between the forms of matter are governed by physical laws, we can simply say that matter and energy affect one another.

If a system, say the earth and moon, is operating within a guideline of construction interference, those actions created by one source complimenting another, a balance is struck and a norm is created.

Enter to that system an extraneous source of mass and energy and a new balance must be established. If the source entering is of a sufficient magnitude, that the existing balance is raised by a power of ten,...the constructive interference will remain and the system will be in phase. However, any change of a lesser magnitude would create a situation when a destructive interference would exist.

As the addition to the system of Haley's Comet would be considered a positive addition, it would be logical to assume that the energy added to the system would be equal, if not greater than that available at the time when the earth and moon have their greatest attraction (by energy here, I am speaking of a magnetic flux).

As we add matter in that system, any change associated with a change in magnetic flux will be dealt through the entire system.

The question then becomes, to what extent? Will the "good vs. bad" dichotomy be broadened? Or, will left-handed people finally get the respect they so "rightly" deserve!

S.W.H.

June 14, 1996
Section 17 Cabin

Ohhh...ahhh...wow!
Whoa...yeah...hooray!
Alright...spectacular...stupendous!
Excellent...super...far out!
Neato...keen...fabulous!

What else can I say???

Di

August 31, 1973
Lily Pond Cabin

Lots of moaning and groaning on the trail, but now that we've had two good days here, they all agree that it was well worth the effort. This has been a tremendous experience for the children. Not only does it provide a sharp contrast to urban living, but teaches them self-reliance as well as many other things; increases awareness of the world of nature, and of their places in it.

I was reading from a novel last night, something well worth quoting:

"...knows nothing about isolation and nothing about silence. In our quietest and loneliest hour, the automatic ice maker in the refrigerator will clink and drop an ice cube, the automatic dishwasher will sigh through its changes, a plane will drone over, the nearest freeway will inhabit the air. Red and white lights will pass in the sky, lights will shine along the highways and glance off windows. There is always a radio that can be turned to some all-night station or a television set to turn artificial moonlight into the flickering images of the late show. We can put on a turntable, whatever consolation we most respond to, Mozart or Copeland, or the Grateful Dead..." *Angle of Response*, Wallace Stegner, 1973.

Alienation from the real world and from ourselves! How far away we've come from simply sharing this world with these creatures. We've removed ourselves entirely from any kinship with them at all. The retreat here restores that feeling of belonging that is basic to well-being....

How wonderful are these ledgers. I love them—poetry, tall tales, practical hints, thoughtfulness, silliness (because it's fun to be silly sometimes)—

but everyone speaking to the same thing. This is a kind of sharing and I love them all.

The P. Family

June 7, 1971
Buckshot Cabin
There are four of us here—in our twenties, from Chicago.... The isolation is both wonderful and disquieting in a sense that we are so accustomed to the noises and lights of other people that it is difficult to give them up. In fact, this pervades my thoughts the whole time here. I have a sense of beauty that comes not very often, and likewise a sense of quiet and history. It's wonderful, and I feel blessed to have such feelings. But again, it's hard to shake off your past, your habits. You are used to doing certain routine things, having conveniences, feeling secure. I guess times like these are worthwhile if only you can realize that most of what you rely upon is fake security and doesn't mean one hell of a lot when you walk to the lake.

Gloria M.

March 27, 1979
Mirror Lake 4-Bunk Cabin
As we spend the last of our three nights in this quaint little cabin in the midst of this beautiful park, I begin thinking of that nearly worn-out statement, "our dying wilderness." But man, it's true. You take away what this country has in national and state parks, national forests, and game preserves—that's it! The rest is farmland, privately owned acreage for whatever, and land prime for developing to the potential of just about any "main street" you can think of, lined with used car lots and fast food joints.

But before I get too far off on that tangent, I just want to say as visitors to this park, we all have to respect it the way we would our own homes and land. There is nothing more discouraging that being in one of the most remote areas and seeing a "ringtop" (or the complete beer can) or an empty cigarette package. And I bet there isn't a single person who has written in this book that hasn't seen some of this.

Everyone, in his or her own life, should have the opportunity to just once see a portion of this earth left just the way God intended it to be.

Jim & Cathy A.

May 21, 1984
Greenstone Falls Cabin
Sitting down here to write by candlelight gives a person some insight on how it must have been hundreds of years ago for the first settlers. Everything is so very different than we are used to everyday. Things we depend on every-

39

day back home are not missed half as much as we first thought they might. Candlelight, cooking over a wood stove, getting water from a stream, and chopping our own wood are just a few things that add to the romance of the whole adventure into the Porkies. I thank God for the chance to be here and for the hope I will return.

Nicholas W.

October 23-25, 1995
Whitetail Cabin
STOP—and listen. You will hear nothing, but silence. Breathe, and you will inhale life. Walk, and do not run, because life passes too quickly.

John S.

June 11, 1975
Big Carp 4-Bunk Cabin
"The equations of animal and vegetable life is too complicated a problem for human intelligence to solve and we can never know how wide a circle of disturbance we produce in the harmonies of nature when we throw the smallest pebble into the oceans of organic life…. This much we seem authorized to conclude."—George P. Marsh

Patrick

August 12, 1993
Buckshot Cabin

People caught—
in traffic
in jobs
in lies
in lores
in a rush to go nowhere
Must come here
Are called here
To remember
How to be people
Amongst the animals.

Sue T.

June 15, 1997
Little Carp Cabin
Had a great stay. Didn't have time to read much of this journal, but what amazes me the most is the vastly different opinions, ideas and thoughts that come from all the cabin visitors. And I'm glad we're not all the same. If any-

thing, we need to be more tolerant of others who we disagree with, as long as they aren't harming anything.

Bob

May 16-19, 1974
Section 17 Cabin

I came not to conquer and
subdue the earth
But to let the earth conquer
and subdue me

Learn as if you were going to live forever.
Live as if you were going to die tomorrow!

Wilderness Studies Club

May 7, 1995
Greenstone Falls Cabin
Wisdom and maturity go hand in hand, neither of which are determined by race, sex, or age. They are rather factors of experience and understanding.

Melinda

May 15, 1979
Mirror Lake 4-Bunk Cabin
Nature here is wonderful and one feels a union with the sky and the forest. But I find this journal the most remarkable part of this place, making me feel yet another sort of union—a bond with the past campers of Mirror Lake 4. Most of us seem to sense that the common experiences and pleasures of this place transcend our individual values and histories. This journal is a window on our times, immensely valuable to a historian of the future.

Rick & Bob S.

July 27, 1968
Speaker's Cabin
Thought for the evening:
To live in the woods—building the campfire, securing shelter from wind and weather, finding warmth and food—provides abounding opportunity for good times and calls for cooperation and self-discipline. You cannot live in camp without sharing generously in the business of living; without learning to consider every member of the group. If anyone is to "go without," it must be yourself and not your comrade, for a wholesome rivalry to be the first in service and the last in self-seeking is at the heart of all good camping. There is nothing in our lives that can take the place of this free "give and take" under

the open skies; sharing in a chosen comradeship, the odors of the pines, the song of the lake, and the quietness and beauty of the stars.

Unknown Author

April 4, 1993
Buckshot Cabin

I looked across the lake from the top of the mountain, and all I could think about was what it would be like to be an eagle flying over top of that wonderful great lake—Lake Superior. The beauty of the shoreline framed by the mounds of snow was peaceful. While out living your life day to day, we often forget the importance of our earth and being harmonized with it....

As I look around me at what this cabin represents, I realize that the simplicity is beautiful and what you create and the attitude you hold is up to you.

Angie B.

September 15, 1992
Little Carp Cabin

I have spent considerable time reading this log...and I must make a comment: I see in these logs the direct results of our right to freedom of speech. We write of our thoughts, feelings, and experiences in these logs. Some may be funny or some may be an account of events. Some are quite personal and some simply offer practical suggestions. Some are spiritual and even poetic, but all are a glimpse into the person we are.

Paulette K.

The Many Faces of the Natural World

October 24, 1992
Mirror Lake 8-Bunk Cabin

When we awoke this morning, the cabin was enveloped in a soft, gray mist. Over the lake, a pale yellow glow tinged with pink offered evidence that the sun had risen. We are two weeks later in the year than when we were last here and the season has advanced much more quickly. The leaves have all fallen and the ferns have arranged themselves flatly over the ground in preparation for the snow season ahead.

When we hiked in, we found that melted snow from last week's early fall had made a slippery tea of the maple leaves on the trail. We needed to take extra care not to slip and the trail is soft and muddy in many places.

The colors of the Porcupines have become muted. A sepia painting with the strokes of bold green from the hemlocks and bright spots of the bracken ferns. As daylight has strengthened, the view of the lake is a double image in soft focus because of the mist. The trees on this side of the lake remain in sharp focus, the maples spotted with grayish-silver lichens and the hemlocks etching green borders.

Unknown Author

June 1, 1985
Little Carp Cabin

For those of you who are wildflower enthusiasts, we found some rare "moccasin flowers," or pink lady slippers along the trail after you go up to the first big hill, just a short distance from the lake. Watch on the left side of the trail and don't pick them. They are very rare and precious. Leave them for others to see...We also saw these flowers in abundance: star flower, clintonia—in the lily family (yellowish-green blossom on a separate stalk with no leaves and two or three leaves at the base), wild lily-of-the-valley (short, white flower with lovely smell), and these were less abundant: cloudberry (or bakeapple), nodding trillium (with the flower under the leaves), common wood sorrel, and mertensia (a blue flower in the shape of small bells and it is in the forget-me-not family). All of these are to be found on the lovely Little Carp River Trail. My daughter and I took our time so we could enjoy these gems of God's creation.... It is hard to decide what to focus on. So much beauty-flowers, river, virgin white pine and hemlock.... It is a perfect place to see the wilderness as God created it.

Kathleen L.

June 13, 1965
Big Carp 4-Bunk Cabin

Dennis sighted a bald eagle while on the beach this morning, and I, Mike, sighted either an oven bird or a water thrush not far from the cabin, as we walked on the beach this evening. Before sun set we spotted some loons diving for fish about four hundred yards out in Superior. We also spotted, much to our bird watching pleasure, some bird foot prints in the sand which were at least eight inches long and were typically three-toed. It might have been a great blue heron. The woods are full of migrating spring warblers, but since they usually inhabit the very tops of the trees, they are hard to sight.

Mike

July, 1997
Lily Pond Cabin
    The most interesting part of this trip was the discovery of the luminescent log by the fire. At night it glows a bright green just like glow-in-the-dark toys. Jim discovered it last night as we were going to bed. The more he peeled away, the more it glowed. It's really quite fascinating, especially since as of yet, we do not have an answer to "why?"

The G. Family

July 30, 1997
Lily Pond Cabin
    The glowing log mentioned from the folks before us is caused by a scientific, chemical process involving phosphorus.

"The Wife"

October 25, 1987
Greenstone Falls Cabin
    I was here Thursday night (October 23). I never cease to marvel and be awestruck by the beauty of the Porkies. I had a great time here. I hiked to Mirror Lake 8-Bunk Cabin Friday. I changed into dry clothes and looked in my pack for my stocking cap. To my dismay, I didn't find it. Thinking back to earlier in the morning, I remembered seeing it last on the top bunk in this cabin. I surmised that I left it here. I was very disappointed since the hat was made for me by my sister as a Christmas present. A glimmer of hope shined, however, since I was hiking to the Little Carp River Cabin on Saturday and back up the Little Carp River to the South Boundary Road on Sunday. Since my trip would again bring me past this cabin, I would stop and check for my cap. To my delight, I found it hanging on a nail waiting for me to claim it. A special thanks to Dennis and Jon and whoever wrote the above log entry for leaving the cap behind when they left, so that it would be here when I returned. The thoughtfulness and honesty of people like them, here in the Porkies, makes the experience here even more unforgettable. Again, a hearty THANK YOU!

Dan D.

Unknown Date
Mirror Lake 4-Bunk Cabin

Unknown Artist

May 19, 1994
Section 17 Cabin

before the birth
of our nation,
my country, 'tis of this tree
i sing
so far beyond
my own birth or
the bite of the woodsman's axe

you are a survivor

of the great progress
that swept from sea to sea
i witness you
with awe and wonder
at what might have been,
touch the foot of your soil
and feel for
sweet forgiveness

Mark & Mary

August 24, 1973
Buckshot Cabin

A variety of weather and activity by old Superior has made the stay most delightful, relaxing, and good for the soul. We recommend the hike to Lone Rock on the trail and also a long hike along the beach to the left as you face the lake. It is possible to get out on some of the huge rocks that project out of the water a short distance off shore. While down that way yesterday, a bird with a good wing span flew past me over the water and landed on a fallen hemlock tree which projected out over the beach horizontally. It blended almost perfectly with the dry, green-gray moss on the tree. I called Mark, who was skipping rocks on the water, and we moved slowly to see if we could get a closer look. The bird was sleeping, but opened its eye to us several times as we inched closer, and it never moved. I was no more than twelve to eighteen inches from it, and I put my hand on the tree and moved it slightly. It looked at me and closed its eye again. I believe it was one of the nocturnal birds; very short beaked, head like a dove, short, compact body, tail and wing feathers merged and fairly long, dull brown and white in a small pattern. While flying it had graceful movement, like a gull, and I noted some red on the wings which was hidden as it sat on the tree.

Clint S.

July 1, 1992
Lily Pond Cabin

Last night was unlike the night before when, after midnight, we watched the Aurora Borealis blaze in the northern sky. The frog rhythm was grooving 'til dawn and beyond (Joanne thought they sounded like distant Native American tom-toms). At dawn, a huge mist rose from beyond the pond and we paddled out to fish. I caught two brook trout. I am always excited by the prospect of trout fishing. Probably because trout are only caught in pure, pristine places like this. Trout don't suffer pollution or stagnation well. There are trout here, but there aren't many places like this left. Perhaps next time I'll pack my snorkel and wet suit and do my trout fishing with a camera.

The parade of wildlife was impressive yesterday. We saw two bitterns nesting on the bog on the south side of the pond. One sat crouched like a grumpy, brown penguin and the other waited with an outstretched neck and blazing yellow eye. It must be a hazardous business to be a frog in this pond. We saw a garter snake whipping through the pond, too, looking for a nice, froggy meal. At midday, we spotted a female merganser with her punk-red haircut swimming up the stream. Trying to stay on board her back was her youngster, a fuzzy ball of gray and white. Mother climbed the beaver dam and started fishing in the pond. She dove headlong into the lilies leaving fuzz ball on the surface. When she came up, a few meters away, the duckling scrambled across the top of the lilies and up on her back again.

Tom L.

September 15, 1981
Big Carp 4-Bunk Cabin

For two long years I have dreamt of returning to this cabin. I have lain awake at night in my small metropolitan apartment and concentrated on the sights, sounds, and smells I enjoyed here in the fall of 1979. My dream went something like this:

After a long day of hiking through miles of virgin stands of timber and unspoiled waterfalls, we spot the tiny brown cabin nestled into the hillside. The sound of spring water rushing over molded rocks grows nearer, and is rivaled only by the sound of the mighty Lake Superior slapping its shore. Our feet and legs joyfully ache, a constant reminder of the miles of breathtaking scenery we have enjoyed. As the path between ourselves and the cabin shortens, the aroma of a small black and white animal arouses our olfactory senses. The intense animal lovers we are, we cross our fingers and hope that the little critter was only passing through and is long gone on his merry way.

Once within the cabin, we fight off the enticing invitation from bunks, and set to work chopping wood. Supper cooked and literally inhaled, couldn't have been more appreciated. As the evening creeps through the woods and reaches our cabin, we sit warm and content. The wood stove contains the blazing fire that warms the air and fills the room with the unforgettable scent of burning birch and pine. Ever so gradually we drift off, snuggled warm in our sleeping bags. Every crackle of the fire seems to put an added weight on our eyelids. And then peaceful sleep.

In a blink, it seems, the tiny room is filled with the soft rays of morning light, the only alarm clock to be found is the gentle sound of the birds and small animals starting their busy day. Suddenly we realize that, although cozy and warm in our sleeping bags, the room is filled with the remaining, brisk evening air. Snuggling deeper into the warmth of our sleeping bags we remember the vast beauties of nature that await us. The excitement of a new day suddenly fills our hearts, and unhesitatingly we arise to meet the riches of nature that await us.

So there you have my dream, a combination of memories and anticipation. I am here to tell you now, that upon returning to the Porkies, I have not been disappointed. And I can assure you that my dreams have only been enriched. The only thing I hope to change is that I return in less time than two years.

I wish at this time to take the opportunity to thank the state of Michigan and all the workers who have labored to preserve the beauty of this area and make it accessible to tenderfoots such as I. The joy and rejuvenation areas such as this bring to me and others, allows us to return to our meager missions in life with renewed energy and enthusiasm. I also wish to ask all who enter here to please consider the long term preservation of such an area every time you are tempted to toss your garbage behind the cabin or flick your cigarette into the woods. Thank you.

Sandy

September 16, 1981
Big Carp 4-Bunk Cabin

Today we are blessed with the glories of yet another of nature's wonders. Rain. I must say though, it gave not only the greenery and waters a period of rejuvenation, but us as well. After three days of hiking, our poor city bodies needed the rest. We spent the day playing with the fish, or shall I say they spent the day playing with us. Watching the determined trout swim upstream was an unprecedented event for me. However, I must add, that being able to see these wondrous creatures swim by, around, under, and over my bait was beyond my frustration point. Soon I gave up the traditional rod, reel, hook, and sinker, and went for strictly man (woman) against beast. Perched on the edge of peninsula rock, sleeves rolled, I sat ready to pounce. You guessed it! Bare hands! I have since come to know and appreciate the true playfulness and extreme intelligence of this aquatic life called rainbow trout. My first attack marked partial victory for womankind. As the carefree trout pranced in the water at my feet, I'm certain they chuckled at the towering 5'5" frizzy-haired creature above. Yet with one quick swoop I tackled the tail fin of one of their ranks. It was glorious, yet I fear as much a surprise to myself as to the trout at my feet. I could not bring myself to yank the being from its habitat and soon (about two seconds) he escaped to freedom. By this time, my gilled friends realized my intent and the tension grew, but not their playfulness. As I sat motionless, ever so gradually did they venture in my direction. Darting occasionally within my reach, they would test my quickness and tempt me to reach further and further over the icy waters. Their goal, you see, was to lure me into an unexpected bath.

My second attack also met with some success. My hand was quick enough to touch the slippery surface of one's shining side. However, my fingers neglected to complete the grasp, another unsuccessful attack.

From this point on, I must admit I continually lost ground, or shall I say water. With each failure I became more determined, with each attempt failure became more evident. After six trials, about forty-five minutes, the cold-blooded creatures won out, if only for the reason that it grew too dark and too cold for me to continue playing. Even though canned corn beef is no match for fresh trout, I must admit I feel like a winner. You see, at least I tried, and I gained. I just hope it doesn't turn into pneumonia!!

Sandy

January 5, 1994
Union River Cabin

I tried to recall, this time, the number of times I have come back to the Porkies. As my age approaches the half-century mark, my memory is beginning to fail me. Thoreau's words are more meaningful to me as my time lessons. It is the little things that I search out now; the marks of others, some inspired, some misled by their own delusions. Their successes and failures teach me, remind me, that the greatest inspiration can come from a solitary chickadee who came to the cabin yesterday, gentle and unafraid. Having lived its life of perhaps two years within a square mile of this cabin door, it knows more than I shall hope to know in my remaining time. Its racial memory contains all of the miners, loggers, fortune seekers, the natives, and perhaps, even the melting of the great ice.

Dave P.

October 29, 1987
Little Carp Cabin

Walked east along Lake Superior Trail from the Little Carp River....

Saw a pair of snow buntings, their colors almost completely changed from summer brown to winter white. Also, a small red squirrel....

We then turned south along the west bank of the Big Carp River, heading for Shining Cloud Falls where we would stop for lunch.

About two hundred yards in, we crossed over to the east bank—a tricky crossing over huge fallen tree trunks. We saw where the ground slid away taking with it these mammoths—a red cut along an otherwise steep, but green, bank.

An uphill walk, gradually gaining elevation. Saw many small falls during the hike, water pouring over these stairs of rock. No critters or birds spotted.

We finally arrived at Shining Cloud Falls. We heard the water before we saw it. Walked out onto a point of rock where a hollow-trunked, but still viable and green, hemlock stood, strong still, though its major parts were exposed....

I've neglected to describe the falls-deliberately—I don't have the words. They are beautiful and powerful and majestic. Make the uphill hike—it's worth every step....

On the way back, now northbound and downhill, I spotted an eagle circling high, away from the river. We also saw fresh deer tracks along the east bank. Probably a small doe by the size of the tracks. She walked down to the water for a drink and then faded away into the forest....

Headed west along the Superior Trail. About halfway, we again saw small deer tracks in the mud on the trail, but no sight of the deer.

A little further along, we spotted fresh wolf tracks in the mud-three pads in front and none in rear and claw marks out from the pads. These tracks had not been there on our way out.

At the mouth of the Little Carp, we watched a downy woodpecker flit from tree to tree, looking for food. Walked down to the water's edge and watched three King salmon lurk in the shadows. One was still, dying where he was born. The other two were splashing along, looking for food.

Unknown Author

June 11, 1975
Section 17 Cabin

Mike says it really isn't raining outside. It's just slightly dripping off the trees. Anticipated locking him outside the cabin to see if he gets just slightly wet.

Doug F.

July 15, 1969
Mirror Lake 4-Bunk Cabin

This space between and around these cabins could be called "Orchid Valley." Found two species of wild orchid: moccasin flowers are very plentiful but are almost gone; also found one rattlesnake plantain, also a wild orchid.

Jack D.

October 21, 1992
Big Carp 6-Bunk Cabin

There is an otter living in the river. He swims through the pond a few times a day. Must have at least twenty pictures of him by now. He doesn't seem to be real afraid of people, he just seems to be in a hurry to go play somewhere else. He went out to Lake Superior one day and was body surfing. What a life.

Lee, Holly, Jeff, & Blondie B.

June 27, 1997
Gitchee Gumee Cabin

How to be...
I am rooted,
strong
expanding
beautiful
ever changing
I move with the wind.
I see everything.
I face the sun.
I face the storm
...and still
I am standing tall,
growing.

Kelly B.

May 25-28, 1979
Lily Pond Cabin
There's a new lodge across the pond that wasn't there last year. Both seem active and we've seen at least four beavers, one of them quite small. It's fun watching these hairy cigars cruise downstream at dusk for their nightly feeding run, and if you can brave the damp evening air and sit motionless on the bridge for awhile, they'll swim right under you. The larger ones are probably the same as resided here last year, for they show little fear of quiet humans. The small one is skittish, however, and will retreat in fright from the least movement or sound.

Unknown Author

July 5, 1967
Speaker's Cabin
The area around here is wonderful for bird watching, especially for the warblers which are nesting in profusion. Down Chicago way, we just see

them travel through for a week to ten days each year. The trick is to find a Canadian warbler next to his nest. He will give you all kinds of "what for" and in doing so, he will arouse the curiosity of the warbler population in the entire township. One needs only to scan the surrounding trees and one sees all kinds of birds flitting hither and yon to see what the commotion is all about. One day I saw at least eight kinds of warblers in a one hour search behind the cabin on the hill. There included the beautiful blackburnian, prothonotany, and chestnut-sided in addition to the Tennessee and the black and white. That's five. I'm not perfect, so I couldn't identify the others. My binoculars couldn't penetrate the foliage. Oh well, the excuse sounds good. Rough-winged and black swallows fly around this cabin all day, and in the evening, the "flying cigar" or chimney swift, are everywhere. They had me fooled for some time because whose chimney are they living in? But they've got to be swifts. Last evening, a whole colony of cedar waxwings were on the bluffs west of the cabin. They've got to be the sleekest bird around. Song sparrows are numerous in the area too. Why, I even saw two robins. Those bald eagles are the memorable sight.

Allan & Judy H.

September 26-28, 1990
Lake Superior Cabin

We took in a beautiful sunset. It's been a long time since I've been able to watch the sun actually go down over the horizon. The clouds took on the shape of a huge bird that seemed to carry the fiery sun in its talons.

Jamie, Tina, & "Jay"

October 9-10, 1987
Greenstone Falls Cabin

Ten years ago, three of us "young adventurers" started making the trip to the UP every October to take some photographs of the fall colors. This year, we did something special and came to this cabin rather than the usual motel routine at Copper Harbor. The experience has been great! Not being a camper, I was up two hours before dawn and ready to go. Can you believe the other two guys complained about this to no end. They told me to go back to sleep, but frankly, the combination of their snoring would make most jackhammers sound quiet. Sleep was out of the question. I sat in the dark until dawn. We hiked to the "big pond" via Little Carp River Trail and back the Cross Trail. About thirteen miles, I guess. Cross Trail is rather muddy in spots. If you go the same route, start early and travel light. Back to Illinois tomorrow, so I'd better get some sleep before the buzz saws start.

Mark

Yes, I am a snorer. I admit that freely. Mark can make a pretty good imitation of a buzz saw, too. Domestic squabbles aside, I did enjoy our days in the park. Some advice: remove all the ashes from the stove before you light the fire. It will make more heat. I hope to return next year.

Michael

I don't snore. The other guys only said I did because they sound like unmuffled diesels. This park is great. Good scenery, good company, good times. We hiked the Little Carp River Trail today. It was beautiful with lots of river crossings. We met four people from the next cabin down. Since we are all married men, I am not supposed to say four lovely young women. Well, we are leaving tomorrow morning so I had better get some sleep. Sleep can be difficult because Mark likes to play with the fire at 3:00 A.M. It is only 9:00 P.M. and he already has it up to about ninety degrees in here. I hope you enjoy your stay as much as we did. We're coming back next year, I hope.

We tried to leave the place in as good a condition as we found it, which was excellent. By the way, we have not seen the terrible ghost that inhabits this place. He probably was scared away by Mark's snoring.

Mike

1963
Lily Pond Cabin

Lily Pond at Dusk and Dawn

Willows wave at sundown
Water lilies fold
Feathered ones wing to rest

Chirping, twinkling, sparkling
Rosy mist surrounds
Creature stir, dawn awakens

Judith D

June 8, 1971
Buckshot Cabin

On the way back...my trail companion and I took it slow and quiet, looking at and trying to identify various trail plants and insects. We ran across the path of a mother ruffled grouse and her chicks. She was ready to cross the path with her family when we stepped into it. She puffed up and started to walk in the woods in a haphazard way, making noises and looking around. She hopped around quite a lot, looking (I suppose) as fierce as she could, but actually she was charming and beautiful to watch. We stood quite still and watched with held breath.... After a long while of this, she headed again towards the path, brushing against my partner's leg as she passed in back of us. Only after she returned to her original side of the path did she call for her chicks, which were hidden under plants. Then the whole brood, Mama leading, went scurrying into the forest. After only a few moments, she was gone. I'm sure we would have missed all of this if we hadn't frozen to the spot. This made the path seem...more part of the forest. Lightly traveled by man, but frequented by the animals of the forest.

Gloria M.

June 14, 1977
Section 17 Cabin
There were four campers here but we got them!!!

"The Mosquitoes"

June 27, 1980
Mirror Lake 4-Bunk Cabin
I believe that the snake that lives around the cabin caught a chipmunk last night. On and off for what seemed an hour, the chipmunk screamed and screamed and then ended in a whimper. I have seen how a snake slowly pulls an animal into its mouth, resting after each thrust forward, and I believe the cry happened after each swallow. Nature's horror for its inhabitants is masked by its beauty. The never ending food chain must be completed as we bask in the serenity of the wilderness.

Carol H.

October 15, 1994
Whitetail Cabin
We...spent a lot of time just sitting on the rock on the shore, watching for nothing in particular and listening to the water lap on the shore. We saw an eagle on the first day, perched on top of a tree located on the point to the west. On the second day, we saw an eagle (or the same one) drift across in front of us then lock his wings and perch in a hemlock east of the point. Then suddenly he was on wing, speeding out over the lake. He was heading to a lone seagull, came upon it, and then the air battle and chase began. Tremendous flying by both the eagle and the gull, but the more maneuverable gull successfully dodged the eagle's attacks, and the eagle finally broke off and headed back to the point. Saw him again on the third day when the wind was building out of the northeast. He dashed out a few times from the point and plucked a fish from the water.

Don & Leny W.

September 30, 1975
Little Carp Cabin
   Autumn colors were lovely—though fewer reds than we had expected at this time of year. The yellows against the azure sky were marvelous—and sunsets over the lake, viewed from the mouth of the Little Carp River, are my idea of heaven. Weather was spectacular—cloudless blueness—and rich, starry nights. Alas, a waning moon, but one can hardly have everything.
   As a city person, I value beyond words the peace and stillness of these woods. Lake Superior has the majesty of an ocean-though I've yet to see its temperament fully aroused. Four nights are long enough to get a sense of the daily feel of such a life; but not enough to really appreciate the more arduous aspects of maintaining oneself in the North Woods. Some time? I need to spend longer, possibly mush longer. But this was sweet, and the feeling of a whetted appetite is not an unpleasant one to leave with.

Jim & Linda

September 25, 1991
Buckshot Cabin
   The night has fallen and we three hikers...prepare to take our rest. It's been a terrific day with numerous "landmarks" to recall since we left Union Bay this morning. Our first hour included a stop at Summit Peak lookout tower. A beautiful path led us to Mirror Lake and then on toward Lake of the Clouds by the northerly route. The path was generally muddy, but all in all, not bad considering the heavy rain yesterday. Before reaching the Lake of the Clouds footbridge, we were treated to a cascading stream off to the west of the path, resplendent with young falls and bubbling commentary. The canopy of trees created a cocoon with the leaf-covered underbrush and runs of baby maples by the thousands. The air was still and moist and spoke to us of our fortune to be part of an ageless wonder.

K.R.

June 17-19, 1989
Mirror Lake 2-Bunk Cabin
   There was a moment this evening at the place where the canoe is docked, in between showers, where it had cleared enough to allow a towering formation of cumulus clouds over the eastern horizon beyond the lake to be colored pink by the setting sun. To the north, there were more clouds, also bright pink, but lighter and wispier in shape and texture. Then, all around, the purplish-blue of the overcast cloud cover, higher up. Streams of mist began to rise up over the waters of the lake. At that moment, it seemed as if it would be possible to take that canoe out from the shore past the high grass and reeds towards

the distant, wooded shore and mountains beyond into paradise—but it was only a moment.

Kim

June 24, 1989
Lily Pond Cabin
Remember when you were a kid and you were watching the Wizard of Oz? And when it got to that one real scary part where you always had to cover your eyes? Remember that's where those awful creatures came blasting through the skies out of nowhere? And when the awful winged creatures scooped down to swoop up Dorothy and Toto, too?! Ever wonder what happened to those scary winged creatures? Well, sit still. Listen. Hear buzzing. See them land. Swat! Splat (if you're lucky)! That is what has become of those creatures. Only they've renamed them. Mosquitoes, I believe.

Seriously, what a lovely place to enjoy the creation. The balance of nature is so perfect and precise that I sometimes feel like an invader. How much I respect the wisdom of its creator! Good company. Good relaxation. Good laughs. Good exercise. Good food. Good times.

Cindy W.

June 26, 1996
Big Carp 4-Bunk Cabin

Thoughts by a Stream

There are no mirrors in this cabin,
Because to see oneself, a mirror is not necessary.
There are no phones,
Because to truly contact takes much more.

There are streams;
I think they tell me my life goes on.
And the woods, vast and full,
As life should be.

And with this place
Inside of me,
Maybe I will be.

John

August 10, 1974
Little Carp Cabin

I spotted some very interesting plants on the Pinkerton Trail coming in. They were very white and about two to four inches tall. As I remember, they're called Indian pipes. They are protected in Michigan because they are becoming rare. They are white because they're saprophytic—they live off the organic material of dead plants. They don't have chlorophyll to utilize sunlight for that reason. Nifty, huh!

Kathy C.

April 6-8, 1996
Speaker's Cabin

Man, this has been a lean winter with all this snow!
Hal just kicked the bucket yesterday!

Here's some salt and pepper for
    your carrots,
    Doris.

Kathy M.

June 7, 1994
Gitchee Gumee Cabin

As we got ready for dinner (fresh brook and brown trout), I caught sight of movement south of the cabin. A red fox came onto the trail at the first hemlock and headed up the trail. I yelled for my six year old son, but he got outside too late. Ten minutes later as we ate inside, the fox passed by behind the outhouse and stopped thirty yards north at the end of a log. He had something in his mouth and we got to watch him bury it. Our whole family watched, then the fox headed back south. I've hunted and trapped all my life and I've never seen a fox bury his fresh kill, though trapping, I've used a similar technique to simulate this with rotten meat. I led the family out and with sticks we uncovered the kill. It was a medium-well done hamburger. No odor yet, so fairly fresh. We laughed and replaced the burger to rot. What an experience! But ten minutes later, we were treated to an encore as he returned for a third time, carrying something white, again from the south. I managed to get out the door before he could see me and got pictures of him as he dug up his burger and left. Why he had a second thought about the burger is beyond me. He certainly had less fear of us than the foxes I normally come in contact with. He didn't look at all sick. Very alert. Stopped him dead the first time the shutter clicked.

Unknown Author

June 14-15, 1968
Section 17 Cabin

As I write, I am listening to the song of the winter wren through the open window. This tiny bird, much smaller than the common house wren of our cities and towns, can pour forth an amazing quality and quantity and variety of music; a series of very fine, lovely, high-pitched trills.

Allen R.

July 21, 1986
Big Carp 6-Bunk Cabin

It was great weather and a great crew; a good chance for all to grow physically and spiritually. Some peak experiences—the refreshing water, three glorious sunsets, blazing campfires, cutting wood, full moon at midnight turning the river silver, warm breezes, and always the rushing water of the river and ceaseless waves. All the rocks tossed into Superior raised the level a foot. We were treated to a marvelous, flashing, crashing storm with a downpour this A.M. Freshened things up a bit. Well, we're going, but you never really leave a place you love—part of it you take with you, leaving a part of you behind.

Jean

May 11, 1975
Buckshot Cabin

We went to Lake of the Clouds yesterday, swam naked in the water, sat in the silence of the hemlocks. The hemlock is such a tree. Lie on your back and take a look. The trunk and limbs, the "body" of the tree, is heavy, real, earthlike. The limbs, however, support the lightest, most delicate statement of joy and peace I have seen. The foliage is dreamy and lace-like, stirring in the forest voices. It is almost as if it is the spirit of the tree, made visible, showing at the same time its permanence, its attachment to the earth and its desire to be away, flying and free.

Unknown Author

May 8-9, 1988
Lily Pond Cabin
I've never appreciated the spring colors more than in the Porcupine Mountains. Even as I was growing up, I noticed the budding trees and shrubs in southern Wisconsin, but the mass of color which is possible with such an event never appealed to me more than this weekend. It is certainly different than fall colors, but I think it is equally impressive.

Eric & Caroline

June 30, 1974
Mirror Lake 4-Bunk Cabin
Our whole self gets bathed and refreshed with the beauty and cleanliness of this place—truly, it isn't only what our eyes enjoy but the smells and scents —aren't they terrific? How long since you rememorized Longfellow's "This is the forest primeval, with its murmuring pines and its hemlocks," from Evangeline? That poem takes on new meaning when one gazes at these huge hemlocks and pines. And then there is our hearing—the birds sing in a perfect symphony or concert, the wind makes gorgeous music as it blows through the evergreens and leaved-trees, and during the night, the great horned owl "owled and owled" and sometimes its call echoed three times across the lake…. I listened at the open window near the stove and enjoyed the gorgeous moonlight shining through the trees and the lake was a dream and the owl music was terrific!

Unknown Author

July 15, 1990
Mirror Lake 8-Bunk Cabin
Reflections on Mirror Lake
The boat glides effortlessly across the mirrored surface, oars making small, creaking sounds as I move along the shore. The only sounds now are the mechanical "whirring" of my reel as it slowly retrieves my lures, and a few birds whose names I do not know. At times, when the birds are quiet, I stop my reel, and a peaceful silence descends. Stillness. Solitude. Nothing and yet everything is there, and for a fleeting moment I sense something of the essence of life. Of smoke wafting across the lake from a campfire where friends are waiting. Of a golden retriever who steadily follows me along the shore, always watching me, unaware that his movement through the reeds scares fish away and annoys me. He watches me, ever moving, following.

Maybe dogs actually are man's best friend. Faithful, forgiving, not scared. A good friend to be valued and always welcome.

Of candlelight on glowing faces, catching smiles that are like no other. Of good food, good drinks, laughter, and telling of stories. Of a gentle peace. Satisfying tiredness. Sweet slumber.

Unknown Author

October 8, 1994
Union River Cabin

I really love these hemlocks. Very spiritual trees. There's a big one, one hundred and fifty yards down the river on the south bank. It curls fairly straight away from the bank, then heads gloriously straight up for the light. That one's spirit is reminding me to keep forth through the twists and turns, towards the light. The tree (and me and you) then blooms out in a massive manifestation; thick branches, leaves (needles), knowing which way to turn. Always with growth. Thicker each year, stronger the branches are.

Unknown Author

July 14, 1973
Little Carp Cabin

Sad Water and Silly Juice

The water has a lonely sound
so far and different from the shore
The land has all its treasure shown
but the lake treasures are out of sight
just this mood for a minute longer
and now you're back on land
The birds talking and wind blowing
so much happier than the Lake
The land in its silly, busy way
and the Lake at its constant part in this play
It's sad how it's held prisoner by the land,
How hard it tries to get out,
and the land stands firm
and pushes it back.

Unknown Author

June 10, 1974
Big Carp 4-Bunk Cabin

Most days start very differently for a wide variety of people. The business man awakens to his radio alarm clock, stunned by the loudness of the morning news, his lovely housewife trying hard to keep it together making the young children's breakfast. Ah, but morning to the great outdoorsman is filled with the excitement of the unknown, but the knowledge that whatever the day brings will be something that will be remembered for the time to come.

Today was one such day for this part-time woodsman. My companion, John, and I awoke in the Union campground to the rather disheartening sound of heavy rain. It's not that I don't like rain, but not when you intend on backpacking the same day. As a matter of factual information, it has been raining for two days running. We decided against tenting for the night and asked the lovely receptionist at park headquarters if there was any room in the inn. Well, Big Carp Cabin was the last one and we took it. The drive down Boundary Road was wet, and it didn't exactly increase our morale. Arriving at the access point to Pinkerton Trail, we lightened our packs, as the cabin would provide shelter and comfort, something to strive for. Starting down the pathway with our ever-constant companion, rain, we were truly held in admiration at the beauty of the mostly virgin woods. The pathway was at times flooded in small pockets, but what do you want with water coming from the sky? Our first real challenge from Nature for the day came from Pinkerton Creek, or as should have been called, Pinkerton River. Not having been here before, we were quite puzzled to see the trail run into this raging torrent, with no visible means of fording it. Taking hold of the situation with a firm mind, we decided to separate and each go a different way to seek some means of crossing the creek. I went upstream, and after two hundred or so yards, I came upon a tree that was fallen completely across the raging water. (As a matter of reference, I've had to ford streams in the Sierras before, but you wouldn't catch me trying to wade across that creek today!) Eager to relay the finding, I went back to the trail where I had agreed to meet John after ten minutes of scouting. Downstream, he didn't see any means of crossing, so we walked up to the tree I had found. Since it was my find, I was the first to go. I unhooked my waist belt in preparation, if by chance I fell, I could easily free myself of the bulky pack. Edging my way out slowly, with the log hugged firmly between my legs, I looked towards the other side with hard determination, and finally made it across. In my concentration on the log crossing, I failed to notice that John had gone upstream even farther and found another log that he was able to walk across, and just as I was walking up the bank, he was waiting. With the knowledge of what a creek had turned into after the heavy rains, we were wondering what the Little Carp River was going to be like. Another hour of hiking soon answered our questioning thoughts. The Little Carp was extremely large and swift. Once again, the trail ran right into the water with no visible means of crossing. This time we both went in search of a way across upstream, as downstream was Lake Superior, and that speaks for itself.

We came upon a log that looked like it was intended to bridge the river, but it was completely submerged in the swift current. We decided to try and wade across at the mouth, but about three feet into the current and water well over the knees, the river proved too strong. Now being quite wet, in fact just down-right soaked, we agreed that we must reach the cabin and the river would not stop us. Starting back upstream, we figured that at some point it would be fordable. After what I figured was a good, honest mile of following the river, we caught sight of a log that looked as though it was completely across. Closer examination showed that it indeed did, but the water was really rushing underneath the log, with whitewater jetting hurriedly over at the far end. It would be tricky, but it was the only feasible way across we had seen. Once again, I struck out across first, being sure to untie my waist belt. I had to crawl across on my hands and knees, as the log was a little on the narrow side and very wet and slippery. Besides, if you put your legs down two inches below the log, they would be flapping in the current. My eyes trained with their corrective lenses right on the portion of the log directly in front of me, I put out of my mind all other thoughts except getting to the other side. Well, I made it, and just to make John's crossing a little fun, he stopped about halfway out to pose for his picture to be taken. Once on the east side of the river, we replenished our body energy with some M&M's and picked up the Little Carp Trail about twenty yards into the woods. Upon reaching the lake, we made a right onto the Superior Trail and rejoined at the sign which said, "Mouth of Big Carp River—1/2 mile." Bull! It has got to be at least a mile. Well, all the way up the trail all we could think about was that the cabin was dry and hopefully some wood would be too…The Superior Trail was, in numerous spots, completely underwater in depths that varied. Already soaked, John and I just walked right through every puddle. We sighted a cabin and hurriedly walked up to it only to see the sign: "Ranger Cabin." Thinking this was a trick to fool the bears, I tried to open the lock with the key I had. It proved to no avail. Then we saw the green cabin on the OTHER SIDE of the river. Needless to say, my spirits were not at their peak when viewing that sight. John hastily pointed to a cabin to his extreme right and on THIS side of the river. Well, that was it, no matter if it was or not. I was to that point. As we went up the trail, we noticed smoke coming out of the chimney and wondered who could be in our cabin, after all, we laid down six dollars to get it. Well a knock on the door proved to be the key to my question. Inside was a detachment of seven explorer scouts with three dutifully bound leaders. Bill, the first leader to confront us, told it like it was. The river, Big Carp, had flooded so bad during the night and that day that the footbridge was completely submerged and half washed away. In fact, Dick, another leader, was sleeping in his tent near the river, and the river flooded over and raged right through his tent, setting him afloat atop his air mattress inside the tent. I feel he was quite lucky. Bill continued and asked how we made it across the Little Carp. He was sure it was as bad as the river right outside. So we related to him that his thoughts were well confirmed and told him our experiences. I had utmost faith in these explorer scouts who were watching us drip water all over the floor, but crossing the Little Carp and even the Pinkerton Creek was not advisable. They said they would leave, as the cabin was rightfully ours, but if they left and even did cross the waters, they would be running into dark, not a healthy thing to do in the woods. We came to an agreement that John and I would get a bunk and they would fill up the floor. Fair enough. All ten of them are very nice, and I'm happy to have been in the same cabin with them.

Most days are different from each other, and gladly so. This one even more so. But I'm just glad to be here, completely surrounded by nature.

John M.

Unknown Date
Big Carp 4-Bunk Cabin

Carl B.

October 2, 1981
Section 17 Cabin

This is my tenth year at the Porkies. I walked these trails years before I started my family four years ago. This is probably the closest thing we Midwesterners have to the Appalachians of the East and the Rockies or the Sierras of the West and far West. I have walked all ninety plus miles of the Porkies over the years except a couple of short, minor trails, such as part of Lost Lake and the east end of Union Spring. By far, the best overall scenery is the Escarpment Trail with the most interesting, at least for youngsters, being the Little Carp River Trail. But again, each trail offers something different to all of us and we each have our preferences. All in all though, the Porkies are fantastic, and based on the care given to the cabins, shelters, and camp sites by most of the backpackers and day hikers, these "mountains" should remain great for many years to come.

Dennis M.

June 28, 1984
Lily Pond Cabin

The stand of virgin white pine towards Mirror Lake have to be seen. They are unbelievable. To see something this gigantic that has survived all attempts to knock down makes me feel there is some stability on this earth.

Ann, Dave, Nancy, & John

October, 1975
Little Carp Cabin

October

They battled the current against rock and now,
what little fight is left in them,
remains to be seen

Instinct was the power, the strength born unto
the fish given to lead them from the big
waters to search to their spawning grounds

Their search carries them on a desperate journey
to inland streams, homeland waters, or the place
of their birth a year ago

Here the battle of their existence now takes its toll,
leaving the surviving parent fish heavy with
the burden of exhaustion and death, to rest

in the shallow stream's water facing the
steady oncoming current;
which will either soothe or recover the
creatures, helpless, battered and worn

They lie there with open wounds revealing a
quest of hardship which for many meets
with death, leaving the strongest
as the few chosen for next years mating and breed

These few suffering their pain to swim waters
of tomorrow lie now so very still,
beneath the cool, shallow, sunlit waters
of their own birth place

An occasional circled motion or weakened
fan of the tail uncovers the unquenchable
thirst for life and total absence of despair,
these simple creatures of the water
possess throughout their life's time

Renee

October 7, 1997
Buckshot Cabin
The tree change is at its prime and I've never seen it this good before.
The colors are simply magnificent. Once in a while you get lucky and the Por-
kies give you their best.

There is a Canadian goose wandering around outside and he (or she)
seems pretty tame. We get the feeling she (or he) might be injured and can't
fly. There is no other reason for a wild bird like that to be hanging around here
when the rest of the geese are heading south. It's obvious the she'll never
make it once the snows hit the mountains. Nature has strange ways of dealing
with its own. When we hiked here last fall, we couldn't believe all the car-
casses we saw along the trails from the deer that succumbed to the deep, deep
snow that fell that winter.

Kevin & Chris H.

August 17, 1985
Lake Superior Cabin
This morning's traditional bath took place on a grey morning, grey-slate
water...warmed afterwards in a grey sweater—all tinged in bluish white. The
description is not a melancholy one, but rather, serene. Our days here have

been restful, full of physical exercise, but restful to overloaded minds having run in high gear for some time. My body is relaxed, my mind is clear, uncluttered by high paced urban schedules. Ahh!

The high that I feel is a balance of body and spirit....Usually only achievable on a quiet mountain in North Carolina where I first felt myself a whole person....This time it is nice to share with my good friend, love, and the Clown Dog.

Cheryl, Dano, & "Clown"

August 23, 1969
Mirror Lake 4-Bunk Cabin
The fishing record!! Sixty-nine trout. Believe it or not. All brookies and rainbows and most under ten inches. Nothing over twelve inches. We had one run in with Rainbow Sam, an eighteen inch rainbow, who is still in the lake after a close call.

Jeff K.

October 13, 1987
Big Carp 6-Bunk Cabin
We've had three beautiful days. Each day a little warmer. Incredible sunsets. Two nights of colors cascading against each other, then last night, a more gentle blending-soft, lullaby colors. The last time I was up here, in October two years ago, I was mourning a recent death and still letting go of an older one. Autumn was difficult for me. It just seemed so much dying, ending, that I didn't want to admit: leaves turning, falling; trees fallen, turning to humus, to earth. Yet at the same time it was healing. For here there is such a sense of generations and regeneration, of the fallen tree creating ground for the next growth.

This year, this brisk autumn, the land has seemed all a richness and celebration.

Sara

July 21, 1974
Little Carp Cabin
This is our last day here. We pack out tomorrow morning. We're ready, after a week of primitive living, for the conveniences of the outside, but we are very sad to be leaving. It's rigorous living here, but it is so simple compared to the stresses of modern life.

Yesterday we hiked up the Little Carp River Trail. It's the most beautiful hike in the park, I feel. The trees back there are so old and big as to defy comprehension. We've never seen white pine as large as those back there. I'd love to climb one. What a view the birds must have from the top.

67

We hiked back about two miles and saw no sign of an eagle's nest. Saw an old white pine blown down (immense!) and broken up which could have been the one mentioned earlier in the log. But we did see an immature bald eagle soar over very high, headed for the lake. It was a rich brown, almost auburn, in the sunlight against a cloudless, outer space blue. We have now seen five eagles between us in the past several years, three of which were immature, which is heartening. It leaves hope for the future to see young. Perhaps our children might see eagles flying free someday.

We stopped near the river and heard the woodlands singing. The combination of water, wind, and rustling of trees sounds, at times, like voices singing.

Saw a beautiful sunset over Lake Superior last night and later watched the stars in the jet black sky. Even small stars look brilliant up here....

It's now late at night, and we've just come up from the shore after our last sunset. It was weird. It quit raining and cleared some. The sun dropped below the clouds and shone a rich orange as it steamed into the horizon. Fog drifted out from the shore and enclosed all. A loon dove quietly offshore. The moon came out in a thin crescent and rode wisps of cloud across the sky. We wondered what joys and sorrows await us and mankind ere we return.

It's hard to think of profound thoughts and presume others care to read them. But this occurred to me as we felt the terrifying mystery of this holy place. No man can presume to understand God until he understands a place like this, and even should he claim to understand a place like this, he presumes a lot.

Work to preserve this place and always try to give more than you take in all that you do.

Our thanks to those who have worked to provide this place. You do an important job.

Steve & Paula M.

August 25, 1991
Buckshot Cabin

When I awoke in the morning after about an hour's snooze, the wind had quit and the trees stood quiet, demure, faintly smiling in the morning sun, as if they had not spent the night rocking and rolling to heavy wind, limbs twisting to its surges, yearning to be free of root, to go with the wind. Then the dawn, and the trees stand with not a leaf out of place, as if (getting) home before (being) caught....

Later on, we noticed another (eagle) fly into the trees by the cedars growing out of the rocks (look left as you approach the shore). Several times we saw this eagle fly out into the lake, beating his wings, as if he knew where he was going. Indeed, he swooped down knowingly, skirted the water, and at his moment, dropped his talons and pulled out a fish, never missing a beat. How's that for eye-talon coordination? We watched him or her do this several times-to our marvel....

This is a wonderful area to study rocks. Just a walk along the beach reveals much active geology over many years.

Leny & Don W.

June 3-7, 1986
Greenstone Falls Cabin

This is our first trip to the Porkies. Reading in the log about everyone's experiences with the bears, I was afraid of being attacked by one. Instead, Rick was attacked by a grouse. It had laid its eggs on the trail to Lily Pond and did not appreciate us hiking by its nest. Rick's boots held up well to the ferocious pecking.

Dottie & Rick C.

May 25, 1975
Section 17 Cabin

I love the freshness of this springtime forest. The violets are my very favorite; these yellow and white and purple flowers stand as a color guard along each path. The jack-in-the-pulpits stand erect just outside the cabin. The fragrance of the May flowers filters through the forest and refreshes us as we hike in and out of camp. And last of all, the river, oh, the springtime river, gushing and flowing, laughing and showing nature's beauty to all who pass by.

Roseann S.

October 12, 1985
Lake Superior Cabin

These are virgin woods, meaning the life cycle hasn't been completely disturbed.... The difference I noticed between this and other woods was the evidence of a life cycle. If you go in an area beyond the trails, the cycle is more obvious. Trees in every, and I mean every, stage of life and death. Hard to tell whether death comes before life. In fact, looks like life springs from death, witness the little trees growing in rows on a rotting, moss-covered tree trunk....

I can say that I truly enjoyed all the stages of tree life and death; the hills and the holes, the spongy, linear mound just barely discernible that yields a reddish fiber when kicked, less rotted specimens that are more layered than the stringy, more newly fallen trees, those leaning on their stronger and perhaps younger neighbors, some dead as the rotting logs on the ground, but still standing straight up so that you'd not notice unless you saw a funny, grayish powder around the base-the sawdust from some woodpeckers work, of course the towering "grandmas" and the aspiring adults in their prime (these trees so much taller than ones we normally see on city streets or in the woods that have been lumbered time and again), and the young of all ages and sizes right down to the hundreds that carpet this woods and that we can't help but stomp down as we walk.

Unknown Author

June 11, 1971
Little Carp Cabin

Now the sun has almost set...beautiful pink flames and wispy, light clouds in the sky off the point. Looking out the windows of the cabin you think of Robert Frost's poem: "The woods are lovely, dark and deep, but I have promises to keep, and miles to go before I sleep, and miles to go before I sleep." We, however, have no immediate promises or miles, so we must simply enjoy!

The L. Family

July 3, 1966
Section 17 Cabin

Got up last night to look for wildlife. Couldn't spot a thing. But found a trail of porcupine quills and a whole mess of them with the skeleton down by the river. Must have been some battle! Who eats porcupines?

The K. Family

February 9, 1994
Gitchee Gumee Cabin

Ravens are the smartest of all the birds. Their capability to visualize solutions surpasses that of their cousins, the crows. They have a very complex social structure and mate for life. They are noticeably larger than crows, up to fifty percent heavier. They fly with slightly down-turned wings. They have wedge shaped tails and have a ruff of feathers on the neck to help distinguish them from crows. Ravens are widespread globally, living in boreal forests, alpine regions, and in the desert, staying away from regions heavily populated by *Homo sapiens*. Ravens are revered by many peoples for their intelligence, longevity (up to sixty years old), and loyalty in mating for life. Two ravens sit at the shoulder of Odin in Viking cosmology. The Pacific Northwest Native Americans included ravens as one of their primary tribal totems.

Unknown Author

May 18, 1976
Little Carp Cabin
The ephemerals (wildflowers that come out before tree leaves arrive) are out, such beauties as trout lily (yellow flower with mottled leaves) and dutchman's breeches (white pantaloons on a stalk). Next year I'll have to bring along my North Woods wildflower books. The trilliums (white, large flowers with three petals) are just blooming—my annual sign of hope for mankind.

Heather T. & Jim D

June 22, 1972
Little Carp Cabin
The most fantastic sound is the sound of tree frogs at evening time. High pitched "beeps" around by the outhouse. Try standing in the middle of the "beeps" and it blows your mind.

The S. Family

June 10, 1974
Big Carp 4-Bunk Cabin
Well, I guess we're back in the Big Carp Cabin. My father was almost swept to his death in the rushing, roaring waters of the Big Carp River last night! He had sought refuge from the chaos of our cabin (we thought we should make our last night on the Big Carp a good one) and had decided to tent on our site of last night. He stayed in the four-man tent and blissfully slept until the wee hours, oblivious of the storm. Then, at the fateful hour of 6:29 A.M., the river broke its course, rushed around a giant rock, and came cascading right into his tent, sleeping bag, and even underwear. The tent immediately began frolicking gaily down the river towards Lake Superior at the average rate of ninety miles per hour, with my father still inside. He, aroused by the commotion, was madly freeing himself from the tent which grappled and stuck to him like a peanut butter cracker. Eyes bulging, he madly tore the tent off, gathered stakes, poles, nylon, sleeping bag, and one thong (the other was eaten by the hungry, brown torrent), and came up to the cabin at a gallop. His feet never even touched ground. His poundings and rantings on the door awoke one member of the party who immediately dove into his bag, thinking father was a bear. And there he cowered, shivering until we coaxed him out by offering him a bit of smoked sucker with garlic cheese. Anyway, when my father finally got in the cabin, he was warmly received and offered a steaming mug of hot chocolate, which unfortunately was not made yet! He then commenced stumbling about the cabin in his underwear mumbling gibberish to himself. We are stranded. STRANDED!

Isn't that exciting? It is all great fun. The world (where I live at least) has become so tame, I am in dire need of adventure, and this fulfills that wish. We are stuck here for at least another day and if the party scheduled for the cabin shows up, we will put up quite a fight. We will offer our services, sleep on the floor, cook the food, or ambush them. Anything to stay in the cabin and out of the chilly drizzle or downpour, depending on your point of view!

Lauren S.

May 21, 1982
Buckshot Cabin
When the days are cool...this place is full of wildflowers to appreciate. There are "meadows" of trillium, marsh marigold, trout lilies, and if you look hard, Jack-in-the-pulpit. Also, in the higher areas, wild columbine and wild strawberry. Instead of getting to a destination, every half hour of hiking we stop for a few minutes to look at nature closely. This area seems so ancient and permanent, but everyone should realize what a fragile balance there is between nature and its destruction.

Elizabeth & Michael

March 2, 1997
Whitetail Cabin

Seasonal Woods

Interior of Knotty Pine boards
Exterior of White Birch stand

Yellow Birch bleeds the snow yellow
Rustling leaves identify the Oak

Melted snow holes encircle each Tree
Nature's perfume breathes from Hemlocks

Winter Wren skirts, among branch bottoms
Deer runways meander through stark Forest

Ashes burn orange to gray

Crazy

September 22, 1986
Big Carp 6-Bunk Cabin
A morning walk, up, through river mist,
Air wet with moss, and earthy smells.
Time well spent at trail side,
For `neath loose bark salamanders dwell.

Unknown Author

September 9, 1987
Lake Superior Cabin
The forest was clean and shiny; the hike to Shining Cloud Falls is awesome through the virgin pine, the magical hemlock, the age-old moss—cov-

ered stones, the soft needle carpeting.... Two nights we feasted on the rainbow, lured from the dancing pools and eddies of the babbling Big Carp. The constant thunder of the Shining Big Sea Water keeps us lulled and hypnotized by the greatness of Nature.... We'll carry with us the memory of a time when we came together for a few brief moments of magic listening to the sounds of the Earth, and seeing how, even though our lives move on, that, for now, "this" remains.

Ginger S.

September 23-24, 1979
Lily Pond Cabin

At 8:10 P.M., the beaver dam in front of the bridge cracked and broke, sending a tidal wave down the creek. Within twenty minutes, five beavers were on the scene to examine the damage. They immediately began their emergency repair efforts, and by morning, the water level of the pond had dropped several feet. The beavers had constructed two new dams and repaired the old!

Dave & Betsy

August 28, 1972
Section 17 Cabin

I don't even know
the names of these greens
that sit on the arms
of this river so tame
or the moss that sheets
with a browning hue
the river-bands door
of the muskrat dam;
but I feel the swoop
of the sparrow's glide
as it catches winds
that comb the tree's crowns
and it folds my lips
in a cameo moon
that smiles so glad for
this place that I've found.

Bob S.

October 7, 1988
Little Carp Cabin

We saw the most spectacular sunset about one mile down the lake shore. Walked back at twilight and it's easy to see how Longfellow could have gotten his verse for Hiawatha. By the shores big sea water pounding, the park forest of hemlock silently witnessing as they have for thousands of years. This place seems quite magical, with beings living in the rocks, sea, trees, and earth, and all being animated to the same primeval song of the rapids.

L.M.

May 21, 1966
Mirror Lake 4-Bunk Cabin

Stone can crack, whose quicksilver will never wear off, whose gliding nature continually repairs; no storms, no dust, can dim its surface, ever fresh; a mirror.

John S.

July 26, 1976
Section 17 Cabin
Dear Log,

This is the most enchanted forest I've ever seen, probably because of its breadth and depth, and the magnificence of the stands of hemlock. The splendors of Section 17 remind me of a song I learned in Girl Scouts: "I saw a little log cabin with a river that flowed by its door, and I heard a voice within me shouting, "This is worth living for!"

Kathy B.

August 10, 1983
Big Carp 4-Bunk Cabin

Majestic Historians

Towering over the hillside,
Reaching up to touch the clouds,
What a story to tell if they could.
Every ring a page of history of God's creation
...Gnarled branches struggling against the elements,
Rugged bark tightly protecting...
Hungry roots reaching deeply into the dark soil beneath them.

Massive giants and yet gentle in their own way.
Cradling nests of baby birds in their loving branches.
Making a canopy of protection for wildlife beneath.

Watching over owls, squirrels, all the woodland creatures.
Even in death housing God's little animals.

Majestic historians, what song are your lacy
branches singing in the breeze?
Are you laughing at us oh-too-mortal-beings,
or smiling down on us?
We can watch for hours as your father
sun plays through your beautiful branches.
Will you help him to peek through to
the forest floor?
Let him find it and a seedling will one day
tower with you.
Don't change, majestic historians!
We are in awe of you and want to gaze
upon your beauty another year, when
we visit you again.

Karen F.

Gitchee Gumee: The Lake

September 26, 1988
Big Carp 4-Bunk Cabin

> A quest for the greatest of Great Lakes
> And here we are,
> Superior!
> You were good to us this time,
> Idyllic weather,
> A rain only in the night.
>
> But we know, oh yes we do,
> That we could easily have been
> The subjects of your
> Windblown banter,
> Your gusty laugh,
> Your haughty waves.
>
> You've taken many a man
> In your seas,
> And for those of us on land,
> We would have sheltered ourselves
> In meager tents and cabins
> From your fury and your energy,
> Should you have chosen to show it.
>
> Renie

June 7-8, 1968
Speaker's Cabin

Hi! Spirited Lake Superior has been angrily fierce since we arrived yesterday. I've felt for her. Sometimes my mood matches hers! All night we listened to her scoldings! What a temper! She's lashed out at everyone and doesn't spare a soul! She won't let me rock hunt. Oh, us! She whips me with a mean wave and I have to jump out of her way. I tried pretending I wasn't afraid and stood ankle deep looking for agates when she threw a nasty wave with rocks in it and hurt my ankles. She won!

M.M.

October 5, 1987
Lake Superior Cabin

James has this thing about storms, and wanted me to suit up in rain gear and all our warm clothes and go watch the giant waves crash on the shore. It's freezing out there and the winds just about to blow you away, but I agreed. We went out for about two hours — it was really scary. I've never seen Lake Superior like this. Huge whitecaps for miles of giant waves. The shoreline we walked down only yesterday has disappeared. The water has reached the tree line of the woods. Very awesome and powerful. Watched a lone gull struggling to fly. The high winds whipped it around like a piece of paper. Looked like it was having great difficulties remaining airborne. When it flew out of our sight, it was still holding its own, though.

Maggie J.

September 20, 1986
Buckshot Cabin

Amy Jo

August 19, 1975
Little Carp Cabin
Today is Tuesday, and so far we have enjoyed it here even more than expected (and we expected a lot). The lake just awes you—it's so vast. In a

village or city setting you never see so much space or different types of weather at once. The shoreline is fascinating—jagged rocks jut out at forty-five degree angles. There is virtually no beach—just rock and toppled trees. The flat area along the water (where the Lake Superior Trail is) has a tortured look to it. The lake conjures up visions of raw power. Wow!

Larry F.

August 10, 1983
Big Carp 4-Bunk Cabin

The Superior, why do you rage so?
Just when we think we will play on
your beaches,
You twist and you turn and gust wind at us,
as if to say, "I'll decide!"
Maybe we won't have such a perfect day!

We look out our window to such a calm,
smooth water, blue sky, billowing clouds,
and then...
You rage your ugly head in the giant waves,
the sky darkens, and our own "perfection" is
no longer so.

What can we do to soothe you, oh Lake?
Are you God's anger at us, oh-too-imperfect mortals?
Maybe we won't take things for granted
so much anymore, at least not about
you, oh Lake!

Karen F.

July 22, 1988
Buckshot Cabin

As I sit here, the Great Lake is as still as a mirror. I never would have believed it could be so tranquil. I don't want to leave this place yet. It is so quiet, and it smells so fresh and good.

Carol, Bob, Jamie, Brent, Mark, & Shelli

September 11, 1993
Whitetail Cabin

The Porkies are great. I've been hiking many other places, including the Grand Canyon and Hawaii. But there is a magic in Lake Superior. A cunning beauty in that big, blue, glorious reflection of the sky. It's like a mirror; then a whirlpool. Also, in short bursts, it changes tone, color, and texture. When hiking, I like to keep finding ways to see the lake from a new perspective. Take care of this place on Earth!

Jim

August 17, 1982
Buckshot Cabin

Buckshot from the Lake

Susan M.

November 28, 1994
Whitetail Cabin

The lake isn't angry anymore. She's still mighty damn violent, but the nasty part is over. Now she's just reminding us of her power. There's nothing out there that's truly evil, but she does have a mean streak about her. Tonight she's demanding respect. There was almost no snow when we got here, but the storm moved in yesterday afternoon. We've gotten well over a foot of snow in the last eighteen hours and they say there are places with well over two feet on the other side of the road. I haven't been able to get out far today because I don't have skis. It's not going to be easy packing out on foot tomorrow, but it's not that far.

Winds are gusting forty to fifty miles per hour and it's a good night to go out on the rocks in a kilt. Waves are up to fifteen feet and it's a refreshing and reaffirming experience to stand on the rocks wearing boots, a coat, and a kilt. Nothing else. Lake Superior in all her force and blackness and a man standing on the shore, free.

And if you do stand on the shore in a kilt, stand quietly and watch the lights in the sky. You may be lucky enough to catch a glimpse of the Big Man in the sky, his face looming over the water. And if you are pure of heart but still slightly twisted, he may just give you a Big Man look. Go from here knowing that the Big Man has looked inside you and he knows more than you think he does. And spread the word about the glories a man can have in a kilt. I've got to get out there now. It's a good night for kilting.

Unknown Author

January 15, 1988
Big Carp 6-Bunk Cabin

These hemlocks are out of this world! Tall and stately. The lake is yet another story. A frozen, swirling mass. A climb to the top of the ice mass, built up along the shore, reveals the lake. The rhythm of the tide pushes ice chunks upon the already icy shore. The ice sheets appear like glass, breaking and sliding with the rhythm of the tide. We humans are pretty insignificant compared to such power. I bow in its presence....

The Great Lake has done it again. It revives the soul, replenishes the spirit, and instills a fear of nature's power all at once. My heart goes out to you Lake Superior.

D.S.

July 17, 1977
Speaker's Cabin

If you do not have the extraordinary privilege of seeing a thunderstorm move in across the lake in early evening, mixing with the "normal" glory of the sunset, you must plan your life to somehow do so. The black clouds filled with lightning become translucent, as the electricity does battle with itself. Or see the long, low storm clouds that run horizontal to the top of the lake, not touching, but sending down stiff, jagged spears of lightning that disappear into the darkening water.

Marly H.

December 15, 1995
Whitetail Cabin

How happy we all would be if we could fantasize at will with no one to tell us we are foolish, to bring us back to reality with a bump. My dreams are like these snowflakes I see drifting slowly into the lake—untold, countless. Dreams drawn inevitably back to the Mother, that cold, gray expanse of water from which they originally came, where they now return to enrich. This sense of spirit, like this lake, cannot be described. You must stand on its shores and feel its winds for yourself.

Don S.

October 1, 1993
Lake Superior Cabin

Lake Superior is rough this morning. My husband says "she's rockin' and rollin'." It's funny how most everything in Mother Nature is referred to as "she." I guess it has a lot to do with the magical beauty of things. Although I am not a devoutly religious person, I do believe in the natural order of the world, or should I say, the Earth. No matter how hard man tries to recreate those things in nature (the biosphere), he will always be inferior to the wonders of nature, no matter how smart we think we are! If you have any doubt, just take a gander out the front window of the cabin and witness the power of Superior.

Ann P.

August 7, 1989
Lake Superior Cabin

This is why this cabin stay has been such a nice respite. The consummate peace of the location, the constant sound of Superior's waves, and the performance of simple, basic tasks all serve to create a sense of deep relaxation.

Jim & Sharon F.

May 25, 1991
Little Carp Cabin

Breathing

The breeze
it does intoxicate.
The gulls carry a cry
to the lull of the lake
breaking shore
Leaves dance—

seeds sail and fall,
one not to grow
on my sweater
the sun it does warm
me—
against the forest wind.

Pauline

June 5, 1993
Buckshot Cabin

Kevin & Shari

April 1, 1988
Buckshot Cabin

The sun is down and a bright, full moon is shining in the east window. Lisa and I just took a walk out to the edge of the shore ice. It's really calm now, but earlier the east wind made some waves and currents out in the lake. As we stood at the top of the ice cliffs, we could hear the ice cracking— moaning—crunching—groaning. The moon is so bright it's hard to see the stars. There is a bright planet in the northwest; it's either Jupiter or Saturn. This is a fine night, the fitting end for one of the best birthdays I've ever had.

Steve

March 7, 1977
Little Carp Cabin

The beauty that exists here need not be mentioned by me. Words fall far short in their capacity to describe the experience of being here. This is what has always been good about life, and hopefully will continue to be. When a man forsakes what is simple and good about life for what is dirty and corrupt, he is sacrificing part of his soul and well-being. This is hardly an equal trade, yet so many of them permit themselves to do just that. To sell your soul, heart, and your mind to the city is the ultimate sin. To be here once is to know beauty, harmony, and peace; beauty in the peacefulness of a winter's day among tall pines and shimmering cedars, or to see the ferocious beauty of a Superior storm. Harmony in the way that nature balances herself, and peace, that restful inner peace that comes from doing for oneself, for depending on you, me, I, to get things done. Or from watching the sun set on the frozen waters of Lake Superior. To appreciate, one has to understand. One has to experience.

William S.

July 18, 1992
Whitetail Cabin

Sitting by the lake
So calm, so neat
Seeing in all directions
Water never ending
Seeing blue everywhere
So clean is the water
Clear like crystal
Sitting on slabs of rock
So peaceful is the lake
Minus the cool, light breeze
The waves rolling gently on the surface

And below on the rocks
Dance golden snakes
The gentle lapping of the waves
Against the rocks of the shore
Put the mind at peace
Man and nature combine

Eerik B.

February 21, 1998
Whitetail Cabin

Unknown Artist

February 28, 1992
Whitetail Cabin
We have seen many faces of Lake Superior since arriving. The 24th was calm, almost eerie, with the sounds of silence. The 25th and 26th we spent walking along the shore in our snowshoes, taking pictures of the ice caves and watching the lake throw blocks of ice into the air. The sun came out in the

afternoon to enhance the photo opportunities and we got a lot of good pictures.

Yesterday we walked along the shore where I broke one of my snowshoes, slipping on a piece of ice covered with snow. We also gathered a large woodpile to restock the cabin as well as to burn at our traditional evening fire outside.

Today the lake is showing its temper with huge waves pounding relentlessly against the ice pack and spray going forty feet into the air. Be VERY, EXTREMELY careful down on the ice! There are many crevasses that have snow drifted over them and are hard to see. When we went down, we wore snowshoes in addition to tying a twelve foot rope with hooks at each end around our waists. Better safe than sorry when dealing with Lake Superior. The closer to the edge you get, the more dangerous it is, so be alert at all times.

We hope you enjoy your time here and have a safe trip home.

Bob & Debby M.

August 11, 1975
Buckshot Cabin

The churning, icy waters
crash against the
clay wonders of nature,
Its seething foam carrying
minute particles of
the day's left-overs
back into the sea.
Is my life not like the
churning waters, trying
to bring back past memories
which will only corrupt
my new found purity?

L.L.

August 29, 1984
Little Carp Cabin

The oddest birds have stalked our little cabin since our arrival. Though I have yet to see one, the percussion and woodwind sections of the forest have been quite happy playing a regular accompaniment to the rolling Lake. One sounds like it is pecking on wood. Another sounds as if it is a short-winded seagull, and another chirps just like the birds that used to chirp outside my bedroom window when I was growing up. But, ah, the Lake!

Having never been on the shores of such a lake before, I was easily seduced by the soft sand and the beckoning waves which were crashing against the shore with unusual vigor. So completely seduced was I, that casting aside my fear of cold water, which has plagued me since the start of our sojourn, I rushed headlong into Superior. But Superior was not to give up her charms so easily. The sandy beach turned into slippery stone and what was alluring turned challenging. The waves that I had "bravely" faced, with the legs of my corduroys rolled up, now threatened to topple me. I headed slowly into the lake, several times almost losing my balance as the waves jostled my feet from their place amongst the rocks. Minutes passed, and I was no further into the center....

Finally, after several minutes had passed, and I seemed no closer to swimming..., I began to crawl along the rocky bottom. Ah, a challenge I could face. My legs dangled behind me as I grabbed the stones off the lake floor to propel myself. Then, as each wave threatened to reach the shore, I clenched my jaw and stiffened my chest, challenging Superior to knock me down. It was a most pleasant experience. Each wave seemed cooler than the previous one, and my heart braced itself for every shock. As I held my head up high, and faced the horizon, I smiled. I had conquered Superior.

John

Friends, Family, and Strangers

May 29, 1966
Mirror Lake 4-Bunk Cabin

After acting as guide, instructor, cook, outdoor expert, teacher of the fine art of fishing, I finished this camping trip true to form. I got lost, burnt the fish, explained the details of a set of bear tracks (turned out they were made by my daughter's bare feet), and last but not humiliatingly least, I was the only one who didn't catch a fish. In spite of all these events, the camping trip was enjoyable; and the next one will be too, because by then I will have forgotten—or tried to forget.

C.J.S.

October 6-8, 1972
Section 17 Cabin

I am writing this from the creek bank, seated upon the seared birch which leans out across the stream, almost at right angles with the aged cedar, an admirable backrest. I have termed this natural throne "Arthur's Seat," for surely Arthur Pendragon's "Camelot" was no more wonderful a kingdom as this.

The late afternoon sun now backlights and dapples the golden maples and birches, setting off in bas-relief the trunks of the straighter, darker trees. The "four o'clock" wind alternately shakes and rustles the branches and leaves of the slender maple to my right causing the foliage to drift downward in a golden cascade which gently kisses the surface of the stream. There it is gently carried downstream until the individual leaves are swept into the seething vortex of the rapids and whisked away.

As the force of the wind grows, its tone becomes more strident and more demanding. The leaves in their tumbling, twisting, headlong fall, pause, turn, and chase the shouting wind along.

In the three days I have been here—it is "I" now for my son is asleep in that deep, dreamless land that one only visits after wood chopping, a six mile hike, and a full stomach—so it is "I," and in the three days I have been here, I have heard the heart-stopping rattle and whir as the grouse leaves her cover to become an elusive, brown projectile. I have heard the incessant drumming of the flicker, or yellow-hammer, on the dense bark of the Norway pine. I have watched in mixed anger and amazement as a skunk made a mockery of human intelligence by imprisoning a grown man in the outhouse. And I have heard and appreciated the ceaseless flowing of a wild river at my doorstep, one so clean and undefiled that its sweet water may be drunk without treatment. It makes me pause to think that some sixty-five new power plants are being installed or are in current operation around the Great Lakes. I also understand that at least six of these are or will be of the nuclear variety. When I go home tonight, I plan to shut off all of my lights, and in the silence of my darkened house, listen to my wild river, and a thousand others murmur their thanks.

I hate to leave this wilderness home of mine, but I am not entirely sad, for soon I will see my wife. You see, I am very fortunate, for she is also a good friend, and I will go with her and other good friends...for a last canoe trip before the snow flies.

And so the day ends for us. But to you, my fellow traveler and next occupant of this cabin, I leave a residence as clean as I know how to make it, a supply of wood double the size left for me, a supply of candles for the previous party used the last of the kerosene, and my best wishes for a pleasant and peaceful stay. I hope you were as lucky as I have been, for I not only watched the animals that the others who have written in this log described, but I also got to watch, for a brief period, a man return to his youth, and more importantly, a youth becoming a man.

Wayland & John (father & son)

September 5-7, 1983
Speaker's Cabin

Ted (Wilderness Smoker)—Experienced wilderness man who smokes Camels (no filters). Likes peace and quiet and not seeing other people in wilderness. Especially annoyed by rude packers who pack too close and linger too long.

Carol (Wilderness Nurse)—After being married to Ted for four and-a-half (?) years, now an accomplished wilderness woman. Uses a sani-fem to pee with (saves butt from mosquito bites). Constantly wearing down coat and booties to keep warm. Poet and nurse—loves purple, hates bugs.

Zorra (Geriatric Woofer) —A geriatric German shepherd. Mellow dog who loves wilderness trips. Drug four foot branch a quarter mile down beach and then slept rest of day.

Merlin (King Goon)—Golden retriever who braves waves and undertow to bring back his sticks! Powerful swimmer and just goony enough to fly into lake for stick after stick. Repays people by violently wagging tail and spraying lots of water. A red dog-boy who's as goony as they come.

Randy (Great White Hunter)—A tall person who loves to eat. Professional recreationist and it shows! Wants to be remembered for his bushy mustache. One of the last "Great White Hunters," Randy swatted over two hundred snotty-looking flies today (see ceiling for body count). Favorite phrase: "Is it time to eat yet?" Likes to wash dishes but hates to cook.

Charlene (Farmeress and Star Finder)—Also a professional recreator. Reads star charts with professional accuracy. Rugged farmeress who rises early and hits the sack first. Favorite phrase: "Randy, why don't you do something to help out here."

Charlene & Carol

August 1, 1981
Lily Pond Cabin

I normally report the news at a TV station in northern Indiana when I'm not looking for tranquility in the woods. With the kind of work I do, my viewpoint on humans ends up getting pretty out of proportion, and I find myself really needing to get away from the world of bank robbers and pre-teen rapists, and folks hating enough to kill (or just not caring). When we got here I began to feel the familiar wilderness-induced calm settle over sore bones bruised by the backpack in. And on the grandest scale ever, the recuperation commenced amidst the splendid Porkies. But even more healing than that, the logs from past visitors showed me a different proportion of people—people that were loving and open. Ones who share. Swapping stories and survival hints all with the same joy and exuberance. The Porkies soothed my spirit—its lovers healed my soul.

J.G.L.

August 7, 1994
Gitchee Gumee Cabin

Twenty-eight years ago we came here for the first time! This is a great experience! The Porkies are a special place for us. Every family should have a special place.

Ginny

May 20, 1975
Buckshot Cabin

Had a beautiful thunder and lightning storm tonight; very little rain, however. All four of us sat down on the rocks by the lake. The sight was incredibly beautiful. Some of the bolts seemed close enough to touch. The heat lightning lit up the sky like flash bulbs. A very warm breeze came in from the lake making everything fantastically unordinary.

To increase the already eerie quality, the moon came out in full and the clouds drifted past us as if attempting to suppress its illumines life. The atmosphere of suspense and of a supernatural presence was enhanced by the slow chatting, swaying of the trees, much like mourners at a funeral. Each tree seemed to sway its own salute to the ghosts and the lost souls in what once was the lost giants of this land.

We told ghost stories, each one of us; not so much because of the stories, but some unspoken, ever-present, intense fear of what we don't know; feel, maybe, a little emptier and a little less self-confident than we would like to have admitted.

The feeling of loneliness is never stronger than in a vast crowd of people, and the feeling of inferiority never so strong as when presented with the greatest powers on earth: wind, water, and fire. Has man a chance to conquer these timeless, endless forces of nature? If he tries, he will certainly fail. But to live in harmony with them is far easier and more successful.

The wind has increased adding to the endless flow of natural powers, for what has man ever made that has lasted or that he, himself, has not destroyed. Being here is a far greater thing than just a night or a day. It's seeing a place that will outlast any human civilization now in existence. With this I close and hope some of this feeling may be passed along.

David H.

August 29, 1970
Lily Pond Cabin

Good morning. Randy, Harriet, Art, Jeff, and I arrived last evening. Randy and Harriet went to get water. It's a little harder to get to than it was at Big Carp. Jeff was teaching Art karate, and I was inside, crying my little head off. I suppose it was a combination of being tired, knowing today was to be my last day in the Porkies, and two things a little more important. My little brother (is six feet little?) Tom, who is now with God, was the first person to tell me of the Porkies. As I got into my bed, I saw his name carved in the wood above. And I'm sure I also cried because I'm going to have to leave all this beauty after tonight, and I want so strongly just to bring all of my loved ones and live here forever. My tears weren't sad—perhaps just nostalgic.

Marlene

September 7, 1986
Mirror Lake 8-Bunk Cabin

I'm the one that is supposed to keep everyone sane. What a joke! I'm the one that yells the loudest! I don't feel very sane right now, anyway. We went for a six mile hike with three, three year olds! Erica has turned out to be a great hiker! I'm the one with tender feet. The walk would have been better if I wasn't looking for all those bears! All we saw was a chipmunk! This place is great! We are already thinking of things to bring next year, and things not to bring next year. Never doing this before, I was not at all sure of the things I would need. So I brought everything I didn't need and nothing I did! I sure am looking forward to a shower and clean clothes! I'm afraid to give Erica a bath. I might not find a kid under all of that dirt!

Tammy J.

October 19, 1992
Greenstone Falls Cabin

I am the spokesperson for the five of us. We leave a leaf for good measure. We ate a lot, hiked a lot, ate a lot, and used Johnny-the-Outhouse a lot. We are five female college students....

The candles are burning, our sight is dying. We will all need focals when we get back home. Our six mile hike today, to and from Lily Pond, was a silent journey going, full of old tunes bellowing through the wild on the way back. The oldest in our group is twenty-one. Yes, twenty-one. We are the future, independent women leaders of the world, as soon as we conquer Jen's fear of "Johnny's" bottomless pit. Although the pit is filling and we foreshadow some unhappy, nose-pinching campers, we have all had fun. I know this because I can feel it radiating from the other four around this table. We bonded, bathed in an ever so chilling stream, ate lots of gorp, read, wrote, wondered what a pasty tasted like, hugged trees, got our periods, and saw nature how God intended—with open eyes.

Cheri

September 11, 1987
Mirror Lake 8-Bunk Cabin

Hi! My name is Dori. My nickname is Pixie because I have striped PJ's.

My name is Kali. I'm eleven years old. My sister's nickname is not Pixie. It's Pixie-butt. My nickname is Slug-a-bug. Oh, be careful if you walk on the log out front. I did that and fell in. Be careful by the creek. I fell in there also.

Hi. My name is Genna. My two little sisters are weird. Kali's nickname is Slug-a-bug because she is the slowest one of all. The last to reach the cabin and probably the last to leave.

The W. Family

June 17, 1982
Section 17 Cabin

It is about time to leave the Porkies, tomorrow. After five days, it has been an experience which will not be forgotten soon. Jack is well versed in the natural aspects of the forest, names of trees, plants, etc. My special interest is photography, and I am using more film than I thought was possible in five days. Water seems to draw our attention, and the photographs of the different waterfalls, plant life, and trees will make an exciting album when we return. That's if I can afford to have it all processed! The natural beauty of the area is a photographers's delight.

Tom F.

July 3, 1982
Section 17 Cabin
Hi Log—

Thanks for being here. You provided a lot of laughs and lots of hope. It's very warm and good to see, or read, people taking care of each other through these pages. To those folks, thanks, you've touched me.

Tom F.

October 19, 1995
Big Carp 4-Bunk Cabin

This marks the tenth year my brother-in-law and I have come to the Porkies. We use the excuse that we are coming to fish (salmon in the fall, steelheads in the spring). Sometimes we score big, sometimes we get skunked fishing. Always we come away with a special experience. This is a very special and beautiful place. Even in the foulest of weather we gain something unique. The damp smell of the forest (not something you experience on the expressway), the savage power of the lake, and the stillness of the forest are all a part of this experience. There are many other elements. You must stop and take notice of each in order to realize the whole nature of the Porkies.

Jeff D.

June 24, 1976
Mirror Lake 8-Bunk Cabin

Wow! Where do you begin when every feeling and emotion inside of you is just going crazy. This place is incredibly beautiful. The only real word is contentment. Nothing could bother me now. The view is nice and there is somebody rowing along, fishing.

Everybody I've met so far on my trip is just so happy and nice. It's too bad that those feelings can't be that way all the time. It is amazing what nature can do for you.

As I sit here and look at this cabin, it makes me feel so good—one of my greatest ambitions in life is to build a log cabin on a lake away from it all. When I saw this place, it was like a dream come true. It makes me realize that my dream is even more promising. You must realize yourself what it's like to have a fantasy come true. It's a great feeling. Hey!

I wish I could sit down and read these logs all the way through. The stories they would tell! As you read, you get so high off of other people's words. It's really a great idea.

It's getting pretty late and the breeze is cooling off, but that's alright. Going to bed in a place like this is a trip itself. This place could also be dangerous for you. It makes you feel romantic, or should I put it bluntly, cuddling up to someone. And I don't really think Ben would say the feeling is mutual. But still, I can't think of anyone in this whole world I'd rather be with. It's great to have friends that you really love, especially ones who get into your ideas and hopes as much as you do theirs. I have, or should I say Ben and I have developed...feelings of love and understanding so strong, that it's a lifetime thing. And I really thank God for such people. Without them, I'd be lost. I'd like to share this with them and maybe someday it will happen. Well, I shall go wake Ben up. By the way, Ben is the reason for this whole mind-blowing trip. I wonder what he'd do if I gave him a kiss to show my deepest and whole-hearted appreciation. See you in the morning, only unfortunately it will have to be "so long." But I'll be back, my heart says.

Cindy H.

August 25, 1978
Buckshot Cabin

We came here to reintroduce ourselves and our boys to the woods—we had some success. The older boys, Alan (thirteen) and Mike (eleven), have finished off these Scout badges: hiking (a ten mile and a twenty mile hike), cooking (five days of same), bird study, mammals, insects, nature, environmental science, and odds and ends of camping. This was no vacation for them and I admire their hard work and dedication.... They handled themselves with courage and reason. Our boys are becoming men.

The Y. Family

August 9, 1995
Big Carp 4-Bunk Cabin

After cleaning up the dishes and cabin, I sat for a while on the bench on the bridge. Butterflies were working the wildflowers along the river, while a mother merganser and her two young lounged around the swimming hole. I think that I'm alone here as everyone appears to be on the move and not at this oasis yet. I spotted two, twelve to fourteen inch rainbows in the river below!

I think the Porkies are a special place, but are there too many people here? So far, the conservation ethic (wise use of our resources) is working well here. Preservation is an integral part of conservation, and not a mutually exclusive term in the Porkies. Hug that bunny if you want, but don't forget that he tastes good when you're hungry.

Wayne K.

August 9, 1995
Big Carp 4-Bunk Cabin

I don't know what Dad's talking about. We didn't eat any bunnies during our stay. We've probably whacked enough flies to make steaks of them.

Ryan K.

August 20, 1986
Greenstone Falls Cabin

Tony & Ev V.

June 3, 1984

Lily Pond Cabin

I have spent many days in the cabins over the years and have always wondered who reads these words I write. Are you male or female? Young or old? Where do you come from? Why are you here? Is your life happy or filled with pain? Do you seek solitude here or do you come to be gregarious? Where will you go from here? Are you in love? Are you here with your lover? Do you long to go back to your lover? Are you under 5'6" or above? Do you have the full compliment of appendages? What is your favorite food to eat, to drink? What is your favorite color? What is the average air speed of a swallow? What is your quest?

Well, I could go on and on, but you already probably think this is all really quite foolish. Here's an idea, though, if you're interested....drop me a note sometime. If you live in the Milwaukee area you might even give me a call (I hope I don't regret this)....

Somehow, I recently have been thinking about some things my mother told me:

Example of the absurd: Columbus discovered North America.

Example of the useful: Don't crap your pants.

Landall L.

June 14, 1967

Big Carp 4-Bunk Cabin

Today ends for us a very wonderful vacation. We spent five days here and loved every minute of it. We didn't catch any fish, but the fact that we were here was more than enough for us both....

Many memories lie sleeping here in this, God's country. I'm sure some of my fondest as well as my brother's.

Here we have found much solitude and enjoyment. We've also found we are very good friends, as well as brothers.

Outside of a badly cut finger and some other minor discomforts, these past five days have been the most wonderful days I have ever known. This place, this cabin, and the Big Carp will be foremost in my mind, as well as Craig's, for many, many years to come. Thank God there are places such as these where people can come and get away from the monotony of life. May God bless these woods forever (no two more sentimental people could be found anywhere)....

I hope the next occupants collect many memories here, as we have done.

Jim & Craig

June 10-12, 1988
Lily Pond Cabin

Joe walked out today; has to go to church tomorrow. I told him I would preach to him, and that made him leave quicker. He claims I'm the "sucker king." Truth is that Joe wouldn't know the difference between a sucker and a trout. He now realizes that I am the "fisherman."

Andy is cooking breakfast. I think he's trying to smoke us out. There's more smoke in this cabin than a smoke house. I call him "long distance cook" as he stands about five feet from the stove and drops sausage into the pan, grease popping all over the place. I brought him along to be the chef. Big mistake. Bacon—crisp (burnt), eggs over-easy (fried), etc. Last night he cooked venison steaks outside. We left some of it out for the bears and Big Foot. I figured if anything would keep the creatures away, it would be Andy's cooking. I was right—nothing touched it.

Gary "Savage" M.

August 7, 1983
Mirror Lake 4-Bunk Cabin

It was really special to come back to Mirror Lake after twenty-three years! That was 1960 or so and I was about ten years old. A lot more people here now, but still one of the most beautiful and peaceful places a person could ever find.

Joe B.

December 29, 1987
Mirror Lake 8-Bunk Cabin
CABIN NOISES: Being a Compendium of the Counterparts of the Mirror Lake Symphony
A) The Basics
   1) Coughs
   2) Sneezes
   3) Sniffles
   4) Farts
   5) Belches
   6) Sighs of contentment
   7) Groans of agony
   8) Snoring
B) Nocturnals
   1) "Whoosh" (sleeping bag farts)
   2) Assorted giggles and guffaws
   3) Clunk!
   4) Curses

5) More guffaws

...a triplet signifying that someone tripped over a sleeping dog...

6) Groan (canine version)

7) "Clump, clump, clump" (footsteps)

8) Minor roar (male occupant at thunder pot)

9) "Pish, pish, pish" (accompaniment to minor roar)

10) Sighs of relieved urination

11) "Tinkle, tinkle, tinkle" (female occupant at thunderpot)

...may be minor roar given enough preparation, i.e: partying before bed...

12) "Thumpa, thumpa" (shutters banging)

...originally thought to be a bruin...

C) Expressives

1) Dog whines and groans

2) Dog barks

3) Squeak of male dog in proximity to bitch in heat

4) Assorted mumbles and gurgles (dream noises)

...Note: May also be listed under "Nocturnals"...

5) Curses (general)

6) Uproarious laughter (funny jokes)

7) Retching laughter (sick jokes)

8) Cooing and murmurs (you figure it out)

9) "Brrr" (a winter part)

10) "Whew" (a summer part)

D) Naturals

1) The wind in the pines

2) Chirping

3) Scratching (the bear at the door)

4) Skittering (the mouse on the counter)

5) "SNAP!" (the deceased mouse on the counter)

...Note: May also be listed under "Nocturnals..."

E) SILENCE

A.J.

August 5, 1996

Big Carp 6-Bunk Cabin

This is my first backpacking trip. My husband and son do it often, but wanted to share the experience with me and the girls. I am not an avid outdoors man (or woman), but I am married to "Indiana Jones" and our son is exactly the same. They have spent hours and days trying to talk me into spending part of our summer vacation here in the Porkies. This is one of their favorite spots on Earth. Whenever "Indy" talks me into something like this, he invariably leaves out small, important details that might damper my enthusiasm. Little by little, after I am committed to the trip, he begins to drop little tidbits of information that slipped his mind in previous conversations. "Sometimes the trail may be a bit muddy in places, but don't worry. There's planking." When we actually hit the trail he says, "Don't worry about your shoes. They will get sort of muddy anyway." SORT OF MUDDY!?! I nearly lost my shoes of several occasions. I slipped, slid, and slogged through slick, slimy mud all the way here. At least I didn't fall on my fanny! Close, though. Very close.

L.A.

August 6, 1997
Big Carp 6-Bunk Cabin

Last year was my first time here. My husband and son have been coming for years and really love this place. After last year, I never wanted to come back (mud and flies). This year has been picture-perfect. We leave tomorrow and I can't believe I don't want to go—like everyone else these days, we are so busy day in and day out that we forget to enjoy "the moment." Being here makes us stop our frantic running to and fro. Makes us take time to find joy in the moment. God doesn't want us to let life pass us by—the shimmer on the water, the butterflies, the zillion stars at night—they are meant to enrich and fulfill us. So take time to focus. Yesterday is behind you and tomorrow is beyond your reach. Today is yours for the taking.

L.A.

October, 1987
Mirror Lake 8-Bunk Cabin

My wife is something special. I dragged her here to do something she has never done before, and she is handling this rustic environment with her head held high and her spirits up. You see, she would really like to be at home, but she is here with me—if that's not love, what is??

She won't do this again.

I love her for trying.

Unknown Author

September 11-14, 1988
Greenstone Falls Cabin

Walking through the wilderness, rich with lush greenery, facing the perils of the outdoors with each step, we made it safely to the cabin. The cabin, as we best remembered it, appeared the same as it did four years ago. Yes, four years ago, and our son who is now three years old, was a mere embryonic beginning of a human being. Tonight he sleeps soundly in the lower bunk.

After a hard day of exploring the dark forests for bear with wooden sticks as guns, he has settled in for another deep sleep with puppy.

Today's rain brought a dampness and chill to the air. The wood stove, however, provides the warmth that removes the nip of fall that otherwise may seep into the bones. It is, at the same time, refreshing to anticipate the awakening to morning's coolness.

My time in the Porkies, whether it's merely sitting on the bench gazing down at the river or meandering through the forest, allows the necessary rejuvenation of the body and soul. The absolute silence takes me away from the exhaust-filled, rat race of the freeway. The Porkies give me time to move inside myself. To reflect on the events that have formed my life as I know it today. For the few days there is nothing to be given or taken. The forests do not demand from me. They only ask for respect and the right to be unharmed.

I find myself, as with previous visits, wondering about the value of career, etc. Here, I am allowed the time, that precious time, to appreciate and to enjoy life's pleasures. It's a wonderful feeling to awaken to the sound of rushing water, to slowly meet the day, and to carry on however the spirit moves me.

> FE FI FO FUM, I smell a small boy
> And his name is Colin
> Walking through the dark woods within
> His gun made of wood, a present from
> A pine
> Oh, what does he see—a small toad
> What is that toad doing? He's looking for
> His mother and father, or so he says
> What? Another toad!
> What is he doing? he asks
> He's looking for his small friend—so he says

After yesterday's rain, today was warm and sunny. We had a good day of hiking considering Colin is only three and has short legs. I figure he's good for about a mile. It's nothing like our previous trips, but still a new type of adventure. Captain Colin took us through the woods on his spaceship. We looked for lions and tigers and bears, OH MY! We flew through the woods on our wings of fern leaves.

Colin renamed the outhouse, "the smell house." Made sense to me. He would walk out to it, but wouldn't use it. Fortunately, we brought a potty with us. Think about it. Plodding through the woods with a potty attached to your pack.

I'm glad that Colin had the opportunity to come. I believe that this experience will increase his awareness for life, give him a different view on living from our "normal, everyday" routine.

Tomorrow we must leave the forests and return home. These few days have given me a good feeling. They have refreshed me for the demands of work. I know that I'll return to these woods to receive the gifts that Mother Nature has to offer.

David, Nicki, & Colin

October 17, 1988
Mirror Lake 2-Bunk Cabin
Wet wood does nothing to boost one's confidence in his outdoor skills. Davey Crockett I ain't!

Steve

October 20, 1996
Lily Pond Cabin
Today I hugged a tree, and I think it hugged me back.

The Great Frankdini

Unknown Date
Lily Pond Cabin

Artist Unknown

October 3, 1982
Section 17 Cabin

Little Carp River— Last Will and Testament

TO CHAD: I leave my Little Carp River soaked hiking boots, complete with foot pads, foot odor, and worn down heels. They're standing by the wood burner attempting to dry, which ought to take a weekend by itself.

TO ROB: I leave my entire assortment of sweated, "stand-by-themselves," T-shirts, briefs, and socks. Also included in this package is the smell. YUK!

TO PAT: I leave my entire collection of Daniel Boone look-alike clothing. Even though I certainly looked the part of a pioneer, from the leathers on my back to my coonskin cap, I stumbled on too many rocks, roots, and mud patches to bring me back to reality.

I must be leaving these valuables in all good conscience, because the warmth and smell of the fire is all too real, the gentle roar of the river is all too close, and the fond memories of this weekend all too vivid.

Chip

September 22, 1995
Buckshot Cabin

I've been studying the martial arts for sixteen years and have really enjoyed performing my patterns on the rocks and on the beach.

Matt K.

October 13-15, 1972
Lily Pond Cabin

We are still here. Woke up this morning to cold stoves and cloudy skies. The quiet is starting to sink into my thoughts and I love it. To go to the woods —laugh, shout, dance a jig, and just feel how you feel—is so terrific. The beauty is so indescribable, there is no use even trying to explain how it makes you feel. The people who come here must certainly all share certain ideals. Though, anyone who will walk with twenty-five to fifty pounds on their back three to four miles back to a cabin with no "modern conveniences" has got to be a "throwback." Thank goodness there are a few of us left.

Who would believe it—it's sleeting outside, really coming down. Ger made the seasons first snowball. We hiked this forenoon. Need to walk off all this food we are consuming. Apparently everyone gets hungrier with outside stimulation.

"The Ontario Six"

September 4, 1982
Mirror Lake 4-Bunk

It has been a good stay here for me. I've learned how to find wood, cut wood, stoke up the stove, cook with wood, and feel more self-reliant. I feel strong and healthy. I've never backpacked before and it pleases me to find that my body is able to handle the extra stress. Not drinking, not smoking, and eating healthier has really made a difference. I've read a lot about people coming in and drinking or doping it up, and I know that one year ago I would've done the same. It is a very different experience, though, without it.

My partner and I are lesbians. I say that because this journal seems to be a method of developing camaraderie between the cabin users. We share some common experiences—the water, the food, the big rock, the stove. And we have different experiences—we're hunters, families, newlyweds, newly engaged couples. I want other gay people to know that we have been here, too.

Kathy

August 21-23, 1972
Lily Pond Cabin

For a few moments after dinner we ran naked and wild through the wilderness. What a fantastic feeling to be so free.

Jeff & Arlene G.

September 1997
Mirror Lake 8-Bunk Cabin

The Sight of Sound

Waking from a restful slumber, a calliope of sounds caress her ears; the quiet whisper of the wind as it rustles through the trees; the melodious song of the morning birds as they flutter to and fro; the busy buzz of the little bees while they sashe' from flower to flower drinking of their nectar.

Sliding back the curtains, she sighs from the sheer beauty of it all and cries silent tears from the sheer sadness of it all.

"Why the tears? Where's the sadness in all of this beauty?"

"I shed tears because I cannot see this beauty with the sight of my eyes. I can only see it with the sight of my ears."

So fill yourself up with the beauty that you can hear and see, and when in doubt, think of me, as I can only hear what beauty is all about.

Lenora G.

August 14-16, 1995
Mirror Lake 2-Bunk Cabin

Where do I start? First of all, it would be helpful to know my idea of camping is staying in a hotel with no free HBO. So packing in the first night in the dark was a bit of a stretch for me. If my girlfriend wasn't 6'2", two hundred and thirty pounds, and an ex-professional wrestler, I might have even been scared.... The fishing was great although the wrestler is also a better fisherman than me. But she carries a lot of water. The flashlight got a lot of use last night scanning the woods at the campfire. I wonder if I was the only one to carry an axe to the lake at night to watch the stars? The wrestler thought I was paranoid. Better to have it and not need it I think. All in all, had an unforgettable time.

Alan

November 21, 1995
Gitchee Gumee Cabin

As a parent, I want to thank my son, Cory, and his wife, Sarah, for a most incredible experience. To be invited by them was an honor I treasure. I shall always have memories to feed my soul when things in civilization get rough. You gave me peace within, strength, and the beauty of gentle silence. Very special.

Brooke C.

September 10, 1987
Little Carp Cabin

The boys were so cute in the hemlock forest by Shining Cloud Falls yesterday. They ran around under those huge trees—it was perfect for them. A matted forest floor with virtually no "understory" and just enough branches to keep it interesting. So tiny against the towering trees.

Unknown Author

May 19, 1968
Lily Pond Cabin

In order not to have to help the others prepare to leave, I decided to record our thoughts in the log. This has been a very special time in our lives. We have been here less than one day, but our memories of Lily Pond will last a lifetime. Our stay here has been a contrast from our every day lives as university students—well known for loud music, wild parties, and revolutionary thoughts—this time and place and solitude are special. We came here for a trip and really blew our minds! We found the real life as it really is. It has been a long search, but the pot at the end was worth the wait. We are on our way now, free at last. Ready to face the new day with a new peace. Thank God for this place!

George, Fred, & Cher S.
E.J.S.

August 25-30, 1969
Lily Pond Cabin

We had a good time in unusually warm weather, with only one night of rain. We saw a porcupine and chipmunks, plus reptiles and BUGS, but no bear (sniff!). The longest and best of our many hikes was along the Little Carp River, past rapids and small waterfalls.

Water is across the lake; the sign can be seen from here. Don't give up— once across the lake the trail is longer than you think. We put a lot of brush and sticks down to cover the extremely muddy area at the boat landing across the sea, and more would be helpful. For cooking, we found that leaving the stove door open helped greatly. As there is no lime for the outhouse, putting salt down once a day keeps the smell down....

I have a new kind of respect for my grandmother, who did all her cooking on this kind of stove. Also, I'll appreciate electric lights and running water in a new way when I get back home. Now, if I could only take the beauty and the solitude with me.

The B. Family

1978
Mirror Lake 8-Bunk Cabin

Doris M.

April 16, 1987
Mirror Lake 4-Bunk Cabin

It's early, but not as early as I'd hoped. I had wanted to watch a sunrise on the lake. It's been overcast, and so it has been a beautiful, still morning with no dramatic change of light for over an hour. My guess is that it is after 9:00.

There are fish in the lake. I see them surface and leave their gentle ring of waves just twenty feet behind the rowboat. Who is baiting who?

The fire is warm and this stove deserves all the praise it has received. It's wonderful!

Mark and I hiked in late last night under threat of rain.... Since we got a late start, we made a quick trip of it, as we didn't want to be caught in the dark on an unfamiliar trail. We did pass someone's emergency camp about a quarter mile back. It looked as though they made an overnight camp right where they hoped someone would step on them. A brush lean-to and remnants of a fire were all that remained.

Beautiful walk in though. A little muddy, but excellent. I had an easy trip with practically nothing to carry, which is probably why Mark is still asleep. Mocha java and birds singing, the last of a good book and the Porcupines. This is Heaven!

We were teased by a pileated woodpecker for a good portion of our walk, but never saw him and were awed by the partridge drumming in the underbrush. I was sorry to read that some campers actually hunted them. I thought that hunting was off limits here. Hmmm...

Mark saw a crane on the lake and we went to sleep to the song of an owl (amazing how BIG everything sounds at night). But no stars. Full moon was covered by this thick fog that literally rolled in as we rowed on the lake earlier. But we could still see the silhouettes of the magnificent trees through the windows....

All in all, a beautiful morning. The sun is becoming imposing and must mean that sleep beyond this point would neglect an adventure, so I am going to shake someone's cage.

By the way, two people fit just fine in a single bunk. You just have to like each other a lot!

On to a day of hiking and the next camp at Lake of the Clouds where we join friends.

Oh, this place is good for the soul!

Robin

July 4, 1997
Big Carp 4-Bunk Cabin

The sound of the river is our music. We both walk in accord to the quiet stillness that surrounds us. Lots of times, we look out at the rushing river and sit, each lost in thought, respectful of the other's solitude. Each time we come to the Porkies we get better at backpacking and trying to leave no trace.

Our respect for this beautiful place is immense. We hope our now too-little grandchildren will be able to enjoy these sights with us one day. I can't think of anything better than the continuum of this as a legacy.

Because this is being alive.

Being in wonder.

Being full, complete.

Nancy & Sam

May 10-16, 1989

Mirror Lake 2-Bunk Cabin

It's time to make our entry to these tales of mice and men. After a week, we have seen no mice and few men. There was a family in the 8-bunk when we came who have been here every spring for twenty-four years. Pretty good, huh! Now they come from Florida, California, and Indiana. The father first came with his father some forty years ago, shortly after this park opened. Bet he knows the park!

This is our third trip to this park, second time in this cabin.

The hike in Wednesday was a surprise. We came expecting wildflowers, but found wet snow to our knees. Much has changed since we arrived. Most of the snow is gone, the trout lilies are blooming, and green life springs from the ground every day.

My wife, Wanda, is blind, and it came in handy this trip. We forgot our fishing poles in Minneapolis, but her fiberglass cane, adapted with tape and safety pins for line guides, made a serviceable rod. We had reels and light tackle so we were set.

Justin A.

October 1993

Gitchee Gumee Cabin

What a place! This is my first time to the Porkies. Nature is a beautiful place.

My first deer camp with my sons. This is what memories are all about.

Izzy

July 2-7, 1995

Lily Pond Cabin

I (Tom) began working painstakingly for four evenings to provide you with plenty of light. I (Tom) also designed and implemented the drawings and construction on the hand-crafted ash receptacle for those who choose to smoke. As you can see, I (Tom) spent most of my time providing for your comfort. I hope the least you can do is give me (Tom) a good report to the park rangers and the Michigan Department of Natural Resources.

We have a busy day planned for Sunday. I (Jim) have to take Tom back to the home. He seems to get along with the other patients quite well. Then I'll take Steve to his 10:00 A.M. appointment with his parole officer. I hope you have a great time. We did!!

While Tom worked on his "candle," my other brother, Jim, and I (Steve) took care of things like water supply, wood for drying our wet clothes, and most of the cooking. We got drenched several times on the pond while fishing and making a trip to the spring for fresh water.

Well, I (Jim) have to go now. Steve is out running around naked again. I think his therapy is failing! I have Tom strapped to his bunk just in case he has another fit. This has been a long week making sure these two looney-tunes stay out of trouble.

Brothers Jim, Tom, & Steve

June 10, 1987
Mirror Lake 4-Bunk Cabin
   I came in as a frenzied woman of the '80's. I left as a docile child of the '60's.

Shari B.

April 7, 1994
Lily Pond Cabin
This One's For You Son
   Returning to this cabin is a great joy, although with it comes many memories. Our group comes here every year for Spring Break and this is now the seventh year. Last year, as group leader, I decided to bring my nine year old son. We hiked eleven miles to Mirror Lake the first day. Anyone who has hiked here in the winter will very well understand the difficulties of travel. After arriving there, my son spiked a temperature. We hiked down here the next day and then we returned to Mirror Lake to await the others of our group. I did not know until we traveled home that he had double pneumonia and mono.
   After that experience, I thought he'd never desire to return. However, about Christmas time, he began making plans to return (something special here). Anyway, to make this brief, three weeks before leaving he got pneumonia again, and so he is sitting this year out. I'm glad that I'm not his mom listening to his complaints at home.

111

Ironically, his last pleading statement to his mother before I left was, "You just don't understand what you're keeping me from." He's right—she's never been here. Sad, but true.

Bill

June, 1989
Speaker's Cabin
We were able to watch our four year old boy catch his first frog. Something no parent should miss.

Bob, Laura, & Mike

September 14-15, 1992
Mirror Lake 2-Bunk Cabin
Took a slow, rambling walk to Summit Peak today and returned by Carp River Trail. Thought about many things, but especially my son who is in college now. I miss him very much when he is away, and when I think about all the neat stuff we've done together, it brings tears to my eyes. I don't know why, but I feel so sad thinking about the past even though he brought me great joy. It's like an era in my life has ended. You parents with young children take note and regard every moment with your kids as precious. I have to quit writing now because I'm crying again. Sorry for dumping on you like that.

Unknown Author

July 25, 1998
Section 17 Cabin
Five Filipino women traveled eighteen thousand miles and twenty million smiles to get here. Two of us live in Chicago, one in New York, one in California, and one in Texas. Major bonding at work.

Tet—our Mother Superior. Everything is organized and well-planned when she is around. She brought everything for "just in case" purposes. From band-aids, to tupperware, comforters to insect repellent. We could not survive without her...except when there are snakes. She freaked out when one passed her while we were trailing. Our Macho Mama ceased to exist.

Elsa—the Planner. She planned this trip thinking that doing "hard work" would bond us forever. Of course, it never happened with her, because exactly at 8:00 P.M. (sun still shining), she was off to dreamland. She, however, bonded with nature, swimming in her birthday suit in twenty degree water. She probably thought she was Eve in the garden of paradise.

Lisa—our Gourmet Cook. The lack of a kitchen does not stop her from whipping up a good meal. We were, however, disappointed that we didn't have chocolate mousse cake for dessert. If we didn't have to walk for a mile and a quarter carrying our things, she would have brought her wine rack and caviar. Luxury camping is what it's all about.

Victoria—the Entertainer of the Year. Every occasion is a chance to sing, dance, and even do gymnastics on the beams. Her constant visits to the outhouse give us great pleasure. She has a New York state of mind.

As for me, the beautiful scenery and weather makes me want to cry. Texas is hot, dry, and flat. The mountains and rivers, the magnificent lake, makes me think that God is the Artist of artists.

We're now packing our bags. Moving on. On Tuesday, we go back to our lives—husbands, kids, boyfriends, and soon-to-be boyfriends. The memories here will last forever. We plan to do it again.

Quote of the trip: "Sometimes quitting is a victory."

Unknown Author

July 17-20, 1976
Section 17 Cabin

The log...is a way of getting insights into other people who find this way of life appealing, at least on a part-time basis. It's fun imagining what the people are like now, a year after the honeymoon, weeks after returning to "the old grind," back to school, etc. It's like an unfinished story, and your fantasies take over after every entry. The log is such a real way to become introduced to people, so unlike the usual ways in which people's homes and jobs seem so important. I don't think the occupations of more than one or two people are mentioned in this log, and I find that very interesting.

"Being one with nature" to a three year old means being covered with God's good earth or standing in a waterfall and crowing with delight as the water splashes over her.

Dave, Carolyn, Eric, Andy, & Allison U.

July 30, 1972
Lily Pond Cabin

Thank you my friends for sharing with me
Your love and your warmth, I'm grateful you see
For all of this wealth, I never could find
Best riches in life are born in the mind
They grow 'til they light on someone in time
And I've been made warm, for friendship is mine.

Sally, Deb, Terry, Lee, Carol, Karen, Pat
Counselors Puck & Pumpkin

September 24-27, 1994
Union River Cabin

Kate

July 25, 1997
Buckshot Cabin

INJURY LOG:

Mike:
- Nearly fractured shin bone after slipping off a rock while fishing
- Split toenail (which I believe will fall off in three days)

- Scarred forefinger and thumb from touching a red-hot stove
- Blistered shoulder from chafing pack strap

Tank (Trail Dog):
- Severely chafed groin area from being continuously wet
- Pack strap sores from carrying pack beer, wine, and vodka
- Mild hypothermia from trying to fetch setting sun

Lou (a.k.a. Danger Boy):
- Burned index finger while trying to extinguish cabin fire caused by improper stove operation (operator error)
- Burned stomach while trying to remove boiling water from stove and spilling (operator error)
- Bitten by spider while fishing — middle finger swelled so it could not bend
- Four long slices on left palm caused by the following sequence of events:
  Sawing wood
  Growing impatient
  Set saw down behind
  Set log between two stumps
  Tell Tank to clear out
  Jump on log
  Catapult off log into air
  Fall hard on ground, palms hitting saw blade — hard
  Bleed as "friends" look on, laughing hysterically
  Girlfriend bandages injury
- Bitten numerous times on back of left knee — caused large swelling that inhibited ability to bend knee

Jen (a.k.a. Cautious Jen):
- No reported injuries for Trail Girl yet, except for minor marshmallow burns to the mouth.

Shannon:
- Severe singeing of nose hairs from the strong odor emitted by Mike's smelly pits.

Mike, Lou, Jen, Shannon, & Tank

July 1, 1990
Lily Pond Cabin

Tomorrow is a big day for me. Ten years ago, on July 2, I quit drinking and have been totally clean and sober for that whole time. I've gone through the deaths of both parents, a divorce, and financial problems in that ten years and have come through it all, feeling everything that happened, without dulling it with booze. Lots of good payoffs including custody of my two boys, peace of mind, not to mention less weight in my pack without an extra bottle.

115

My goal is to quit smoking completely tomorrow, on that tenth anniversary, and I'll be able to do it if I approach it the same way I did drinking.

We're (Jeannie and I) heading back to civilization today, and as always when I'm up here, I hate to leave, but the boys need a father, the dog and cat need their freedom from the kennel, my business needs somebody to run it, and I need to celebrate tomorrow with all the friends who have made my sobriety possible. For all those who come to this place after me, my only advice is, "If you believe this life is a good life, it will be, but only if you live it one day at a time."

Ray

April 7, 1993
Mirror Lake 8-Bunk Cabin

We have come to the end of our journey. After tonight, we start hiking to park headquarters to pick up our vehicles and start that twelve hour drive home. What a place to end such a wonderful experience. Mirror Lake. To me that seems appropriate, as I stared over the lake at the trees on the opposite side, I couldn't help but see a reflection on the top of that snow-glazed "mirror." Many thoughts came to mind, memories flashed, and my heart just let loose. My thoughts were coming just a mile a minute, from thoughts of this trip and the magic it produces, to my very loved, belated grandfather. I could not help but reflect on his life, the way he helped my mom when we were struggling, or just the encouraging notes he sent once a week all the way from California. With questions like, "How's Angie? Does she need anything? Is there anything I can do to help her make the best of her ability?" The legend that man left in my heart will never be forgotten. I pray to God every night that this very great man wakes up in the morning in God's land, looking over a "Mirror Lake," thinking of me, his little Angie!

Yes, this place is a happy place, but it is also one of reflection. The last chance that we have as hikers in this great park to take a look in that "mirror" and reflect upon our lives. As I reflect upon my life, I see all the things I do in one day, and I ask myself, are any of those things important? Do we forget the importance of the simple life?

I know I sure do. I ask you to read this, find the incentive to go out to that lake, Mirror Lake, and look at your reflection. It isn't called Mirror Lake for nothing. The beauty of the trails encourages me. Really start to deal with nature on a heart to heart basis. You'd be surprised at how important the little things really are.

If I could ask You for one thing, I would ask for a few days of my life back. Maybe this time Little Angie wouldn't forget to write a return letter to that man she calls "Her Man," the only man that loved her.

Thanks for taking the time to read this, and I encourage you to go and reflect on that wonderful, peaceful place called Mirror Lake.

Angie B.

October 7-9, 1979
Lily Pond Cabin
This morning after relieving myself out at the wizard, I opened the door to see eight men in blue jackets staring at me. What could I say? They had come to move our outhouse. So beware—the totally unexpected will always happen on a true wilderness experience!

Lona, Bunga, Skudge, & Tenderfoot

March 2, 1994
Whitetail Cabin
I was told the true meaning of life this time. That we are all 92% water and that we are created as a vessel for water, so that water could dance, sing, feel, and love. This was another gathering of the great-great-great-granddaughters of the ancient ones, the keepers of the water. A gathering that nourishes the innermost places of our souls with the power of this grandmother water, Lake Superior. Our time here has been shared with the giant lynx whose head is carved in ice on the lake and whose tracks we saw in the snow. Also, we visited with two eagles, and a herd of deer came to the cabin to greet us this morning. We have skied until we couldn't move and then devoured yummy, yummy food. Then some enlightening conversation. It doesn't get any better than this.

Llona

March 23-26, 1997
Whitetail Cabin
We women of the grandmother moon have gathered in this place to celebrate women, life, and joy. We have been here many times. Our spring gathering near Lake Superior has always been a powerful experience. This gathering was very special. As we gathered on the lake, comet Hale-Bop streaked across the northern sky. A beautiful brush stroke of cosmic energy painted across the energy of this mighty lake. In the opposite section of the sky, a full moon entered lunar eclipse. In the crystal clear air, only a tiny sliver at the top remained lit, as the bottom of the moon turned an orangy hue of red. The energy of many women danced here for this special occasion. We dance for the power of women, the keepers of the water, for the return to balance, and the healing and nurturing of our planet. We spent days laughing, skiing, and returning to the spirits of our childhood. At night, eating and sharing.

One enlightening thought from the week: Do not keep fretting over what is your purpose in life. Instead, put purpose into everything that you do.

Llona

October 17, 1997
Whitetail Cabin

The harvest grandmother moon, just like this fall, has been warm, mild, and gentle. This years gathering was very special. We have womyn from many areas, but this year we have a mother-to-be, a girl about to enter her years of becoming a womyn, and two young womyn leaving today on a quest that will take them traveling to all points of wherever. We sat down on the rocks and witnessed the full moon coming up from the lake. It was huge and red and beautiful. And so we gathered and danced and sang and celebrated. It was totally powerful and energizing. And so, I am grateful for this place and leave it with only those spirits that are good.

Llona

October, 1998
Whitetail Cabin

We are the women, the keepers of the water. We gather here for the full moon each year, as we have done for many years, as others before us have for time eternal. We gather by the power of Lake Superior, to honor all the blessings, and ask for the healing of our planet. Words cannot express the blazing experience of explosive colors we experienced, as we feel we have never experienced before. We sat down by the water last night as the moon rose red, then bright orange, and the Northern Lights briefly appeared to display a delicate dance in the northern sky, as a shooting star dazed through the display. It is a sacred place, Lake Superior, and a true honor to be able to come and renew.

Llona

August 18, 1993
Little Carp Cabin

Rosie, our dog, is in her element up here, swimming and hiking through the woods. As a Newfoundland, she does quite well climbing and diving into the clear, cold water. Today, after the children spent many happy hours going down the rock water slides just past the bridge, Rosie would swim across the biggest of the pools, Paul or one of the children would hold onto Rosie's tail, and she would proceed to swim them across the length of the pond. Newfys have that water rescue instinct bred in them and Rosie never seemed happier.

The K. Family

August 30, 1993
Buckshot Cabin

I did joke to my friends that I was going to get back to nature and run naked through the woods. Well, I was naked for over an hour. I walked about a quarter mile on the trail, then went down to the beach and sat around the campfire. It was an ugly sight, though, and I hated to spoil the natural beauty of the area, so I did get dressed.

Author unknown

May 22, 1993
Little Carp Cabin

This visit here is a very meaningful one for me. My last stop here was August 12 to 13, 1992. Ten days after, I suffered a massive spinal disk extrusion, and by September 1, I was paralyzed from the waist down. The past eight and-a-half months have been a long and difficult road back for me. All through that period, thoughts of the Porkies and other such places have sustained and encouraged me. The fact that I have been able to get in here alone, with a full pack, is due in great part to my love for this park and this place. May it remain an inspiration to all of us who draw strength and renewal from it.

W.S.C.

May 15-18, 1996
Little Carp Cabin

My help is in the mountain
Where I take myself to heal
The earthly wounds
That people give to me.

I find a rock with sun on it
And a stream where the water runs gentle
And the trees which one by one give me company.
So I must stay for a long time
Until I have grown from the rock
And the stream is rushing through me
And I cannot tell myself from one tall tree.
Then I know that nothing touches me
Nor makes me run away.
My help is in the mountain
That I take away with me.

Earth care me. Earth receive my woe.
Rock strengthen me. Rock receive my weakness.
Rain wash my sadness away. Rain receive my doubt.
Sun make sweet my song. Sun receive the anger from my heart.

W.S.C.

November 25, 1995
Gitchee Gumee Cabin

Coming to the Porkies is always a special thing. After several days of "airing out your brain," the real peace of the place and the solitude can be enjoyed truly. The girls enjoy every little thing—the top bunks, skiing, hiking, and enjoying the family. Jennifer (my wife) is a good sport for doing these things with us when she'd probably prefer warmer climes and hotels. But she enjoys the outdoors, watching the wildlife, and enjoying the family. In these times, one needs to keep in mind that life is a journey, and the constancy of the Porkies wilderness is an important part of that process. Hope you all enjoy it, too.

K.H.

November 25, 1995
Gitchee Gumee Cabin

I am the "mom" and the "wife" to the previous entries. In spite of what my family thinks, this has been a very enjoyable and memorable experience for me. It has been very rewarding for me to watch my children enjoy the simple pleasures of life, being together as a family, cooking together, playing cards, laughing, listening to music.... Over the past few days I have done some "soul searching" and have come to the realization that the most important thing to me is my family, and their health and happiness. An experience like this forces one to set their priorities straight. As someone once said, life is a journey. Hope to return again sometime with my family.

Jennifer H.

July 21-23, 1974
Big Carp 4-Bunk Cabin

Our thanks to the G. family...through whom our son, Kurt, discovered this cabin on Easter weekend of this year, which in turn led us to the world of backpacking and the Big Carp Cabin. The logs have been fascinating to read, so much so that little time is left to make our entry. We've made friends in absentia with our predecessors, sharing many of their opinions and experiences, becoming familiar with families whose names reappear, as we hope ours will in the future. We, too, shall write the DNR in Lansing, adding our plea that the cabins will not be phased out, hoping that enough of us will speak so that someone will listen. We feel that this park should definitely enforce the rule that no bottles or cans be carried in, which is not in force at present, though suggested. The Quetico canoe country in Canada is extremely strict in this regard. It is the only way to deal with litter, as there are always some who will not abide by the honor code.

We, too, would like the complete privacy of our isolated cabin, but can't begrudge the passing hikers and campers, as they seek the same as do we from this unique wilderness area. We find their cheery greetings on the trail and the exchange of experiences interesting. There is a camaraderie here which is lacking on the city street, and it is reassuring.

The campers whom we have met are young people. A "plus" for the cabin is (reinforced by reading this log) that they have introduced family groups with young children to the backpacking experience. Having dared this and found it successful, they will undoubtedly continue to camp, to enjoy and reinforce their skills having gained confidence. The Porcupine Mountains are unique in the midwestern U.S. in this regard. The Appalachian Trail in the east, the Rockies in the west, but here in the central U.S., this is it! Plus the Superior/Quetico area.

We briefly visited Lake of the Clouds twenty-three years ago and said we must return! Time flies—we finally made it. Three nights here and tomorrow we pack out, and in again, to Lily Pond Cabin. We've chopped lots of wood, mastered the small black stove, and supplemented dried foods with delicious trout (sixteen in all, the largest being about a twelve inch rainbow, measured against a roll of paper towels, which we'll recheck at home). Have suffered no ill effects with minimal use of halizone. We've watched a family of merganser ducks sporting in the rapids. Last month's entry records twelve ducklings; happy to report all twelve are still active and growing. The hike to Shining Cloud Falls was a real treat. The largest hemlock on the high point seems to be making a valiant struggle to survive after fire damage. Lovely Turks-cap lilies en route. Also, northern green orchids, and others. Such magnificent stands of hemlock, cedar and yellow birch. Sunsets, reading by candlelight, and falling asleep to the sound of the rapids. What more could one ask for?

The P. Family

June 28, 1975
Buckshot Cabin

The idea of backpacking is not to see how much mileage you can accumulate in the fastest amount of time...backpaking is a means to an end. The walking in the wilderness is physically demanding, but stimulating satisfaction. Backpacking brings you to an isolated wilderness area where solitude and privacy can be had (we skinny-dipped at Shining Cloud Falls without the slightest fear or inhibition that we would be intruded upon)....

Our last thought—backpacking people are good people. All the people we met these last three days have been great—very kind and friendly. It is such a great feeling to see people and not be afraid to talk (there seems to be a natural rapport between backpackers). It makes a mockery of city and suburban life where we pass so many people each day, even without a word of greeting. It is so sad and lonely.

To all of you who come here to share this cabin, I wish the best. There is no real place where anyone can physically go to gain ultimate peace; it's a day to day search that the experiences in your life either strengthen or destroy. For me, the wilderness is the only place where I have been the most happy. The experiences that I have had, have I think, strengthened me for when I return to civilization. Backpacking is like taking a bath and just soaking in the water, so relaxed after being so sweaty and miserable.

Tim & Terry V.

July 3, 1987
Big Carp 4-Bunk Cabin

It's been a perfect trip! We could not have planned a greater exposure for the kids' first time: backpacking a good number of miles, being responsible for their gear, chores at the cabin, staying safe, seeing new animals and sights, living a different way for a while, forgetting time for a few days, exploring the forests, and the shorelines of Superior....

I sure have enjoyed sharing this journal with you. Thank you for sharing with us!

Paul H.

July 3, 1987
Big Carp 4-Bunk Cabin

I'm boiling water, so I thought I would take a few moments to add my thoughts and insights as I come to the end of a three day visit to the Porkies. First of all, the people who have taken the time to keep this cabin as charming as it is, I wish to thank each and every one of you. Of course, you will never know. I have dreamt of a trip with my twin brother to the Lake Superior area for nearly twenty years. Thanks to the people who have preceded us, and the beautiful wilderness, my trip has been everything I would have hoped for. Both the simplicities and complexities of nature have been experienced.

I have come on this adventure with my brother's daughter and son, two people I admire and respect greatly. Being one of the people who has decided not to have children, this has been an unbelievable joy for the five day trip. To watch and listen to them talk, discuss, clown, be serious, etc., has proven to be worth every moment hauling in supplies, fighting the flies, and of course, boiling water.

I hope those who follow experience whatever they are hoping to experience in their hearts.

Philip H.

August 7, 1996
Buckshot Cabin

4:00 P.M.—Just arrived. Nice scenic hike in. Sure is peaceful.

5:10 P.M.—I hear some loud cussing spoiling the peacefulness. Must be my wife with the sixty quart cooler of beer and the one quarter cord of split firewood from town—what a gal! I don't know what she's been complaining about. Me and the dog's been fighting the flies around my bunk for over an hour!

6:30 P.M.—It's getting a little dark here in the woods. Maybe I should wake her up from her nap by the front door to get a fire going.

7:00 P.M.—Sure is quiet in here with the wife running back to the truck to get matches. Flies are still bad.

8:30 P.M.—Finally! A beautiful campfire. Wish she was awake to see it. She always sleeps so much when we go on vacation!

10:00 P.M.—We'll have to turn in now, me and the dog. This clear air sure makes a man tired. The cooler is lighter for her when we hike out tomorrow. Hope she's got the bed made for me.

7:00 A.M.—Must have been sleepwalking. Woke up with an axe in my pillow. I was probably chopping wood in my sleep just to keep her warm. I hope she realizes what a great guy I am!

7:30 A.M.—My wife really knows how to have fun camping. She wants to play a new game to prove how virile I am. She wants me to put on my knapsack and boots and see how far I can swim out into the lake before I get tired. Just last year, in Yellowstone, she put bacon grease in my shirt pockets to see if I could outrun a Grizzly bear. What a gal!

Unknown Author

May 5, 1998
Lily Pond Cabin

Most said that I was either crazy, stupid, or brave. Perhaps a good mix of all. The woods call me home and I must obey. Being a single parent can't stop that. So this year, I (twenty-seven) set off with my four year old daughter and six year old son, not to mention a seventy pound backpack. The hike in was good until I realized I overshot our cabin. The Lily Pond Cabin sign should have been my first clue, but I only saw the Lily Pond Trail which went the other way. The river should have been my second clue, but oh no, I rock hopped across with each of the kids and on we went. Finally I got the map out (novel idea) and realized my mistake. So a three mile hike turned into five. The kids were very brave and although Brianna shed a few tears the last one and-a-half miles, she kept walking. I couldn't have been prouder of them, and my fear that I had ruined them for life in the woods was quickly resolved as the cabin came into view and they both took off running. Neither have mentioned it again.

Our days have been full of amazing adventures. Frog catching by hand, beaver watching, canoeing (it counts as an adventure with one adult and two children), hiking, and our best adventure, catching fish in a bucket! We actually caught a dozen fish with bread crumbs and a bucket (all of which we'll return to the river later today)! They are safe in the bucket of water for now as all families need a pet, according to my son.

My spirit is feeling more intact and my mind cleared of so many burdens....We leave tomorrow and head back to Escanaba. I'll go back whole again. My children seem to thrive here and that's the best gift of all. I will keep in my heart and mind the brief but true statement: You never really leave this place, you just go home for a while!

Tina

August 24-26, 1982
Mirror Lake 4-Bunk Cabin

Came in this afternoon by some trail. The scenery was beautiful, the scents were new and abundant, and the chipmunks were plentiful. Crystel and Jay look pretty beat, probably from those heavy packs they had to carry. Glad I travel light. The clothes on my back are all I need. And food? Well, Crystel and Jay provide that.

Got up this morning and climbed some mountain. It was pretty high and it took a long time. The way there was real fun—bounding over logs, splashing in puddles, and chasing chipmunks. Of course, there were responsibilities, too. Finding the right trail, making sure Crystel and Jay were behind me, and watching for wild beasts to name but a few. When we got back, all I wanted to do was lay down. I didn't feel very well, probably due to all the puddle water I was drinking all day. But no. Crystel and Jay wanted to go fishing, so they hauled me out into the middle of the lake in the rowboat. And I've never been in a boat before! They kept throwing little balls into the water, similar to the one I've got at home, only on a smaller scale. I'm glad they didn't want me to go get them because I was already tired, and the rocking of the boat was really making me queasy by this time. As soon as we got back to the cabin, I hit the bunk and was fast asleep.

Had a rough, but long, night's sleep. First it got real smoky in here when Crystel and Jay made supper. Then when the lights went out, the little mouse was after my food. Then I got sick. All the puddle water from the day before came up. Stayed in the bunk until afternoon, after finally getting a sleeping bag. Then we walked down another trail (I stayed away from the puddle water this time). When we got home, it started raining, which was fine by me because I wanted to take a nap. The rain quit for a while and Crystel and Jay went fishing, which gave me time to get my paws on this book and give my account, as Crystel and Jay weren't going to write in it even though they enjoyed reading through it. Well, we had fun but we have to go in the morning, and I suppose when we get back to Madison, Crystel and Jay will want to give me a bath. Farewell, great outdoors!

Ebony, the dog

Sorry our dog wrote in this book. Crystel and I had fun, too.

Jay

November 8-18, 1979
Mirror Lake 4-Bunk Cabin

To come to the Porcupine Mountains in wintertime is a supreme test of an individual's stamina.

To hike the trails is simple to say the least, for no one can get lost on a trail.

To pit oneself against Mother Nature at her wildest and most dangerous time, wintertime, is to find what amount of intestinal fortitude you have established within yourself.

To leave the known and well marked trails to travel cross-country in 57,000 acres of wilderness with only a compass and your common sense to guide you is a task befitting a voyager of old.

To explore unknown rivers deep within the complex intricacy of this park, photographing them as they dash over frozen rocks and cascade from one level to another for two hundred meters and more.

To look at the wintertime splendor of a total forest blanketed in an ermines trappings.

To not be able to discern one valley or hill from another because the mantle of white encompassing the trees makes everything look the same.

To hunt the elusive Virginia Whitetail from dawn to dusk, pitting your skills as an expert hunter against his skills as an expert of camouflage, an expert who knows every nook and cranny of this land, an expert who will not lead you down trails but will ford streams, cross mountains and valleys, double back and even use the fresh remains of a fellow deer to mask his trail, to elude you.

To do these things my friend, is to hunt deer. To see these things is to leave the trail and set out across the wilderness with compass in hand and a well-defined map of your locality.

To do this is why I have returned. The Porcupines are my country. They belonged to my people long before the white man set foot upon this shore. For I am Cree, and educated, a dangerous combination. But every year I return to the land of the Great Manitu by the shores of Gitchee-Gumee, by the shining deep-sea waters (according to Longfellow). I return to capture in my heart and in my eyes the sights that Manitu has bestowed upon this land.

To destroy these sights is to make a sacrilegious alteration to one of Mother Nature's most prized areas.

To put a road across the northern point of this park from east to west would be just such a sacrilege. Keep them from doing this, to protect our park for our children to walk and see the sights which I have seen and my children have seen.

My next few days are the most enjoyable of each year, for now is when I see what I am made of. Now is the time for the hunt.

Was it Mephistopheles who roamed the world looking for an honest man?

Was it an honest man who cut live timber for firewood for the Yukon stove?

Was it an honest group of people who have created the unsightly garbage dumps behind the cabins?

Are you an honest individual? Did you leave enough wood for the next honest man?

Did you clean the dishes?

Did you sweep the floor?

Did you take your garbage with you?

Most people who visit this park and reside in these cabins for but a few precious moments leave here with but a mental impression of how beautiful it is. These same people have thoroughly neglected their fellow individuals and Mother Nature by disobeying some or all of the few, simple, general, easy-to-follow rules stated above.

The only honest individual which I have encountered within the domain of the Porcupine Mountains has been Mother Nature.

Honest in all respects; infinitely merciful and forgiving, she has succeeded today in hiding from view all of the garbage, new cut branches which will never see another spring, and all of the natural wastefulness which man and his "exploring" has created.

Today, Mother Nature made it snow. Six inches down and more coming.

It's invigorating to watch the sun through a forest of hemlock, bowing their branches with the weight of tons of snow, and every once in a while, the glistening of a snowflake, setting the branches ablaze with myriads of diamonds twinkling before the eyes.

The only sounds heard today were the lonesome tap-tap-tapping of a woodpecker looking for tree insects, the frightened sounds of rapid wing beats from a pair of startled grouse, a solemn honking of a flock of snow geese late on their winter departure to a warmer clime, the yap of a dog some two mile or more distant, the sound of my blood pulsing through my temples as a lonesome walk is made to the South Boundary Road.

These are the sounds of nature, no fancy frills has she, but most people cannot hear her special callings because they do not want to hear. They are not trained to hear.

No sound from Kisla. He moved today within the confines of his natural realm, as it he need not touch ground.

Only the raven saw Kisla today, as he soared high overhead looking for a meal. Possibly a small squirrel was disturbed while eating his meal, as Kisla walked past.

Tomorrow I hunt for him. Tomorrow he hides from me with cunning.

The lake has a cloak of white today. The freezing process was completed early this morning and with the intermittent flurries of snow throughout the day, a master artist could not paint a scene as perfect and extravagantly beautiful as the one from my doorstep.

Kisla evaded me today. He left his tracks for me to follow and then laughed at me from hiding as he watched my futile efforts to catch him at his game.

I saw where he had lain under the hemlock boughs and watched as I tracked him through the valley below.

Kisla the smart one, ever vigilant.

I am alone. It is now my time to put mental occurrences together, a time for deep thought, a time to measure the solitude. This is the time I appreciate the most. Alone, with no one near during daylight or nighttime. Only myself and nature. Pitting wits for survival in a wintertime wilderness.

Think! Can you do it?

Complete solitude.

The cabin is so quiet. The wood mouse is afraid to come out.

Time to hunt again for Kisla. He beckons from the wilderness for me to play the game a little longer tonight.

I will oblige him. One half-hour of daylight left.

Maybe he will falter tonight and come upon the arrow.

Dishes cleaned, food prepared for tomorrow's hunt. Cabin is warm and the bed beckons to me.

Very late, must arise before dawn.

Kisla has formed a pattern. Very dangerous thing for him to do.

Hunted long and far today, but did not see him. Only the pattern.

Hope he was not baiting me. Tomorrow will tell.

Found today that a new North Mirror Lake Trail has been made since last I visited this area. It traverses west and north of the previous trail. All identification plaques from the old trail have been taken out but you can still see the trail if you look hard.

The weather is warm. Good sign for more snow. I do not expect much though.

The cabin is lonely but it still leaves me with many moments for thought. I need that very badly.

The rest of the men will be in tomorrow morning.

When they come, the cabin will be warm, but I will be away, with Kisla.

As the last rays of the sun managed to creep across the mountain tops, the sound of a rare specimen, a robin in a wintertime wilderness, echoed from one tree trunk to another until it finally fell upon my ears, deep within the hemlock forest as I waited in silent seclusion for Kisla to appear upon his trail.

The song was like vespers being said to a silent forest where the only ones to hear were the trees, the wildlife, and I.

Kisla didn't appear today. He plays the game very well and from some unknown glade of fern-laden forest nook, he lay, silently laughing about our game and how he is winning.

The night is upon me, the stars are out and shining in a cloudless sky. Tomorrow night is the first semblance of a moon. The nights will then start to brighten.

The other men are in and relationships are once again being renewed. Everyone who came in today is tired and looking for bed.

They will have to learn to acclimatize themselves to the strict regimen which is carried on is this camp.

Arose at 6:30 A.M. to an overcast sky, the small sliver of a moon passing its rays of reflection through a screen of heavy, moisture-laden clouds.

The ether is very heavy, it has been all day. The cloud cover was a good sign of snow coming in, and just as predicted, the snow came.

From early morning 'til after nightfall, the snow came in waves of one time heavy and one time light showers.

Toward the twilight of the evening, as I was moving down a steep ridge, Kisla appeared from under a group of cedars. Each looked at one another for more than ten minutes, eye to eye, never blinking, never moving, and each knowing full well of the other's whereabouts. The distance separating us was one hundred yards and he knew that the bow could not reach him. And so his stand was firm and his senses alert, for he knew that the game for today was won by he.

Before the blink of an eye, he was gone, vanished into the cedar swamp as if he were a ghostly vapor and the slight breeze and snow blew him to shreds.

The only trace was the footprints left in the snow as he laughed on his merry way to his bed upon the mountain.

He knows that to play the game means to survive, for all too soon will come the day when white men will use fire sticks to hunt him down.

Today was exploration day, across and around the lake. Up and down the mountains and walking through ankle deep snow. Across swamps laden with snow and ice and following forgotten trails up on forgotten ridges.

The river was exquisite in every detail. Intermittent snow and sunshine, but generally overcast.

The view from the mountaintops must be splendid in early spring with the new formed buds and flowers upon the trees and ground, and also in the fall with the color change. I will have to return here during one of those times with camera in hand and loads of film.

Today at 7:00 A.M., Eos with her magnificent steeds, drew her chariot and pulled the sun towards the horizon. She blew away the gossamer veil of darkness and slowly, down, crept over the Porcupines. At 7:15 A.M., my blind was in order and with rifle in hand, I waited for Kisla.

At 7:30 A.M., he appeared upon my left, so close that I could hear his rapid breathing. The wind was in my face and not a sound made I as he walked in front of me.

With rifle to shoulder and safety off, he suddenly sensed my presence and stopped, turning only his head in my direction.

Fifteen feet separated us and with scope crosshairs upon his lower right shoulder, I watched him with my unscoped eye.

He knew that he had lost and an aura of fear slowly crossed from him to me.

With the slightest of movements, I safetied the rifle and moved it from my shoulder.

He watched me with a death stillness, and then I said to him, "Today I win my friend for I cannot find it in my heart to kill you with a rifle."

He looked away, and suddenly, with a flurry of bounds, he moved out of vision, only to be heard stomping his feet and snorting in anger over having given in to the game so easily.

I silently looked at my bow, which I had taken to the vehicle parked upon the roadway. It was just out of reach, hanging on a branch.

Larry V.

Unknown Date
Lily Pond Cabin

Jim H.

130

May 27, 1995
Mirror Lake 2-Bunk Cabin

Words and styles of writing seem to describe, define, and characterize all who have committed themselves to paper. Though simplistically, I'm sure, your faces and thoughts revisit me in this cabin, on the lake, while swatting flies or enjoying the fire. I'm describing a haunting, a fraternity shared by all that have borrowed this place. You all have left a mark and piece of personality in this book. Writing this, of course, my audience might as well be dead. They are gone. But you who have come will continue the legacy and hopefully be haunted by me, someone you'll probably never meet, except on this page.

Paul

Friends, Family, and Strangers

Nightscapes

August 28, 1997
Big Carp 4-Bunk Cabin

It is so odd at night here—the blackness, the silence! Being used to the constant hum of noise in the city, I have to admit that Dana and I were scared out of our minds in the pitch blackness whenever we would hear a twig crack or the water gurgle! Today I laugh at our silliness, but I'm sure tonight will be the same deal.

Tricia

May 29, 1980
Speaker's Cabin

Unfortunately, there is a cloudy sky this evening and no stars. However, if it is clear, Venus is about thirty degrees above the horizon in the northern sky. It's the brightest object in the sky other than the moon so you can't miss it. Presently, it's going through phases, similar to the moon, and it's about one-quarter now. Jupiter is almost eighty degrees above the horizon in the western sky, and it's almost as bright as Venus. With a small scope, you can see its four Galilean moons (Io, Europa, Calypso, and Ganymede). These moons were first observed by Galileo, thus their names that he gave them. Close to Jupiter is Mars. It shines with a red hue that is unmistakable. Saturn is also in the near vicinity and its rings are "edge on," that is, in the same plane as the Earth, which means they can't be seen except in very powerful telescopes. On June 1, Venus and Mercury will only be one degree apart. This is an excellent opportunity to view the elusive planet Mercury. This will not happen again until 1993. To test your vision capabilities, check out the bird in the handle of the Big Dipper. It's actually a double star, and it should pose no problem for you. General constellations of the summer sky include Cygnus, the swan, which is in the shape of a lips, and Cassiopeia, which shape is similar to an offset "W". Should all of this seem too confusing or uninteresting, remember that if the stars came out only once a year, it would be an honored event we wouldn't miss.

Terry, Jan, Dan, Heather, & Toby

January 19, 1998
Union River Cabin

It was uncanny dark last night. There was no moon. There were no stars. We directed our flashlights to the heavens and, within the beams, snowflakes appeared as if materialized from the void, motes of the universe. They fell off-kilter, entering the illuminated shaft acutely and exiting the same, as if the world were tilted. In that moment, nothing else existed. The passage of time was marked only by the passage of the snow, and was measured by the whispering staccato rhythm of falling powder striking grounded matter. How much time passed? A million beats, or perhaps a billion. After some time, we switched off the torches and the stygian deep returned. And the patter of the falling snow remained, counting past, present, and future. We awoke from our revelry, found the footpath, and were gone.

D.N.

October 10, 1988
Buckshot Cabin

Geoff G.

September 13, 1987
Buckshot Cabin

The last rays of sun made the yellow and orange of the trees along the shoreline reflect extra crisp color and the sky was pink, red, and orange when the sun finally crashed into the lake. At night, every one of the stars was out and the Milky Way was clearly outlined in the sky. Later, when the half-moon was rising burnt brown in the east, the Aurora Borealis, the Northern Lights, were forming a small, green amphitheater in the northern sky. The area of pale green grew until it reached the Big Dipper. At first, the lights appeared to be like two parallel tubes of bright light with an ethereal film between them. Then the show started. The tubes undulated like a giant ghost snake in the sky. Then, vertical beams shot up within the tubes and appeared to light off and on in sequence, as if someone was shining a flashlight up and down a tube of green panels. At times, hints of red outlined the tubes. Towards the end, the tubes seemed to tail off in the distance like twin, parallel roads winding up identical mountains, side by side.

Fritz & Pam

August 25-30, 1991
Gitchee Gumee Cabin

Oh yeah! One last thing! Swimming in the buff under a full moon is one of the greatest feelings on earth! Give it a try!

Heather A.

May 16, 1992
Mirror Lake 2-Bunk Cabin

Out on Mirror Lake with the full moon rising over the trees seemed to reconcile the grand scheme of things for me. There are many things in life we cannot control—many losses and difficulties—but the sun always sets and rises again, the moon goes through its lunar phases, and the wildlife here seems barely to notice our presence. Thank God for those things that are pre-dictable here in nature!

Laurie

April 19, 1976
Buckshot Cabin

Now I know why Monet wanted to capture the difference the light of day makes. The sun and starlight painted a different picture for us every few min-utes. We saw a stark, rugged birch forest in the early light, a white, white bright one, contrasting with the bluest, blue waters at high noon, and then at sundown another forest reflected through a pink-blue sky. Twilight was also beautiful to watch as the sky became a mottled gray and blue behind the stark white birches. And then, more and more darkness. Then, the stars added later, like an afterthought, a pinch of salt.

D.

December 28, 1993
Gitchee Gumee Cabin

Jimmy

August 21, 1982
Little Carp Cabin

Went back to Superior for sunset. Beautiful, multi-faceted, serene. Shortly after sunset, we saw the most magnificent meteor (did it land?) streaking all the way across the sky from west to northwest 'til it disappeared over the trees east-northeast of us. Incredible! It appeared to be very close at about forty degrees elevation. Burning chunks of it broke off as we watched it. I have seen meteors (shooting stars) before, but nothing like this. A most apt climax to our last night in the North Woods.

Tom

September 14, 1988
Speaker's Cabin

The scariest part about camping on Mother Superior is the sky at night. Of course, it is a beautiful, wondrous thing to behold. Even the Milky Way, a hazy ribbon stretching across the void, is visible. Tonight, Peren saw a bright-red shooting star arriving above the northern horizon. However, the vastness of the sky makes one realize what a flyspeck humanity is in the universe. All of our fighting, wars, loves, goals, histories, and monuments to ourselves are insignificant. No man likes to feel insignificant. I came across a quote today by Frank Herbert that sums it up:

"The universe is God's. It is one thing, a wholeness against which all separations may be identified. Transient life, even the self-aware and reasoning life which we call sentient, holds only fragile trusteeship on any portion of the wholeness."

Unknown Author

April 1, 1997
Mirror Lake 8-Bunk Cabin

Artist Unknown

September 15, 1985
Big Carp 6-Bunk Cabin

What a night! Last night the Northern Lights were changing slowly and subtly with one ray beginning on the northern horizon, arcing clear across the sky and crossing the Milky Way in the process, and ending on the southern horizon. The Northern Lights and Milky Way crossed right above us on the beach and this arc ended behind the cabin. The night air was warm, balmy even, and the sky clear! A sweet smell in the air.

Doug A.

September 23, 1980
Buckshot Cabin
Moon shining so bright, shadow dancing in its light to the rhythm of waves and rocks as they rendezvous upon the shore. Slender birch luster white in the moonlit night.

Shining moon
Dancing shadows
Waves upon rocks
Lustering birches
All beckon the well-fed, warm, and sleepy cabin dweller out into the magic of night.

New worlds are seen through widened pupils of the night. Thoughts, like shooting stars, emerge and glisten in all corners of the sky. Some live only as long as an initial spark—others take the unlikely turns of a cedar's roots upon a rock.

Unknown Author

June 12, 1975
Section 17 Cabin
Do you know how black it is when you shut your eyes inside a closed closet? Well, it was the same way here last night. It didn't matter if your eyes were open or shut, you saw the same thing—absolutely nothing. Joe said it scared him when he first woke up during the night. He thought he had gone blind from drinking the river water!

Doug F.

June 12, 1997
Mirror Lake 4-Bunk Cabin
What a beautiful night out on the lake!! A wonderful blanket of stars and a couple of "puff" clouds dancing near the half-moon. Crickets chirping and the gnawing of beaver keeping time with the patter of waves on the boat made heavenly music. The moonlight and reflections on the lake were truly stunning. You could almost read out there!

Joe, Justin (age twelve), & Jordan (age six) L.

September 6-7, 1994
Little Carp Cabin

Had a super hike in, light packs and fleet of foot helped move us along fine. Enjoyed dinner by the lake, listening to the symphony of calling crickets and the crashing of waves on the shore. The sunset which followed provided the perfect cadenza to the music of the glorious day. As the colors faded away, we reveled in the cold light of the stars which hung in the indigo sky. The night which followed was semi-restful. Unfortunately, city ears become attuned to the nighttime noises other than nature and it is sometimes hard to adjust to the new silence....

Something amazing always happens here. You become. If you allow yourself, you slip into a state of calmness and oneness with the world that can be found in few places. At that point, finding the meaning of life is not a problem or a concern, because you just are.

Pam & Rich

September 8, 1975
Little Carp Cabin

The summer Milky Way and the fainter stars stood out so strongly that it took some time to recognize even the familiar constellations Delphinus and Cygnus. Nova Cygui 1975 has definitely faded below the level at which it can be recognized by the naked eye.

Audrey & Homer D.

July 14, 1991
Little Carp Cabin

Last night we saw the most awesome Aurora Borealis show. Incredible lights. Started as a bright band from northeast to west, then twisted and broke, and reformed across the entire sky. Blues, violets, greens...lit the water and the woods. Directly overhead it flickered and pulsated. Words fail to describe the magnitude and variety. Might have been the show of a lifetime.

Douglas T.

January 5,1995
Gitchee Gumee Cabin

It's cloudy now. Earlier in the evening and last night it was pretty clear. The stars are incredible! Most of us rarely get a glimpse of that many stars. We live in cities and only get to see the brightest stars. We get the haze from the city lights and we obscure the nighttime, we block it out. It's an eerie feeling to be outside and be in complete darkness. It's awesome. We are less in touch with the nighttime now than any group of people in the history of mankind. Most people cannot even name all of the planets that circle the sun.

Ancient civilizations used the stars and their position in the heavens as markers of the seasons. The major zodiac constellations were known by people on the street, not just by astronomers. Their lives were ruled by the stars. So much was imbedded in the culture, that it lives today in the horoscopes on the page with the comics. Funny to some, but just think of Nancy Reagan and the joke is no longer humorous.

Right now the moon is in its first quarter so there are still plenty of stars to see. A meteor shower began on January 3. I can't remember the name of it, but there are as many as one shooting star per minute. If you get a clear sky, you should be able to see some.

The other fundamental astronomical event which occurs daily (actually nightly) is the rotation of the stars. The stars appear to move counter-clockwise during the evening, all maintaining the same relative position to one another. If you imagine the sky as the rim of a bicycle wheel, the North Star is the hub, and all the stars rotate about this hub. You can find the North Star by first finding the Big Dipper (at this point, it is right above the lake in early evening). The two stars that make up the end of the bucket point to the North Star. As the evening goes on, the Dipper, as well as all of the stars, will swing around the North Star while it does not move at all (actually only slightly).

Well, enough blabbering already. My candles are almost gone and the mantles in the lantern blew out earlier in the evening. Peace.

Unknown Author

January 18, 1988
Speaker's Cabin

We saw a strange star on the northern horizon that flickered red to green irregularly. Diane thought it moved left, I thought it moved right, and Mike thought it was stationary. I sat down on the beach and watched for several minutes with the star's position referenced behind a branch...until my vision blurred and I got quite spaced out. It never moved in reference to the branch, but is seemed to move down and to the right constantly. Weird?

Robert T.

June 12, 1995
Big Carp 6-Bunk Cabin

I skim stones across the water as I watch the dragon stare at me. Burning bright red, she slowly descends into the lake, her multi-colored aura trails her exit. Standing still, I listen to the sounds of nature change. Walking back to the warmth of the distant fire, the night air moves across the sky, touches my bones, and whispers "wish to the one-eyed owl." Who? Holding my hair away from the flames, the river's current carries a cry. I arise, startled. I turn and there, hovering overhead, flying so low and steady, casting light upon the lake, the river, the bridge, the trees, and me, I make my wish.

Unknown Author

November 1986
Section 17 Cabin
We were all resting peacefully after a scare with a skunk. Kino (one of the dogs) had a real bout with the striped kitty just before bedtime last eve, and miraculously escaped the spray. So we went to sleep with visions of anything but sugarplums dancing in our heads!

Fran

1981
Lily Pond Cabin
Saw the Northern Lights, and couldn't go to sleep, for the sake of them. All nature, all colors, all strength and harmony dancing in front of you on a night sky.... Thank you Lily Pond and lovers for offering such a pure and serene haven to us both.

Unknown Author

Romance 'au Natural

September 22-24, 1992
Gitchee Gumee Cabin

Debbie and I came here to celebrate our third anniversary. What a beautiful, romantic choice! We spent most of the two days here hiking through forest trails. The sense of time and history is awe-inspiring. The rock formations along both Lake Superior and the trails give a glimpse of a period long ago, of hot volcanoes, blowing sands, running streams, and a big lake. A long time later, glaciers came through and cleaned out the lake and shaped the hills, perhaps to look like it did during that time, long before, with volcanoes.

While hiking around, we can see evidence of the last several hundred years of the time line. The various copper pits, tree stumps, and abandoned mines attest to the joining of people with the marching time line of the Porcupines. Our arrival here two days ago, to celebrate three years passing on our own time line together, seems to join us with the ancient and majestic time line which has been marching on through this place forever, one billion years.

Eric

August 30, 1985
Lake Superior Cabin

We enjoyed the evening very much—light winds, calm lake, magnificent sunset, and full moon! We are both far away from "home," but we are finally together again after many months apart, and that is where we're really at home. We built a fire near the beach last night and enjoyed the shadows dancing in the trees.... We've enjoyed the tranquility of the forest, rivers, and mountains. It is a wonderful place for a reunion of two hearts which have been lonely for so long.

Michael S. & Mary B.

August 13, 1976
Big Carp 4-Bunk Cabin

Jan and I arrived yesterday afternoon, walking a long four miles down from Pinkerton Trail. Prior to this, we spent the night at Lily Pond. So far we've been having a great time.

We were married last Saturday, so this is our honeymoon. It seems slightly out of place to call it that, because we have been planning this trip since January. We feel that this is a good way to spend time with each other. This type of situation helps to foster an atmosphere of cooperation and closeness. It also helps to realize that our lives have very much to offer, especially to each other.

I think that most everyone should do this type of thing every year (at least). So often we get bogged down by all the complexities in our lives that we actually forget what our priorities are. It almost seems obvious that when people become unhappy, confused, depressed, etc., that it is simply because they have lost track of their positions in this world. The greatest word that I have ever learned is "ecosystem." It's the ability for all things (animate and inanimate) to get along in the environment on an equal level. In short, it is harmony. Just look out of this window. Nature is our biggest example because so many different things can live here, and yet do little to harm each other. Our own main purpose in life is to become harmonious with the world about us. After this achievement, the benefits will become obvious. This occurs on every level: from a complex situation such as Jan's and mine, to one that is very minute, such as the harmony of atoms. And yet when approached in this fashion, who can say what situation is more complex or more necessary. Everything becomes equally important because one cannot exist without the other. This is one reason why we are here today. Nature is our greatest teacher.

Tom S.

September 23-24, 1995
Mirror Lake 2-Bunk Cabin
The canoeing was great, even with just one paddle. I got to be Cleopatra, ushered around the lake by my man-servant, slaving in the back.

Judi & Bill

October 5, 1994
Big Carp 6-Bunk Cabin
Last evening, I witnessed what I believed to be the beginning of a long romance. A Canadian goose had been hanging around the cabin, all by itself, for about four days. I walked past it, desiring to catch a view of the beautiful twilight rainbow colors on wispy clouds from the bridge. I saw the silhouette of a lone goose at the mouth of the river. It gave a honk, and "our" goose immediately swam out to it. They seemed to take to one another so.

Jan

August 13, 1995
Big Carp 4-Bunk Cabin
I was looking out the south window of the cabin, towards Lake Superior, when he asked me to turn around and open my eyes. In his hand he was holding the most beautiful diamond that I had ever seen. "Will you marry me?" he asked. So long had I waited to hear these words! Of course I said, "Yes,' and we both started to cry.
This is day two of an eight day hiking and backpacking trip through the Porkies. I've coined it our "engagement trip," and we're looking forward to

time away from jobs, phones, dogs, and bills! My only frustration is that I haven't been able to tell anyone that I'm engaged! The first packer I encounter tomorrow will have to endure having my ring thrust in his or her face, and will (hopefully) agree to take our official engagement photo. If it happens to be you, thanks in advance for your understanding!

Barbara G. & Marty O.

June 27, 1987
Big Carp 4-Bunk Cabin

Honeymoon in the Porkies! We were married one week ago, today, and this is the place for a honeymoon. It's like starting our married life by going to heaven. Coming up here doesn't solve life's problems, but it sure makes them lose their significance. Here we can focus on our love and relax in the beauty around us.

George & Robin V.

September 24, 1979
Buckshot Cabin

Rick & Martha B.

July 19, 1991
Gitchee Gumee Cabin

There are so many different sensations and expressions to feel that it's hard to put into words. The cabin has charm and beauty. Our first night, the lake had a stiff breeze blowing. It was so invigorating that it blows right through you and stirs up the blood in between. The sunset lasted long and was haunting. It was mellow, fiery, warm, and contrasting. Only a true artist could create such a miracle. Sunsets aren't like this in Battle Creek. They don't have Lake Superior to mirror and try to rival their beauty. We jogged along the beach and felt the sand pull on our tendons. All three of us were the Three

Stooges by sitting (or trying to sit) on our inflatable raft. It's really fun to float on one of the rivers and into the lake, doing a face slapper into all the waves. I wish life wasn't lived and governed by memories. There's a sweet sadness to that somehow. My husband is sitting here across the table, softly waxing and buffing our rock collection. Each rock chosen we agreed upon, our ideas of beauty in harmony. We are good, close friends and it's intimate to watch the shadows and light move over the planes of his face. I recommend a stay at this cabin to every married couple! What adds to the appreciation of this place is the comfort of knowing that the very person who created all of this, the one who gifted it, has promised that it will really be here forever...I am grateful for that promise. It won't be broken. This has been a wonderful stay. People cared who stayed here, and the cabin reflected it. Thanks! We'll try to do the same.

Kathy H.

August 28-September 1, 1967
Little Carp Cabin

I heartily suggest that many more new brides suggest a honeymoon of this type. It has its advantages, girls! He'll be so hungry that he'll rave about your cooking, and when you get home, he dare not say otherwise!

Kathy S.

October 12-14, 1985
Mirror Lake 2-Bunk Cabin

Cookie and Dick came here in love; with the woods, the mountains, the quiet, and each other. We canoed a bit, hiked a bit, breathed the fresh air, cut a pile of wood, cooked some neat food, loved, laughed, groaned (some of those trails), and wished the mice would be a bit quieter at night. We leave the way we came; in love. With the woods, the mountains, the peace, the quiet, and most of all, with each other.

Cookie & Dick

October 4, 1981
Lily Pond Cabin

First of all, I would like to say that this has been our greatest anniversary ever. It's our twenty-fifth (that's not months, but years), and I have enjoyed every minute of it. For those of you who are spending your honeymoon here, all the effort and work that a marriage involves is well worth it. Think of it as a bunch of peaks and valleys; there are highs and lows to every relationship, and with age, those highs just become higher and the lows don't seem so major. Right now I'm on the biggest high anyone could ever expect, all due to a wonderful husband and children (we have three, all in college) who have all contributed to making my life very meaningful...For all of you—enjoy the cabin, this beautiful spot, and your marriage, for the benefits are far greater than the effort.

Pat & Len P.

July 28, 1968
Buckshot Cabin

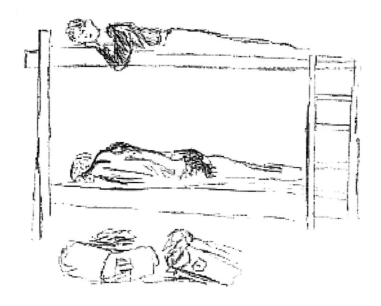

Jo J.

June 28 - July 1, 1975
Section 17 Cabin

I really like the idea of a logbook. Reading people's thoughts helps me relate to them.... So many of the thoughts expressed in this book have been our thoughts, too. There is something mysterious and almost magical about this place that sets your mood and way of thinking.

This one room cabin has been a blessing to our relationship. I think that it was an excellent way to start our life together. It has been a time of growth and sharing. Starting out from scratch as a young, married couple, I think that this cabin has helped to prepare us. For this I am thankful. I can appreciate everything a little more. What we have is going to look greater than what we don't have when we set up house. It also helps me to realize how much you don't need. We've found happiness and peace here that transcends the material aspect of life.

When we came here, we noticed that the people who stayed before us each contributed a little something to this cabin. If these walls could talk! How many secrets, experiences, and memories would they reveal? Like a good cheese, this cabin will get better with age. We'll leave something, too, but will carry away our memories.

Mr. & Mrs. Mark D.

September 6, 1983
Greenstone Falls Cabin

After having camped at Speaker's Sunday with Bryan's parents, sister Dana, and brother David, we arrived here yesterday afternoon to Bryan's favorite place of all places, which he wished to share with me. This is a very special place to both of us now, as I learned last night that it's not the only thing he wants to share with me—he proposed!!! What a perfect setting—beauty, serenity, and very romantic, only interrupted by our eight month old lab, Stinker, and our ten week old lab-collie mix, Sierra, playing tug-o-war with an old shirt. It was truly a night of bliss....

Until next Labor Day, enjoy this place and its beauty!

Carol

August 10, 1991
Gitchee Gumee Cabin

I've been kind of depressed today. This is stupid, but my very first boyfriend that I ever really cared about was married today in Minneapolis, and it bothered me. I know it shouldn't, since I know I don't love him anymore, but it still left a certain twinge of melancholy.... Alas, life goes on. Tomorrow is another day. Time heals all wounds. And who, I'd like to know, came up with those sayings? Did they ever work for them? I think I need some sleep.

Dara

June 1, 1997
Speaker's Cabin

I am sad to write, but as time now steadily moves onward towards the start of a new day, it is time to depart from this wonderful world and back into the mainstream that everyone calls life. It is here, back to where it all began, that calls for the soul and meaning of every individual, and mounts their searches for all of life's happiness.

This is not my first trip here to this wonderful and majestic place. I have been here well over ten times throughout my life. This is the first time I have been here with such a beautiful and truly special individual (Shannon). Her beauty, as well as her inner warmth are enough to warm the heart and soul of any man as the chill of night settles in. Whether it was the gentle smile on her face after she caught her first trout (Presque Isle) or the gentle curiosity in her eyes as we explored the bear tracks so alarmingly close to our cabin.

These are the memories that will always stay so close and so dear as we live our lives the only way we know how. It takes a place such as this to help make an individual who he or she is destined to be. The raw and untouched beauty of such a land is something that can touch us all. There simply are no boundaries. It is on this note that we bid this heaven good-bye until yet another time...where we can all come together with Mother Nature again.

Craig

May 2, 1992
Greenstone Falls Cabin

AH, SPRING! Love is in the air. Or at least lust. You want proof? I hiked down to the river today, and as I lay down in the grass for a nap, I caught sight of two flies copulating! The male (I assume), who was a full third smaller than the female, shamelessly mounted his lover from behind, proudly doing his duty as I stared in amazement. I hope they enjoyed it, considering the short life of a fly—I pause here for a moment because my cabin mates appear to be near to starting the place on fire—not to worry, all's well again. Anyway, considering the short life of a fly, that may have been their last hurrah, so to speak. But now they can die happy and fulfilled. They will have left a legacy behind in the form of many baby flies. They'll be long gone by the time the kids are born, though. But I guess that is not unlike many human (so-called) parents. Perhaps they'll have left their world in a little better shape than when they entered it. I hope I can say the same for myself when I die. I also hope that I can do what they did today, sometime, again.

Scott D.

November 1, 1978
Lake of the Clouds Cabin
To my husband—

May our love be as beautiful as the days spent at this cabin and as the woods and lake outside. May it last forever and may our children be happy and loving like you. You make me very happy and lucky to have you. I think our love will last forever and our feelings be as free as a bud and a carefree deer. My love I cannot explain or begin to explain to you. Like I said to you on October 10, 1978, I Rose, take you, Dave, to be my beautiful wedded husband, to have and to hold from this day forward, for better or for worse, for richer or poorer, until death do us part. I love you!

Rose

June 20, 1996
Lily Pond Cabin
　　The weather is really calm and gray, a little bit rainy even. It's perfect for making love in a cabin all day.

John & Erika

June 6, 1993
Buckshot Cabin

Kevin & Shari

June 21, 1996
Gitchee Gumee Cabin
　　The skies are clear! What a glorious day, all we can do is hope that this continues into the evening. What a beautiful place! I was walking along the roadside and a bald eagle swooped down towards the water, right in front of me. What a blessing! Today is my wedding day—how very strange. My new husband (to be) lays asleep still. I think he's pretending to be asleep. My wedding dress lies hanging in a bag across from me. I'm very, very happy. All I can say is, how strange—.here I am—to be married—really nothing changes—just a piece of paper with our names on it, a contract that we will be together "'til death do us part." I'm happy.

Becky

October 1, 1992
Greenstone Falls Cabin
　　Our third anniversary and it couldn't be a more glorious day here in the Greenstone Falls Cabin area. The sky is a clear blue, the foliage a contrasting, fiery gold, and the bark of the trees a deep black. I'm taking all of this beauty

151

in from the hammock strung between two trees and warmed by the sunshine. My husband and I are going to spend all of our anniversaries up in the Porkies. It seems that the "time crunch" and nonsensical chaos of civilization gets worse each year! Our annual trek up to the Porkies is a needed rejuvenation of the soul each year.

Deepak Chopra, M.D., in Magical Mind—Magical Body, calls the intrinsic happiness that man desires, "bliss." It is very easy to find bliss among the natural beauty here. Why is it so difficult back home?

Mike & Kate W.

May 4, 1992
Mirror Lake 2-Bunk Cabin

A great way to spend a birthday!... I keep looking out the west window, seeing trunks that look like elephants (pun?), tree limbs like snakes, and rocks with raccoon faces. I almost expect the trees to come to life—not like the Wizard of Oz, but more like the magic broomstick in Fantasia, walking up and down the hills, dancing and pivoting across the forest stage. And every time I glance up from this book to check out the entertainment, the trees stop, in place, and pretend nothing ever happened....

For a birthday adventure, I can think of nothing better than to spend a day hiking through the woods, watching the birds from the wood bench, hearing the sizzle of steak, and feeling my wet, frozen toes turn warm in front of our little "fireplace."

As the sun drops down and the bands of light wane in the woods, I still keep looking out the window, expecting once, to catch and see the dancing grove of trees! Sweet dreams to your night and day, and thanks for the memories we carry on our way!

To my wife on her thirty-fifth Birthday:
Everything
depends upon

the wildness
of her eyes

the solitude
of her hands

and the galaxy
of her smile.

Sue & Phil

July 2-3, 1994
Mirror Lake 2-Bunk

The cabin is secluded, but not as private as it seems. Upon finishing my business in the outhouse, I returned to find a pair of hikers talking to my boyfriend at the front door. Unfortunately, all I was wearing were shoes and socks. One of us thought it was funny.

Unknown Author

September 21, 1973
Big Carp 4-Bunk Cabin

After reading and enjoying many of the entries in this log, I have come to the realization that hikers have a "common bond" consisting of weather conditions, firewood, and the condition of the cabin,...but no matter what the status of these things are, I have noticed that all who have shared this place over the years have seen and enjoyed its beauty. Tonight, the beauty of a warm fire in the small stove, with the rain on the roof, occasional thunder and lightning, writing by candlelight, and an occasional warm and loving hug from Greg, bring to a close one of the most naturally spent days of my life. I feel most happy to be alive and able to share in this experience of nature.

Mary

Romance *'au Natural*

The Spiritually Inspired

Unknown Date
Whitetail Cabin

WAKANTANKA

Save me and give me all my wild game animals,
And have them close enough
So my people will have enough food this winter,
And also the goodmen on earth will have more power
So their tribes will get along better and be of good nature
So all the nations will get along.
Well, if you do this for me,
I will sun dance two days and two nights
And will give you a whole buffalo.

Unknown Author & Artist

October 21, 1988
Speaker's Cabin

Being here among the huge balsam, yellow birch, the many kinds of rocks, and the lake have again made me aware of the shortness of our lives and the importance of living fully everyday. This is a spiritual, eternal place. A place for reflection and peace. Enjoy it as we have.

Gene

September 13, 1992
Big Carp 6-Bunk Cabin

All in all, the time spent here was quiet and peaceful. Learned a great lesson this morning about God's love—watching the waves roll in upon the rocks allowed me to understand how God's love works in our lives. Daily, He gently washes over our lives smoothing off the rough edges and polishing us for His glory. When you know God in a personal way, a trip and time spent like this in the Porkies becomes so meaningful.

Men's Group, Northwoods Assembly of God Church

August 23, 1973
Little Carp Cabin

It has been interesting to note everyone's distaste of the usual life compared to the stay here. I guess that is a sign of a good vacation. The change of pace does everyone good, I am sure. The relatively unspoiled surroundings brings up the question of just how much better our personal lifestyles are in our modern society compared to that of two centuries ago? However, we must remember that the happiness of the individual is a product of the internal environment, and the external environment is only a vignette to which the soul responds. We may be happy in any situation we find ourselves. In the present surroundings, though, the happy soul finds new pleasure.

Tom D.

April 27, 1999
Whitetail Cabin

I came here to heal my soul, to nurture my spirit. The deaths of my sister and grandmother have shattered my world beyond belief. My life has changed forever.

In the woods, in the sounds of the water, in the rising and setting of the sun, I have found energy, love, and have been held by Divineness in the most tender way possible, and I have begun the road of healing. For now, I know that the spirit of my sister, my grandmother, live on in me. And I know, too, that the universe demonstrates the Divine love in every blade of grass, in every drop of dew, in every grain of sand. For time is merely just that...time.

And soon enough I will see their faces again. Until then, I will dwell in the love that the world gives and heal my heart and spirit in the love of the world.

J.W.

October 2, 1997
Mirror Lake 8-Bunk Cabin

Dances With the Wind (Ruach)

A fire burns deep inside
Time stands still for an eternity
And that is...is
And always will be
Creation bows her head
In respect of her Creator
Love abounds
To spill forth her passion
The heart dances to a silent drum
Water...water
Ever cleansing the earth
Forever singing a new song
The Word speaks to her...
She listens
The moon shines her light on the darkness
To comfort the one whom is lost
Dust at her feet
Sweat on her brow
A fire burns deep inside
The wind lights her way
As night gives way to the day
A new beginning
Ever changing...ever changing
She dances with the Wind

Note: the word Ruach is Greek for "Holy Spirit"

Kelli K.

August 6, 1995
Lake Superior Cabin

What an awe-inspiring place. I don't know what it is about places like this, but they always seem to strike a contemplative urge within me. I think that the simplicity of it all is so therapeutic. I mean, what could be more simple than the sun setting over the lake, or the fire chewing away at a log. To me, these things seem so simple, but in the midst of the chaos and confusion of my other life, I often find myself getting away from this simplicity. It is difficult to describe what this place has done for me, but with a little urging from my brother, it's time to get personal. I am in a very important time in my life, because I am making life decisions that no one else can make. Back at home, these decisions seemed insurmountable because I was hung up on the little trivialities of my life. Laying on the rocks by the river and sleeping in a cabin full of mice has helped me to regain focus on my life, and I somehow feel that there may be a happy ending. When Thoreau talks about nature and its soothing abilities, he sums it all up with one descriptive word. Simplicity. I think that a chance like this does not come along often where one can be so in touch with nature. Who would ever think that swatting that mosquito there would have any sentimental effect? This may sound strange or just plain messed up, but I honestly believe that we as humans have an indescribable bond towards nature that not everyone realizes, which leads to unhappiness and unfulfilled aspirations. This trip has given me a refill of sanity and a new aspect on life. Simplicity!

I hope with all my heart that someone else reading this may feel the way I do about this place, because they will probably leave feeling the way I do—fulfilled!

Drew M.

March 30, 1994
Whitetail Cabin

Sleep, eat, clean, ski, sleep, eat, clean, work. Enjoying the basics of life. Attention to detail, gratitude, family, devotion. Sympathetic joy for children's mastery, compassion for children's suffering, and everybody gets a hug. I love you whether you fall or stand. It takes more courage to fail in a said thing and to forgive yourself and try again. I see my faith: in myself, in my children, in their children. Unbroken line of life, interconnected and interdependent. Even grateful to the mole in the cabin. We are all bodisatvas—forest, children, deer, father, majestic, frozen lake. All of us helping each other towards a gentle dawning, awakening. I'm gratitude and sobriety. May all beings be happy.

Unknown Author

October 5, 1988
Greenstone Falls Cabin
Friends—

We who stay here are of a certain kinship. All people are Children of Earth, Supreme Mother of everything. All creatures are our relatives—trees, animals, birds, fish, soil, water, insects. We are the family of Earth.

Nothing is so sacred as Mother Earth untouched. Respect her as you would your own natural Mother. Do not take this place for granted—this is the "real" world. Our artificial, paved world is not the true Earth. It's a falsehood we've created for our own ease and convenience. This "real" world is cleaner, purer, saner than anything Man has ever created, except in this; her dreams. Here, the waters laugh, the animals play, the trees grow strong and give oxygen, the Sun shines and gives Life.

Listen to the laughing river. Feel the gentle rain on your face. Smell the spice of the forest. Laugh with the coyotes and the woodpeckers, alike. Be warmed by the Sun above.

Help others like us teach these others who are less thoughtful of the Earth Mother, to respect her and not harm her. Help us stop them from cutting forests, polluting soils and waters, turning all of Earth into a vast desert for money, vanity, and greed. Be proud of places like this. Protect them. Each person can do his/her part. This is not a valuable resource for human use. This is our Mother.

Listen to the rush of the river echo the ocean within.

Krista

May 26, 1975
Little Carp Cabin

This cabin is beautiful. The peace that silence creates within the soul gives your mind a chance to rest and a chance to grow in any way that you might want. I hope you see the beauty I have felt up here so deep in the forest, not knowing there are friends all around. When I think of how this place and every place came to be, I can only look to God and thank Him for letting us feel His emotions.

Ellen D.

July 14, 1985
Big Carp 4-Bunk

The gods have been good to us. We have had three beautiful, hot summer days in God's country, the UP. There are six of us here—Wymmin of the Woods—gathered together by forces outside of ourselves to relax, share, and grow in becoming one with ourselves, each other, and nature. Our backgrounds are varied but we all embrace the same spirit.

Our days here have been filled with daily chores of gathering wood, hauling water, cooking, and learning how to live off the land. We have had many walks in the beautiful woods, ongoing skinny-dipping trips in the stream and lake, sightings of a mother bear and her two cubs, and hours of intimate talks.

We share a common goal—to establish a Holistic Health Center to help ourselves and others get in touch with our inner selves. We have spent time brainstorming about this Center and how to arrange it. The seeds have been sewn this weekend and now we wait for the sun and rain to nourish then and bring them to bear fruit.

All of us have felt the healing and wholeness through this weekend and have re-established our oneness with ourselves, each other, and nature. We thank the woods and the waters and the animals for sharing their home with us and allowing us to get back in touch with ourselves.

May all who follow enjoy their visit here and know that we leave this place sending out energy, love, and peace to all our brothers and sisters.

> sun merging energies
> waters flowing, waters still
> blue heron, kingfishers, bears, and mice
> red squirrel, chipmunks, flies, and fish
> we are happy

Wymmin!

August 29, 1995
Big Carp 4-Bunk

I have waited a year to return here. I've been here many times when I've closed my eyes and let the vision of this place, imprinted in my mind, return me here, although hundreds of miles away. Thank God for memories and landscapes the mind can conjure up when we need them, to help us escape when physically we're unable and mentally we are desperate to. I carry this place and the peace I find here with me and it gets me through another year.

Unknown Author

November 26, 1984
Lake Superior Cabin

> Spurn the religions of security and convenience,
> Warm and sticky sweet,
> Brewed in weak, southern climes.
> Return to the cold, clear, northern light.
> We are as the transient flames dancing high in the frigid air,
> Burning more brightly in the knowledge
> That they must now be extinguished
> In unspeakable, cold, eternal darkness.

Jim

November 30, 1996
Section 17 Cabin

A little more on the serious side, walking through these sacred woods is like walking through the mind of God. Respect them, because they are holding our fragile world together. Try to live in peace within you and without you. Then you will not fear this wonderful place and it will begin to teach you some of its fascinating secrets. Tread lightly, for you are just a temporary visitor, and learn from it, all that your limited time gives you. Maybe you'll find the Naturalist walking about here sometime. Stop a moment to talk. Listen to what the great trees have told me. This is the greatest place to be. Thank you, Michigan, for saving this place.

D.J.

1968
Lily Pond Cabin

People lose so much of what should never have been lost. Society puts too many holds on things. You just awaken the natural instincts out here. You are really out here—there's nothing to stop you. When I leave here I will take more of Lily Pond with me than I leave behind. See the trees, drink the water, breathe the air. Now ask, where is God?

Unknown Author

July 7, 1993
Section 17 Cabin

days are numbered
like notches
on a number line
what is the result of what was
what will be the result of what is
a precious day
to act from the heart
life is the art of drawing
without using an eraser
there where the rivers are nameless
and filled with hush to the brim
choked with creatures like sun and water
it seems just the place to begin
the moon breathes the scent of a mixture
that quickens your heart and your will
the pines are a private elixir
and you love them, oh God yes, still

Unknown Author

November 21-23, 199?
Mirror Lake 2-Bunk Cabin
    here in the woods
    in a log cabin
    wooden table
    on paper

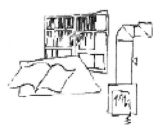

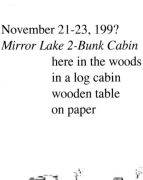

cut chipped pulped
bleached rolled
printed bound
virgin white

trees are strong
non violent
long lived
giving

they stand in grace
in all weather
while we hide
in our holes

such pitifully vulnerable
fleeting mayflies
amid giants and
immortal kings

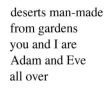

deserts man-made
from gardens
you and I are
Adam and Eve
all over

Unknown Author & Artist

May 20, 1993
Big Carp 6-Bunk Cabin

Serenity. After contemplating this trip for "years," it has finally materialized. We're six men, ages thirty-five to forty-one....

We have all come here for different reasons, some obvious, some not. I would say that we have all come to observe God's creation and try to absorb it. Breathe it, walk in it, and hope that through osmosis, take it back home. Life tends to create a need in all of us to take refuge in a quiet place "beside still waters," to reflect on "who we are, why we are," and thank the Lord for His intervention in our lives. Our society tends to be doing a downward spiral towards Godlessness, therefore we feel compelled to come here to experience Him in ways that seem so distant on a day to day basis. If there is one thing I would like to share with reading eyes, it is this: God is here, very evidently in all that surrounds us. Please take the time to contemplate His world for us. We, as men, honor His work. We're thankful for being here. It truly is a refuge for us.

Randal A.

June 30, 1990
Buckshot Cabin

Monday, July 2, 1990, I will have been sober for ten years. It's wonderful to wake up in a place like this, fully aware and appreciative of all of the things around me. I've stayed clean and sober through a divorce, the death of both parents, and financial problems. My worst days sober have all been better than my best days drinking, and I hope and pray that ten years from now I can come back here and write that I'm still happy, still sober, and feeling everything that happens to me. Enjoy the day and live your life to the fullest.

Ray

October 7, 1988
Little Carp Cabin

The relationship which each individual has with the Earth is the most important relationship he/she can ever have. The Earth is all of our Mother. Every creature, every tree, bird, fish, bear, drop of water, molecule of air is related to each and every one of us. Please understand that we are the family of Mother Earth and it matters how we treat our Mother and cousins. The Forest and the Waters are alive and they are a truer reality than our convenient, artificial, paved world. We can't be in touch with reality there. That world is a false cocoon, keeping us from the truth. Do not take this place for granted. It matters more than us and our little lives. Teach others to help protect the Earth, not to use more than we need, not to give the Earth garbage, poisons, and Cancer in return for the life she's given us. Come here to rejoice in the Spirit of Life. Learn what "clean" and "pure" really mean.

Listen to the waves breaking on the beach, eternally alive, our birthplace. Listen to it echo the Sound of your spirit, the constant flow within each of us, the unlimited depth of all knowing. We are of the waves. We are of the Earth.

Trieta

August 8, 1984
Big Carp 4-Bunk Cabin

Big Carp River

In a hurry, in a hurry
Rushing, rushing, rushing, rushing,
Cool stream, you mimic me.
Your constant rhythm is a lullaby,
And yet an ever-present reminder of
What I must return to.

In a hurry, in a hurry,
Rushing, rushing, rushing, rushing,
When will it stop?
When will you stop?

I laugh when I see the parallel,
But you are too beautiful,
too refreshing,
too vibrant,
too God-like
To remind me of such mundane things.

Ah, cool stream, can we slow?
This place scares me.
Time is my enemy, yet it doesn't seem to phase you.
I guess maybe you just let Him handle that.
Maybe I should, too....

Karen F.

May 9, 1993
Greenstone Falls Cabin

The beauty here is sometimes overwhelming. The constant rushing of the river and the evidence of how powerful (and dangerous) water can be, which is contrasted with the peaceful life of the wildflowers which smile to all who pass and take the time to look. It reminds me to be thankful for and careful with the abilities God has given me.

Nate W.

September, 1983
Buckshot Cabin

Many miles my brothers and I have traveled this day, and many more to go. On moccasin clad feet we travel the paths of our Grandfathers searching for inner peace and a oneness with Mother Earth. With the call of the coyote, the Great Spirit touches us. With the flight of an eagle, the Great Spirit teaches us. Only by seeing with our hearts can we learn the ways of the Earth and Sky. To the four winds we call for help, to understand the wisdom of our Grandfathers. We are brothers of the mountains and although we each have different paths to walk in life, our hearts are one.

Ghost Fox

April 16, 1994
Big Carp 6-Bunk Cabin

"A Fisher of Men"

I pray that we may live to fish, until our dying day.
And when it comes to our last cast, we then must humbly pray,
When in our Lord's great landing net, we're peacefully asleep,
Then in His mercy, we be judged big enough to keep.

Jerry B.

March 3, 1995
Whitetail Cabin

The pages of this book attest to the serenity which is found in this place. It seems to be present in the rustling of the leaves and in gale force winds, in the soft lapping of waves and the crunching of ice floes. Its presence is not restricted to the sense of hearing, but is often associated with the sight of a silent snowfall, a beautiful sunset, or is felt in the vast expanse of Superior.

In much the same light as the thought provoking question, "Does sound exist if there is no one to hear it?" I wonder if serenity existed prior to the cabin. Do animals experience serenity? Do explorers have time to appreciate the beauty of their surroundings when not protected form the environment by sturdy walls and plate glass windows?

I wonder if serenity is a commodity that has to be restored, much like firewood, between cabin usages. Does it fill up the "bucket" with a steady "in-flow" or can it be dipped, a "bucket" at a time? How many people can drink from the same source at any one time? I would be surprised if the level of serenity did not decline rapidly if there were two cabins here, or four or five, some yapping dogs, a few generators, and a couple of boom boxes. Does serenity only come into isolated spots? It's interesting to read that people have traveled many miles from Illinois, Colorado, etc., to find the same serenity that people from White Pine, Michigan, ten miles away, seek.

Do some people only observe serenity while others truly absorb it? Are some satisfied with a "Porkies" T-shirt or a mug to set on a shelf verifying their visit? Do others carry with them a feeling or source of emotional enrichment which can be drawn on in times of need? Does our need for serenity keep pace with our use of this item?

I suspect the same Higher Power which provides mankind with the ability to ramble on in such a philosophical manner as penned above, has also provided "serenity" as a pathway to increased communication with him or her. A better understanding of his or her will and a somewhat direct means of transferring wisdom to our actions. I am grateful to those who have constructed and maintained this communication center, and hope that it will provide many more with the opportunity to touch base with serenity.

Bob G.

August 31, 1983
Speaker's Cabin

Woke up to a perfectly blue day and my first thought was, "I don't want to go." There is something about this place that makes one feel "spiritually centered" and each successive visit forms a separate continuum that has no relation to one's everyday existence. I thought when I came up here I would have great satisfaction in recalling all that I had accomplished this year, but the truth is, any thought of the year's activities I would immediately vanquish from my brain. In fact, it almost seems too ridiculous to think of my existence as a pianist and piano teacher. When one's greatest task is to fetch water and boil it, the piano seems light years away in comparison. It is so easy to get lost in one's reality and that is why this place is so important in realizing there are other existences. Enough on philosophy.

Unknown Author

November 6, 1983
Mirror Lake 8-Bunk

We have been bathed in the solitude and harmony of this spot deep within the woods.

As a group, we have made tobacco ties in the Native American (Sioux) tradition. We have prayed over them as we tied them, and then, this evening, we offered four rounds of prayers for help and health for our nation, and all nations, for our friends and relatives, for the air and the streams and the woodlands. These tobacco ties are now hanging here in this cabin with prayers for the well being and peaceful journeys of all who stay here. There is a separate tie for each of the four directions and they hang on the four walls. In the middle are four more ties, two for both the Earth and Sky and two additional strands of ties done by people as prayers for the recovery and safety of our world.

Gail P.

October 16, 1991
Lake Superior Cabin

For the true seeker,
This path through the woods leads to the other,
Immortal shore.

Paul C.

June 18, 1983
Section 17 Cabin

I sit here, below the falls, searching for words to express my feelings at this moment. Trying to take it all in, almost afraid that I may wake up and it will all be gone.

I feel as a child who has been away from home for a long time and has finally returned. Searching every room, joyful to be home again.

Porcupine Mountains, how I have missed you! You are like a dear, dear friend to me.

This great gift that God has given to mankind is very much appreciated by this one, this Nanacosse.

I look around me and I want it all. I want to own it. But why? So that no other person might have it? Or so that I might live here always? Yes, so that I might live here. I guess, I too, have this white man's character defect—greed.

I regret that I did not bring my dog, but maybe it is better this way. No kids, no dog, time alone, a oneness, getting in touch with the Great Spirit and nature.

The falls are calling to me, they want to take me away. Down the river. Sweeping me off into a feeling of euphoria. The water is so clear and bubbly, it is hard to think that mankind, with his pollutants, could ever harm this river. Eventually!...

I see spider webs glistening in the sun, spun from tree to tree. Little roadways in the sky.

The majestic hemlock seems so familiar, almost parental, towering above. There is a sense of security when one hugs one of these friends. Try it!

They are so stable and almost seem to hug back. I think that trees are the most secure things in life, and they give so much to us.

Fishermen come and bring me back to reality. One begins to feel almost alone up here in this wilderness. I began to feel a little bit like how Eve must have felt in Eden.

Nanacosse (Hummingbird)

August 23, 1992
Union River Cabin

It has been very restoring for me to read this here journal. So many people. So different. All with their own special stories, quirks, and the such.

I came here a bit sarcastic and bitter, disheartened and somewhat down.

All of the writing in here has definitely helped restore my belief in people, and the woods have rekindled my belief in life and the courage to go on.

Their writings have been prolific and rich, full of wisdom and fun.

Thank you all very, very much.

H.R.S.R.

Lake of the Clouds Cabin: A Chronological View

June 16, 1955

Went to east end of lake and found old beaver dam had been repaired recently, so set up movie camera in marsh grass hoping to get a few movies of beaver. After a two hour wait, a big fellow came down stream and looked over a small break in dam. Got a few feet of color film run before he heard the camera. His tail whacked the water like a gunshot, and he took off under water. Waited until sundown, but Mr. Beaver didn't come back.

Earl S.

July 2, 1955

This is our third trip to the Porcupine Mountains in less than a year.... This will probably be our last trip to the Porcupines for a few years, for we are both draft eligible and expect to be IN in a few months.

E.B. & J.B.

August 17, 1955

I speak nor write any other language so I'll just say in plain old English, "It is good, soooo very, very wonderful here." Being a real tenderfoot, I'm taking back a few wilderness scars, i.e., aching muscles, scarred shins, etc. But it was triumphant, including a fourteen inch perch and a two pound bass, even if I didn't take them off the hook. Thanks, Joe! Think I've earned a merit badge. Even reconciled to the outdoor plumbing.

Bev C. & Ann D.

September 14, 1955

Took a walk along escarpment to near east end. This is the most magnificent walk within a thousand miles—never tire of it!... A twilight row on the mirror-still lake to the accompaniment of an owl's hooting from the south woods.

Unknown Author

October 12, 1955

Two cheers for Mother Nature and the conservation department...Each lake has it's own mood and character—a fact we have frequently noted on canoe trips, too. So whatever you call it, Lake of the Clouds, or Carp Lake (as the old miners did), it's an enchanting place—wild, with changeable weather and the bear who comes to dinner.

Bob & Nancy T.

October 13, 1955

Here we sit, cozy around the table, both fires crackling merrily, as dusk settles over the lake. Saw flocks of juncoes, many blue jays, downy woodpeckers, robins, fox sparrows, saucy black-capped chickadees, a flicker, several grouse, and Bob insists, a hairy woodpecker—many birds for this time of year. Oh yes, song sparrow, too.

Nancy T.

August 21, 1956

Did some sailing on "Cloud" by rigging a square sail on a rowboat. An oar for a mast, a poncho for the sail, an oar for the rudder, lots of rope for the rigging, and a load of optimism kept the cruise from being a fiasco.

Judy & Alan B.

August 6, 1960

This evening we read through this book. The children were bug-eyed as the accounts of friend bear were recited.... We awoke at 11:00 P.M. to the sounds of a thunderstorm heating up it's fury in the tree tops and the lake. Daddy got up to close the windows on the windward side and we all snuggled back and let the patter of rain and the gusting of wind in the tree tops lull us back to sleep.

The S. Family

September 8, 1961

On behalf of my associate and me, I would like to take this opportunity to welcome you to the splendorous site founded for the benefit of you, my fellow nature-loving citizen, by the glorious state of Michigan.

These teeming hills, abounding with God's creatures, should not be adulterated or polluted by us humans, who after all are merely visitors in nature's wonderland.

"Smokey the Bear"

July 1, 1963

From 6:00 to 7:30 P.M., a bear circled the cabin. Rick was the one who found him right at the corner of the cabin (towards the lake), just as he was ready to run down to get Daddy's fish. We had been cooking ham, which is what he smelled, and just as Rick went out of the door, he saw his head peaking around the corner at him. Rick came charging back into the house; his eyes told the whole tale without words. For an hour-and-a-half he circled the cabin, his nose in the air towards the windows. We hooked the screen door and closed the front door, and once, when we looked out the kitchen window, we saw him sitting on the front steps. Several times he climbed trees when he seemed to have heard something, and snorted as if he were mad.

After about forty-five minutes of running from one window to the next, watching him circle the cabin, we decided we would just as soon he leave. He became too insistent on finding the ham (and we wanted to go out) so we 1) clapped our hands, 2) shouted at him, and 3) even got bold enough to open a window that didn't have a screen on it and throw a stick at him hoping it would frighten him off. He would stare up at the window with his black, beady eyes, but wouldn't take off. Never did we imagine to find ourselves trapped in the cabin with a bear outside determined to get our ham -- or us.

I kept saying, "Daddy, we've got to get rid of that bear. We've got to find something that will frighten him off."

Once, he went over to the clothesline where Rick's swimsuit was hanging to dry, and tried to reach it by stretching up as high as he could. Another time, he had his paws up against the back window, looking in.

Finally, after an hour-and-a-half, I found something that made him uneasy enough to take off–a frying pan and the stove-poker handle, and beat it with all our might (we already had the back windows shut when he stood up against it). He would run a short distance, and stop and look back. Then we made enough "racket" to be heard all the way to the Park Headquarters, but it finally made him more disgusted than frightened. We didn't come in here with too much fear of any wild animal, and not too concerned about knowing they are in the woods, if fact, very anxious to see them—thought the first one very exciting, but when you see one determined to get into your cabin no matter what, and stare you right in the eye (several times he looked in the back windows and the kitchen one near the stove), you don't feel so safe....

It's 9:00 P.M., our first day, and find ourselves quite in reverse to some of the other families whose entries are found here, who suggest how to lure a bear, setting up all kinds of devices to be able to get a glimpse of them during the night. All we can suggest is, FRY HAM!

The W. Family

October 12, 1963

Boy, this is really living. Read Robert Frost poems to each other and turned in about 10:30.

Louis F., Elanor B., & Lonnie K.

June 23, 1964

We observed a turtle laying her eggs on the path to the boats. Maybe some lucky person will see them hatch if they are left undisturbed.

The B. Family

June 29, 1965

Wind pushed waves and mist down the lake. Heard the plaintive call of a whippoorwill behind the cabin at dusk. The bass are not biting—they seem to be in a lull. Dave, Mike, and I explored the Little Carp in a boat. We pulled it over the beaver dam and rowed at least two miles up the small stream. Saw a gray heron with long neck and orange legs. Climb the rock slide—it's fun! If you see one to five gulls wheeling over the lake, whistle and throw small perch out to them. They swoop, dive, and snatch the bait from the water with an expert snap of their beaks. Saw Mr. Beaver swimming and diving in the lake...With a fire in the stove, it is cozy in this snug, little cabin. At night, the long shadows fall over the escarpment bluffs, contrasting with the golden sunlight slanting on the sides of the white birches. As the shadow moves, dusk deepens, and the wind dies. The lake turns into a glossy mirror that reflects the verdant splotches of green, smears of brown, and other colors. Beautiful!

Kevin L.

August 26, 1965

Caught one bass seventeen and-a-half inches long weighing three pounds, one hundred yards southeast of the dock; lost another one there, too. We went to the southeast corner of the lake to follow up what was already written in the book. About thirty yards offshore, by two dead trees overhanging the lake, is a perch fisherman's dream at about 7:30 P.M.; they would hit on anything! A few trout along with perch; small but numerous.

Jim

September 6, 1965

Felt like a pioneer after I conquered the "cotton-picking" wood stove! Grandmother really must have had her hands full using one for all her cooking.

Dorothy K.

October 15, 1965

So you don't think there are any bears around, huh?! Well, here's how to find them.

BEAR RECIPE:

Must enter cabin early, before sunset. Eat one hardy, hot meal and clean up afterward. Now, open at least two windows and leave door unlocked while you prepare for sleep. Take your socks off. Now, take a jar of honey and proceed to spread it liberally over entire region of toes (these must be exposed during entire evening). With camera or gun close at hand, calmly go to sleep with one eye open. We did it with amazing results, and it will work for you too, if the instructions are followed carefully.

For those who wish instantaneous results, let me recommend that the honey be spread on the front steps and windowsills.

P.S. A word to the wise. PLEASE refrain from wiggling toes during this process, as it seems to disperse a most disgusting odor (phewwwww!), which promptly warns the bears of your scheme. Thank you.

Dietmar

June 20, 1966

Wednesday, we all hiked to Mirror Lake and searched for the mine that is on the map. The location of the mine is not marked along the trail, but we found it! Along the trail, there is a steep hill. On your right is a deep ravine with water rushing from the mountain. The sides of the ravine are cliff-like, and under the cliff is the mine. All the mine is, is a square hole about four or five feet deep. You won't be able to see the mine from the top of the cliff. You must climb down in the ravine and then you'll find the mother-lode of mosquitoes, bugs, flies, and no-see-ums.

Dennis, Janet, & Valerie V.
Tom, Donna, Rick, Mark, & Sally S.

August 7, 1966

This is the second group from Birch Trail to stay in this cabin this summer. Campers have been coming here for the last four years, just to enjoy the beauty of the lake and the surrounding mountains. We arrived yesterday and immediately fell in love with this quaint, little cabin that, as one lady has already said, could have come from a storybook.... We were fascinated by the phenomenon of a cloud rolling in across the lake and mountains.... It is really hard to believe, as we sit here in this wilderness haven, that there is a war going on in Vietnam that is destroying the peace for millions of people. It is a shame that everyone in the world can't come and enjoy this solitude for just twenty-four hours. Maybe then they would realize how valuable peace is.

Ellen R., Tripping Counselor

August 8, 1966

We are the second group from Camp Birch Trail.... I think that for all of us, this has been a restful and relaxing trip. Sitting here in this snug cabin, watching the misty, wet clouds roll down the lake, and listening to the patter of rain overhead, one can easily forget about the busy world that hurries beyond the wooded hills. Here, we have time to stop, to think, and to realize what really is important in our lives. There are none of the comforts of home here, yet we have been more than comfortable. It has rained and rained, yet we have had much fun. Life here is simple and basic, as it is in all wilderness camp settings. But it is here among the hills and beneath the clouds that we learn to know ourselves and find the true meaning of life.

Kath W.

August, 1966

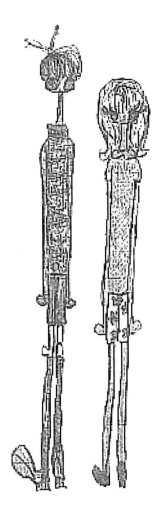

Betsy S. & Kathy S.
Camp Birch Trail

August 26, 1966

    Some people think this is roughing it. But really it's kinda civilized. Even though it is, I love to be close to nature and see the beauty of God's creation. Tonight the lake is pretty with the bright moon shining on it. Last night the lake was very calm and still, but tonight it is rough and rippling.

Darlene M. (age ten)

September 10, 1966

I must say the fishing is great. I have fished just about every place that is known to have large fish, but I have never seen perch as big as they are here. I landed at least ten that would go sixteen to eighteen inches long and weigh between one and-a-half and two pounds.

Jim & Steve A.

April 25, 1967

Getting water last evening, we saw busy beavers across the lake, and several ducks seem to call the lake home. They are buffalo head (the small black and white) and American mergansers. Another resident is a magnificent osprey (a large black, brown, and white, fish-eating eagle) who sat across the lake, just right of the water spring, in the top of one of those three large pine trees.

So far we've seen robins, flickers, yellow-bellied sapsuckers, hairy and downy woodpeckers, black-capped chickadees, myrtle warblers, white-throated sparrows, and little chipmunks around the cabins. We saw a porcupine sunning himself in a tree on the way to the escarpment who just looked at us and went on sunning. Last night, Bob saw a skunk just outside the window — we think he lives under the cabin. We advise leaving him alone.

Rita H.

Memorial Day, 1967

I think this day is appropriately named because it will be long in my memory. Today I had my best bass fishing experience. Five nice bass, one sixteen plus inches, in about two hours of fishing time. The weather has been great. Hate to go back to hot a humid Chicago. One pleasant thought, however, about leaving, is knowing we will return. "Not soon enough!"

Dan N.

June 18, 1967

Our group is a segment of the 1967 Camp Chippewa Bay staff—Boulder, Cathy, Cricket, Happy and Pip—with the purpose of exploring the facilities and trails to prepare for the forthcoming camper trip.... We've sent a telegram to our "boss" requesting she just send the kids and our belongings—we'd like to stay!

We're now ready...to share our experiences with the rest of the staff and prepare ourselves so that we might guide and direct the young scouts with whom we work towards meaningful and personal growth.

Camp Chippewa Bay Staff

September 10, 1967

The cabin and Lake of the Clouds are, of course, ideal for small children who normally live on the twelfth floor of an apartment building. The short walk down to the lake from the parking lot does require a bit of prodding from the parents, however. We hope the kids have been conditioned by their experiences today, so that they might make a swift and uneventful ascent up the trail tomorrow. We anticipate, though, their enthusiasm for the quasi-primitive life will wane in relation to the number of feet climbed.

Dick, Caryl, Guy, Jim & Nik

September 23, 1967

We were all so excited about the prospects of fishing that we failed to appreciate the extent to which the wind had picked up. Gusts were getting very strong and whitecaps started to show up. We rapidly realized that the north shore looked like a safe spot to put the boat in, and that we did. It was decided that we would walk directly north up the escarpment wall, which at that point is steep, but possible for the kids, in hopes of locating the Escarpment Trail and then walk back to the cottage. It was about noon when we pulled up the boat and secured it, and three or four hundred feet higher, we ran into a vertical stone wall ten to twenty feet high. It had breaks and was climbable for an adult, but we feared for the children on it. So, back to the boat.

We rowed close to the north shore, directly into the wind, and made about five feet per minute. An hour later we were back at the cabin with a new appreciation for the wind, the escarpment, and our two little girls who never complained, and hiked with the best of us.

The G. Family

June 8, 1968

In these woods we like to wander,
But the tales of bear make us ponder
About wandering yonder.

Unknown Author

September 2, 1968

Found cabin in excellent condition. I came in by myself on my days off as a ranger here. Last night there was a three-quarter moon which was directly across the lake from the cabin. Its soft reflections and the slight breeze created a truly beautiful scene, one I shall long remember. However, I must admit it stirred in me a bit of melancholy, for I wished my wife and family were with me—perhaps we will return this fall!

Dennis K.

September 24, 1968

Brady F.

October 12, 1968

You can really find good leaves if you like them. Right now they are as pretty as they will ever get. Carrie and I are good friends. She is nine and I am eleven, but we don't care. We each got a leaf collection and we really got the big ones.

Tonee

December 28, 1968

Walking these trails in winter's whiteness proves to be quite an ordeal. More often than not the markers are covered with snow, and after awhile, every snow-splotched tree looks as though it holds a hidden trail marker. The woods are more beautiful than one can imagine—trees laden with snow—branches drooping to the ground—twigs icy and black, edged in white.

Unknown Author

July 7, 1969

Picture yourself on top of hills called mountains with Superior on the far left running off into the pink spotted sky. Turning your head slowly to the right is a giant cliff. Going on in the distance is a fog rolling in. Far below is the Lake of the Clouds, about two to four miles from one end to the other. Across the lake is a forest which is down below you, too. Further to the right is the end of the lake with a windy stream going into Lake of the Clouds. In the distance, on the right, is the fog rolling in again, closing towards the other side. WOW!

Ed G.

July 8, 1969

Sunset, sunrise.
Time is short here.
Live for now,
this minute,
not for what's to come,
like in traffic.
Here, time, space is irrelevant
for what's to come.
Life is for now,
not for the next time.

Bruce L

May 3, 1970

One other thing about the Government Peak Trail; the guys who made that trail liked to play a little game. It's called "Hide the Markers." Great game. We got sidetracked about thirty times. Another little game is, "Put a four foot bridge in the middle of a twenty foot swamp." There is no way you are going to get to the bridge without getting a little damp. The guys who made the trails are a laugh-a-minute.... Overlooking all of our trouble, this was a great trip and we had lots of fun. In fact, without all of the hardships and mistakes we had, the trip wouldn't have been half as good.

Skip C.

September 29, 1970

View the Dock

Let it be said that we
shared an experience here
as overwhelming as the view from
the dock—
for one night and one day
we shared the present
time was unimportant
with no sweet-smelling liquids
no elaborate adornment to give us beauty—
we were beautiful-bathed by the wind and the sun

what is important is that we are here
we are now
can we continue this experience when
the view from the dock has passed?

Don & Dort

December 24, 1970
The Horrendous Winter Solstice Expedition

We arrived two hours after darkness dropped her curtain. Our leader, the infamous wilderness guide, H.T.M., aided by his trusty, Duracell-battery powered mini-flash, led us to the abyss — and beyond. Even unto the valley of the shadow of night. On skis we came, we four, two of each, bearing burdens of better than two stones each. On reaching what seemed the edge of the earth, we, unburdened of skis, fought our ways through the oozing darkness to a place we had never seen before. Weary beyond all measure, with a craven beast unleashed in the pit of the maw and so cold that our thoughts became deranged, we dragged weary, broken bodies to "THAT PLACE" in the distance. Would we make it? Or would we be forced to take refuge under sheltering bows, or in the defactorium made of wood? Only precious little energy remaining in our light, in our bodies, would determine our collective fate. When hark, in the distance, a placard, a signpost pointing the way to that most besought of things — CABIN. Long minutes passed as fateful decisions were made at last, broken to a weariness that permits one only to whine, while we stumbled across the threshold.

Spirits rekindled, we forced weary muscles to work yet again. To gather wood, to make fire, to cook humble victuals, to give praise for our arrival, and at last, to ease throbbing spines into bunks, as though lowering coffins into the grave.

Long past daybreak, the eyelids parted, first quickening part of bodies frozen by locked sinews.

A painful day passed quickly. Pain, this time, of regeneration, of new bodies being assembled to outspan the framework of the old. Difficult decisons. To return in minor agony for abandoned skis or to await the passing of another day, perhaps chancing the loss to furred creatures, of a pack slung low in the trees now hours behind.

The decision is inevitably made to return, and return we do, to a new rhythm instilled by the previous day's hardship. And just as then, we felt new vitality, new juices, new lubricants, stronger muscles, so do we all feel this new vigor with each day. Tasks once difficult are done with one hand. Now the real beauty of all that we do, of everything around us, can be winnowed free of the chaff of inefficient, busy machines, of the suffering required to live as we do now.

We play out-o-doors as nature's children, enthralled with the mysteries of the forest paths. Exhilarated by the biting ice enema on the wind-blasted Escarpment. Uplifted by the snow underfoot, feeling slightly more able to touch those stars that burn down at night from their daytime hiding places in all of the vastness beyond even our huge valley. The heavens at night appearing, from the middle of the lake to be a band wrapped around the earth, bounded on north by the Escarpment and south by gargantuan Porcupines, placed there for our endless enjoyment and always changing. We watch the "Orion" show pass slowly across the screen of our sight.

With each passing day, the wish to stay grows stronger. Here, friends of nature abide. Tomorrow we must leave, to return to...friends, loved ones. To celebrate in our own ways, the birth of a child now 2004 earth-years old. Somehow, these five days have made that event more meaningful.

Craig P.

May 11, 1971

Today began with a large, ominous layer of overcast clouds and a stronger wind than yesterday. I went for water this noon and the wind almost took the boat from me. The clouds lowered in around us and gradually snow began to whiten the air and ground, almost obscuring the other side of the lake. I went up to the cliff view and started a fire close to the edge. It was more than adequate warmth, and the view down was of white, universal lacing and quiet snow. All things held the white calm on their surface. Ravens croaked the silence across the valley with wide, black wings and gurgled at groups of our friends arriving from other parts of the park to meet us here.

Dave

May 25, 1971

All evening I kept getting threats! Dave and the other two guys kept saying, "We'll get up tomorrow morning and out in the middle of the lake you'll go—in the boat, without oars!" Well, I really didn't think they'd do it, but I was awake most of the night in suspense!

Dave and I were supposed to get up at 5:30 to start the fire. Well, the alarm went off and I asked Dave what time it was. He told me "not time to get up." The next thing I knew, I was in the air on my way to the lake, sleeping bag and all. Dave and Allen surprisingly succeeded in carrying me from bed to boat. The only problem was after they pushed the boat out away from shore, Miss P. expressed her concern by telling the boys they had to go get me. So...Dave bravely took off his shoes and "plunged" into the water to my rescue. Boy, was he wet and cold.

All the while this was going on, I was "comfy-cozy" in my sleeping bag.

Marie P.

June 25, 1971

We of Boy Scout Troop 795...have finished our final day of hiking around in these mountains. Some fifty miles in all. We worked and trained all year for this trip.... We lived out of our packs for a week. We enjoyed talking to people on the trail; all ages. There were a lot of young people and this is good. I think that they will be the ones to save and protect this place for the next generation.

Boy Scout Troop 795

June 30, 1972

I scared Mike and Mark by snorting like a bear while they were in the john!

Bob F.

March 21, 1973

Tuesday night Ron carved a chess set out of driftwood, rocks, and carrots, and used soot to color the black set. A game was going well when suddenly the players began to eat each other's carrot pieces, to put a very abrupt end to the game. "You ate my queen!"

Rico S.

April 15, 1973

We nestled into bed and took in the sights and sounds of the night. We could see the checkerboard of the front window against the moonlit sky, and the birch in front of the cabin reaching towards the nearly full moon. We could smell the mixture of burning wood and recently brewed coffee, and listened to the last crackles of the fire and the gusts of wind coming from the northwest, rattling every window of the cabin when it arrived.

Paul L.

May 25, 1973

Being here makes you appreciate the comforts of civilization—and what we sacrifice for them.

Mike & Rob A.
Pat M.

July 18, 1974

We've enjoyed this cabin many times through twenty years. Now, we hear that the cabins are to be removed under a new park management system.

People, too many people, are forcing defensive planning to preserve the natural habitat. It's not really wilderness, but it is a kind of last frontier, the last virgin timber, the last large trail which has been helped to resist civilization....

Maybe this is our last time in this cabin. Many memories are here — the happy family times, eager children, anticipation, fun, food, nature, scenery, excitement — these are part of this cabin for many people. It will be sad to see it go, if go it must. Good-bye, Lake of the Clouds. You have meant a lot through the years to the L. family.

The L. Family

October 27, 1974

Having just recently moved to Wisconsin from Kansas City, I find this the most spectacular place I've ever seen, except for the rolling plains and flint hills of Kansas. The serenity and solitude really blow my mind. I've never seen anything that comes this close to being a mountain. Seeing Lake Superior for the first time in my life was even a greater thrill. Coming from a city with only man-made lakes and then seeing such a wide expanse of bright, blue water really filled me with awe. It is strange to think how God has made a variety of faces, and each one holds an amount of beauty in itself. Wheat fields and the multi-colored patches of crops on a farm will always mean home to me, but I think that seeing new beauty of this sort, with so many fir trees it is unbelievable, will hold a new meaning for me. Just walking through the woods and seeing the bright, blue water and sky blending together really makes me feel closer to God. I only hope that everyone, at one time or another, will be able to behold this beauty as I have.

Anne W.

April 26, 1975

A night, a day, it's not really long enough to appreciate and integrate the solitude into my psyche. It's all too new, too much of an adventure, but the potential for "spirit" renewal seems limitless. I would like to stay awhile longer, to work out the necessities of life away from my packed-full urban environment, in a quiet place such as this.

Unknown Author

April 26, 1975

Moon rose full over the lake, brilliant light, almost white in color as it came up. We stoked fire at intervals during the night...and felt almost spiritually invigorated in standing before the lake and the moon. I would love to bay and howl at the moon for hours. Somehow, in the city, that just wouldn't work.

Unknown Author

April 4, 1976

I had twenty billion thoughts today that chased each other around and around, like an echo, trying to tell me something that came back like half an answer.

I stood there on the shore with a confused grin.

Herald

May 15, 1976

It's great to explore and seek adventure, conquering the confusion sometimes felt when surrounded by tall trees in every direction....

It feels good to be totally relaxed, with the environment conducive to my peace and restfulness. The desire to stay and take more and more inside is overpowering, but at least that taken in will be integrated and available for awhile. Refreshed, perhaps it will renew a creativity to work within the city environment, hyped up as it is, and keep the positive mental energy flowing towards the necessity of my life as it is at present, with the hope and knowledge of a more peaceful existence available for the having.

Cathy

May 15, 1976

Where there is love, there is life.

Stephen

June 3, 1976

This is a nostalgia trip for me as my last trip here was some twenty-five years ago. The scenic splendor is unchanged, the cabin somewhat more rustic, but the trail seems somehow much steeper and more difficult to traverse with the passage of time.... Hopefully, I or my kids will return before another twenty-five years passes.

Steve

September 13, 1976

A man is truly considered great when he is not squeezing his world out of shape. He taps it lightly, stays for as long as he needs to, and then swiftly moves away, leaving hardly a mark.

Pete

April 30, 1977

This is my first trip up here without my girlfriend along. It's lonely in one sense because I really miss Diana, but yet time to collect my thoughts feels mighty good, too. Madison can really wind a person up, and the Porkies act like a sedative. I'm calm and finally able to be myself....

To you Diana, I leave this message. I love you so much and someday we'll be here together to read this old log entry. Happier one person has never made me.

To who may read over this, believe me, enjoy these blessed woods and share the memories that these Porkies offer to all your friends, because the Ghost that haunts these woods offers the enchanting gift of mystery, adventure, nature, and love to anyone who sincerely wants it. Just look beyond the cabin door and before you lies not only the Lake of the Clouds, but the heavens, full of thoughts and life-long dreams.

Gary W.

August 19, 1977

Ode "Ol' Stove," in the cabin of Lake of the Clouds
"Ol' Stove," for three days,
You were a part of our lives—
We filled you with birch wood
And how you replied.
You smoked and smoked
'Til the cabin was blue,
But with Dad doing the stokin'
And Jeff out there choppin'—
We cleared out your eyes
And were in for a surprise.

You heated our water and fried our fish.
Pancakes you fried were the very best.
And potatoes you fried, so even and gold,
We thought you were almost out of this world.
You baked us a cake, and biscuits, too—
And kept our little cabin homey and warm.
We forgave you the smoke—
We forgave you the black—
Because, you were our friend so good
In that little cabin in the wood.

Mom S.

April 29, 1978

The beauty and company up here has made this trip more than worthwhile. College life can never be this good.

Being with Robin up here has really helped me realize how wonderful she is. Somehow, she has really made this trip one I'll never forget. I guess the

187

lack of hustle and bustle of city life has really given me more of a chance to see her, without the feeling of school over my head.

To you Robin...I love you. I love the Porkies. There's a world to dream about, but this is not a dream. It's all for real.

Gary W.

April 29, 1978

Well, Gary, I will always treasure the great times we've had together and hope to have many, many more! I love you so very much, even though I don't always show it. How I ever met some as super as you, I'll never know. My love will always be with you, sweetie, wherever you may go.

Robin B.

July 30, 1978

I am one of the so-called "giggling" daughters. The truth is that our fathers can hardly keep up with us. If fact, my Uncle Jack is now showing me how to chop a block of ice with a hatchet. Another fact is that he just about chopped his thumb off with the hatchet. Well, he put a big gash in it anyway. Me and Lisa are doctoring him up, so with our superior knowledge, he'll be as good as ever in no time, as long as we keep him away from all sharp objects. We really have to keep an eye on our fathers. We stop watching them for one minute, and you never know what kind of trouble they'll be in.

Dawn S.

August 23, 1978

Christy H.

November 4, 1978

Regardless of weather variations, I think fall is the most hospitable time of the year most places, and here in particular.

Tonight, as I make this entry by candlelight and listen to the wind roar and moan through the valley over the lake, I'm struck by what a large portion of basic experience modern, western civilization has lost. I can't but think that we may have sold much of our own human heritage too cheaply. No sensible person would advocate a return to the past, if it were possible, but certain values and experiences are necessary to human sanity. Quiet, darkness, weather, even simple physical exercise are alien to many people.

Unknown Author

October 23, 1979
Autumn's end
lies in golden silence
on the forest floor
under the first winter fleece.

Unknown Author & Artist

October 23, 1979

Gary, Rick, Julie, and little Jesse shared the last of autumn here at Lake of the Clouds in the Great North Woods. Gary and Jennifer, up from Oklahoma, experienced the first breath of winter in the North Country. And little Jesse, just a year, had his first North Woods over-night in the Magic Forest. The weather could only have been shared with good friends—slate snow clouds cozying us in this friendly cabin—and we loved our piece of wilderness—and the snow makes us one with our winter wonderland.

Author Unknown

October 11, 1980

Most interesting aspect of our three days in the Porkies has been the variability of the weather. The warmness of Indian summer, blistery snow, sleet, and hail, light, fluffy snow, all come and go in a short period of time. It was especially fun to sit on some of the lookouts on the Escarpment Trail watching the weather. Small storms and cloud banks could be seen moving in and out and up and over nearby ridges and valleys. The sun was trying to shine on Lake Superior.... Make the time for this trek.

Unknown Author

September 7, 1981

This trip affirms for me the importance of getting away — removing one-self from the daily humdrum — to "let go" of responsibilities and really appreciate the gifts of life and beauty and fellowship with family. May your adventure at Lake of the Clouds be "life-giving," too.

The B. Family

March 20, 1982

Due to circumstances beyond our control, we were forced to enter this cabin illegally. Temperatures of minus twenty degrees Fahrenheit, and fifteen inches of snow in the last twenty-four hours left us with the cold, hard decision; either enter the cabin or perish. If it wasn't for this cabin, they would have dug our bodies up in the spring.

Name Withheld

May 22, 1982

We were all sitting around the table, playing cards. It was very dark and still outside. All of a sudden, there was a bloody scream outside our window. We put the flashlight on a looked out the window. There were two bloody looking eyes and huge jaws snapping at the screen. We were frozen in our seats. With all of the courage we could get, we went outside and killed the biggest Junebug we ever saw. We are going to have him for breakfast, and if there's any left, we'll leave some for the next campers.

Unknown Author

September 29, 1982

Girls — a bit of romantic advice — when coming back from the outhouse, arrive naked under your poncho — works great!

Cathie

May 14, 1983

To play devil's advocate, let me say that I do not believe in the existence of a god, nor in any earthly savior, as so many of the other entries in this log are constantly stating. I am a spiritual person, and believe that this is a beautiful area. It is here, in a relatively untouched state, not because of God's work, but because the land was so rugged to prohibit the economical removal of timber, as had been done throughout the Upper Peninsula, often under the guise of God's work. Our species has also cleared, settled, and slaughtered most of the original inhabitants of this country, again in the name of God. I believe that we are the sole landlords of our destiny, that the only way we can insure the existence of parks like the Porkies is through continued campaigning and support of causes that lobby our governmental leaders for additional land acquisitions.

The Porkies are beautiful, but many other similar areas were also beautiful before we ruthlessly exploited them. People who are concerned about saving this park would be more useful, in my opinion, by supporting environmental legislation, rather than leaving it up to God in his infinite wisdom.

That statement made, I hope to provoke a spiritual dialogue in this journal. Religion is great, but it is a personal thing!

Gary M.

June 2, 1983

And what a fantastic four-course meal we dined on this evening. We began with the house appetizer—perch cocktail—kind of bony if you want my opinion, followed by the special of the day—freeze-dried "Chicken a 'la Cloud." We then progressed to a steaming bowl of lentil soup, which ended up in the campfire, sorry to say, and finished up our gourmet meal with mouth-watering strawberry crepes (they were out of whipped cream). And to think we only drove four hundred miles for such a delectable meal.

Jenni M.

July 30, 1983

We met the resident horde of leeches soon after our arrival. BRAIN-STORM!!! Take the handy rake so thoughtfully provided with the cabin, and rake up some of the debris lying on the bottom where the leeches hide and presto, no more leeches, right? Wrong! I got more leeches on me in ten minutes of raking than I would have in ten days of swimming. Probably revenge for wrecking their low-income housing.

Jeff

September 8, 1986

Last night we saw the most incredible stargazing view I've ever seen. I could very easily discern the spiral arm of the Milky Way. To see it, look straight up and slightly south (towards water spring). The band of haze across the sky that extends forever north-south is the arm of the spiral galaxy that we reside in. Sight of it seems to put minor things in perspective.

So far we have been unable to see the Northern Lights (Aurora Borealis) as our view has been entirely southward. Maybe tomorrow we'll hike the escarpment in the dark and stare into space. I imagine the show will be very good here. In Detroit, it's impossible to get away from the glare of the city, hence, no show.

Sitting here, looking at the stars, I feel at peace.

I have a theory about aggression. I've noticed that when I'm out-of-doors, as now, I feel gentled. I do not wish to hurt anyone or cause them any trouble. Anger is virtually gone. I feel that everyone has a certain personal, human density level, meaning they can only tolerate so high a level of humanity concentrated in so much area. Levels of tolerance vary between people. Mine is relatively low, so that when I'm in the country, where human population is low, my level of tolerance is not exceeded, and life is easy. When I'm in the city, my red-line is exceeded, and I hate. I think the city is a great breeder of hostility and aggression, because so many people are on overload. A return to nature seems to gentle everyone's spirit. I wish we could solve the problem simply, but the problem itself is not that simple.

Adam

March 12, 1988

Seeing as how we are intelligent Michigan Tech students, we thought we would be very smart to plan our first winter trip for the milder days of March. After reading the previous letters of the last two weeks, talking about the warmth and sun, you'd think we were correct in our assumption. WRONG! Here we sit, trying to keep warm, as the biggest storm of the season rages only a few feet away. Weather radio claims that there is a Winter Storm Warning for today and tonight, with six inches or more today and another six inches or more tonight. Wind is whipping around and causing nice drifts up the cabin walls.

Since we arrived last night, after stretching a two-and-a-half hour trip into five hours, about six inches have fallen. During the night, thunder and lightening were abundant. One "boomer" shook the whole place.

Although it may seem sort of crummy, once you get up in the trees, it's super. I was snowshoeing earlier in the powder, and although it was extremely tiring, it was just beautiful. The trees are all bending over from the weight of the snow, making it real scenic.

V.J.

March 20, 1988

My family (maternal) left this area at the time of the Depression (1929). We were of African, Indian, Welsh, and French-Canadian stock. We owned land...cooked, cleaned, went to school, and struggled.

Not only did the Depression hit us like so many others, but we lost a lot more through fraud and swindle. So we left for places like Duluth, Detroit, and Chicago. My branch ended up in Chicago. Mother tells of arriving in Chicago in October. They were already dressed for winter. They had to be the strangest looking "colored" people on the South side.

Now I live in Minneapolis, and made this weekend trip to our "ancestral home." There was a picture in my grandparents' home that looked a lot like a view from this lake, near the bridge looking towards the mountain. Now I know why it was so central to the atmosphere of their living room. This place is beautiful. "I wouldn't give nothin' for my journey." Peace.

Louis

April 1, 1988

i sit here to watch and wait for myself.

one never knows what might happen in this cold, white land.

in five days i saw one eagle twice, and that is enough.

in five days i wrote one poem, and that is enough.

if somehow i could say what else i found in the lost corners of myself,

you would know less than you do now.

Julie S.

June 21, 1988

This A.M. I awoke! Sounds funny to some, but to those of us who have reasons to love life even more because of our closeness to losing it, there's no humor there. I walked to the end of the dock and saw Mother Nature at her finest. A doe and her fawn, across the lake, were casually strolling along the water's edge. What a beautiful sight, indeed! Then my family started awakening, and I, once again, realized just how wonderfully lucky a man I am...This place I call Freedom. I remember our first trip here. The DNR and others call her Lake of the Clouds. I call her Freedom. As a Vietnam veteran, one who does not ask for your sympathy or money, and who has worn the Green Beret, I named her Freedom. She is part me and part you. She is America. God knows how much I love this great, beautiful Country of Ours. Don't anyone ever try to take her away from me.

In beautiful memories, I remain.

Bill S.
Fifth Special Forces Group Airborne
Nha Trang, South Vietnam
'68/'69

July 22, 1988

This is, for me, a dream come true. I didn't know this place existed until a few hours ago, and now I'm here, wood stove crackling with sweet cedar and birch. Nokomis Giishik and Mishomis Wigwas—Grandmother and Grandfather—stars gathering above a mirror-still lake. Creation laughing at the pure joy of creating such beauty.

Ann M.

October 3, 1988

The wind is kicking and the oneness of the cabin, water, trees, wind, and man give it all meaning for singularity. Candlelight and stove allow fire to be a mutual brother out here, along with life and the earth. We only have one planet and each one life. See it and enjoy it. For even as these hills, all things must pass away. Mother Nature gave birth to this planet. Treat it as a new born. Life is what we are.

Ropey & Deb

October 14, 1988

If you love it here in the Porkies, I would suggest that you take that vision home with you to the cities and suburbs:

- Get a sledge hammer and knock out your cement sidewalk, so the rains can penetrate the earth. Add wood chips to your path and enjoy the scent of woodland that you appreciate here.
- Go to the library and research which plants are native to your area. Learn about the conditions that help them thrive.
- Locate plant sources — you'll be surprised to learn how many native plant nurseries are springing up. Avoid digging plants in the field unless you have permission.
- Check out a copy of Marie Sperka's classic, Growing Wildflowers. She'll teach you how to reclaim the soil in your yard.
- Plant a woodland! Plant a prairie! Plant a savanna! Sit back and enjoy - you'll do less mowing and watering.
- When you see a tiny, gold finch perched on a cone flower, eating his fill, the Porkies won't seem so far away!

Doug, Christie, & Claire

October 22, 1988

We started coming here in college ten years ago, and now we've initiated both our kids over the years. Roughing it is not always easy and it takes work to enjoy it, but to me it's not the effort or the work, but the result or reason why we come to this or any wilderness area. There is a spiritually satisfying reward that we can take back with us, that can live inside us, and more important now is give our children the opportunity to appreciate it also, and the seed is planted in their lives, too....

As I look across the lake, I see the last scattered clumps of gold. The lake, indeed, wears many faces of the clouds. The cabin sighs with the peaceful sleep, yet it's always a day too soon to leave....

The R. Clan

January 17, 1989

> To the ophthalmologist who comes back alone—
> To Julie, in search of lost corners—
> To the Green Beret who would die for this place—
> I burn incense in your honor.
> You add immeasurably to the spirit of the wood,
> And facets to me

Mark F.

January 29, 1989

The candle will spare me no more time. Advice is cheap. But if I could have only one thought for you to ponder, it would be this...decide what it is you really want. Decide what you are willing to give up to make it happen. Plan your steps carefully. Work like hell until you accomplish your dream. The joy is in the journey.

Dave F.

February 18, 1989

I came up here in 1974 a troubled young man. But when I realized that you must depend on yourself to find your own way, it makes it easier to accept others and for others to accept you. I'm now thirty-two and have friends I can count on and I rarely doubt myself anymore. Life is great, it's what you make of it, and I owe mine to this park.

Sarge

March 8, 1989

We skied to the lower end of the lake today, and then a mile and-a-half up the Mirror Lake Trail. The snow and the forest were magical. Great, surging shapes draped all the downed logs and stumps. One was a white whale, with its great, gaping mouth formed by the snow above the log hollow. The gentle incline slowed our pace enough so we could stop and examine and wonder at the sheer beauty of our surroundings. The stands of hemlock were like the walls of a cathedral. A gentle snowfall made the silence seem even more profound. And then, higher up, the heavy stands of birch etched a white on white mosaic....

I have also read most of this journal, and am struck by the surprising range of people who come. I am pleased to note that nearly all who came were enriched by the peace and beauty of this place. So long as there are men and women such as these, there is hope for mankind.

Warren

April 5, 1989

As I stood overlooking Lake of the Clouds two summers ago and watched a tiny rowboat dancing across its cloud-reflected surface, I felt the wilderness below me beckoning. I knew that someday I would return and cross that bridge below me. In the past two years I have crossed many bridges to arrive at this place in my life. I have returned with my very best friend in the whole world whom I love more than anything. Events did not happen exactly as I planned—they never do....

I know that nothing is ever going to be the same—and I'm GLAD!

Kathy & Bill

June 26, 1989

We (two female/male couples and Malamute) scared ourselves silly reading on and on, well into the night, about all the bear troubles. We bought the True Bear Tales book at the Visitor's Center and then read back into this log book! We went to the outhouse in groups. After the men fell asleep, us girls considered smearing them with tuna and tossing their snoring bodies out to see how big the bears really are. But it was a hassle.

Cathy J.

October 10, 1989

I find myself wondering...about all the forces of life emanating from these mountains and lakes throughout the ages, and of the tribal peoples to whom this land was sacred. My prayer is that all who step upon this ground, step into the spirit of giving back to the Earth mother with honor and love, taking from her only that which is in balance with our needs. This is the way of our ancestors, and I open my heart to their voices in the wind, their spirit ripples through the lake and rises up the roots of trees, out through the branches and beyond. I feel the beauty of the shaman's drum as my own heart beats its pulse in rhythm with the all-enveloping vibration of life.

To the elements, directions, and all my relations, two-legged, four-legged, finned, and winged.

Denise B.

October 31, 1989

Nothing neater, more cosmic than paddling out into the middle of the lake and giving a great "HALLLOOO!!! Halllooo!!! halllooo!!!"

Unknown Author

April 29, 1990

Like beasts of burden
We maneuvered our way

Through the tall sullen sentinels
Of the mist-covered mountainside.
The soon to be canopy of leaves
Were still huddled tightly together
Except for the slight brush of green
That sprinkled the white birch.
Nestled in the fog stood the refuge
That would be our haven
From the world that now seemed
So far away and almost without reason.
The lapping of waves
Against the now sunken dock
And the distant call of a phoebe
Joined in soothing our weary muscles.
A woodchuck who had chosen the first floor
Of our new home scampered busily
Pausing to woo us with his friendly antics
By nibbling on crackers we offered him.
An overwhelming sense of the
Balance of life and the richness of being
Flooded our hearts.

Shirley C.

October 28, 1990

"To laugh often and much; to win the respect of intelligent people and the affection of children; to earn the appreciation of honest critics and endure the betrayal of false friends; to appreciate beauty; to find the best in others; to leave the world a little better place than we found it, whether by healthy child, a garden patch, or a redeemed social condition; to know even one life breathed easier because you lived. THIS IS TO HAVE SUCCEEDED!"

J.E.B.

May 1, 1991

Sitting back, by candlelight
on a cold, cold night,
Loading up the wood stove,
getting ready for bed,
wondering again how to take
this back to everyday life,
and when I read these stories
it makes me want to cry.

Bo

May 23, 1991
I throw out crumbs for the crows.
My belongings are moved closer to the edge of the escarpment.
Contentedness.

Unknown Author

October 5, 1991
This trip has provided me with a lot of firsts:
- Second anniversary of marriage celebrated at Speakers
- First sight of beavers
- First sight of otters (Mirror Lake)
- First bald eagle
- Most peak foliage ever
- Best sunrise and best sunset
- Made love on bridge
- Heard owls
- First autumn shower, with soap!

Dino & Lisa C.

November 20, 1991
I found an old mine on the southeast side of the lake. The opening is about two and-a-half feet in diameter and drops down on a forty-five degree angle about six feet, then levels out and is about six feet in diameter and goes back about thirty feet. The rocks are pretty rotten inside and crumble real easy. There are a few remains of an old cabin nearby. When I slid down into the mine, I was hoping there wasn't a bear waiting to greet me at the bottom. But it was empty. Whatever the miner found he must have used because there is no sign of the rocks he took out. Just a few rocks with white crystals.

Rex

March 30, 1992
We've hiked the Escarpment Trail, and of all the words in the human language, none are able to describe the spectacular views we've seen. Whether hiking across the edge of a mountainside, or snowshoeing through the glistening valleys in between, not a moment was regretted. I know I'm not the only one to say that, either. Even through gasping, wheezing moments of uphill endurance, never was a moment regretted. This is our second annual trip, taken during our well-earned, high school Spring Break. Many of us are "veterans" from last year, and I painfully say that it is them I shall miss the most, for this is my (our) senior year. I've traveled hundreds of miles and many hours to be here this week and say a spiritual good-bye to my friends. While here, I listen to the deafening silence, and remember all that has

occurred in my life, both the good and the bad. I remember who those friends were that quietly held me up before I had the chance to fall. Words can never express any form of saying farewell, adieu, or anything other than good-bye. That word, as small as it is, has affected my life in ways unspeakable.

So I sit here again, spilling my words to strangers, knowing that we will never meet. However, I know that we may know each other in a different, unique way.

Remember the Porkies, and truly view and listen, not only hear and see.

Melting Snow (a.k.a. Corey P.)

April 19-20, 1992

We are two women in search of solitude and relaxation. That's why we're two women instead of two women, two husbands, and two kids—as you know, we must go in pairs. The outhouse was near capacity and Tierza noted lower hotel rates during the off season. As I held the door for Tierza, we noted two deer (proving the pair theory) approximately twenty feet from our throne. We watched, they watched, etc., etc. They did not seem afraid and must have been notified by the park rangers of our lack of outdoor knowledge. We did have the rare opportunity to witness a deer's bowel movement. The deer ran off when Tierza offered it the use of our toilet paper.

Rachel G.

June 10, 1992

We are a family of five with an Australian exchange student, making a family of six, just sitting around the campfire...having a great, relaxing time.... This trip has been so exciting and it is great to be with my family. It has been such a joy to see us all together again without fighting and competing with each other. Wendy has also made the trip extra-everything. She is such a joy to have in our family, even though I think we are all getting too attached. She'll be moving to another host family in a few months.

Lori M.

After spending two days and nights out here in the wilderness with a very wonderful family, one is overcome with a complete feeling of serenity and becomes quite oblivious to the world that continues to hustle and bustle without us. Yesterday, we took a comfortable hike along the Escarpment Trail, which from the cabin, took us the whole length of the lake. From several rocky outcrops, on one side you could see Lake Superior, and on the other, Lake of the Clouds. It was very impressive. I especially enjoy the evenings/ nights here. It's so peaceful and quiet, you can hear nothing but the sound of the Porkies and see nothing but the silver moon, which last night was bright enough to cast shadows. At night, from the end of the pier, the lake looks absolutely beautiful. In the darkness, the lake and woods appear to stretch forever. I feel very lucky to have spent some very beautiful, relaxing times here, watching the animals and admiring the surroundings, swimming in the lake and relaxing around the fire. Coming from tropical Queensland, Australia, this has been an experience to be this far north and I have enjoyed it very much. I also can't think of any five people I'd have rather spent my time here with. Enjoy it and leave everything in as good a shape as you found it.

Wendy D.

I am Dad, packhorse, and cook. But most importantly and meaningfully, husband of one and father of four. After backpacking the Porkies a few years ago, I have dreamed of bringing my wife and three daughters here. And now am especially delighted not only to be here, but to have our Wendy, our Australian exchange student, with us. Makes these days especially enjoyable. I am so much in love with my family and these forested slopes and the precious creatures...and this wilderness area. I am in my church. My Father the Sun, my Mother the Earth.

David M.
The Wandering Scot

June 26, 1992

I think this is a place Winnie the Pooh would choose to live. It has the beauty of the Hundred Acre Wood. Pooh lives simply—worries never. I hope to take the peace of this cabin with me and try to live more like Pooh.

Unknown Author

July 6, 1992

I came to this cabin thirty-two years ago (hard to believe) with my father, cousin, and a friend. For some reason, the cabin seems smaller.

Now I am here with my children. They complained all the way here how stupid this would be. Right now, they are all across the lake, together, not fighting, and checking on the spring water. It is very quiet here, and peaceful. Can't wait for tonight to live by candlelight. The kids are having fun and enjoying each other for a change. There is something about this cabin. I never forgot it. And the way the kids are talking, they will not either. There is magic here...if we can only keep it in our hearts when we leave.

Bill B.

October 5, 1992

It has been a glorious weekend.... This is my third trip to the autumn Porkies, and the weather could not have been more congenial. Mother Nature surely used her entire palette of colors in decorating the forest. The warm brilliance of the sun added just the right amount of glow, perfecting the display. Have the reds ever been more crimson, the oranges and yellows warmer, and the blues of the sky and water any deeper? Not even the most imaginative and articulate of poets could have captured, in mere words, this awesome panorama.

George K.

April 30, 1993

This is an amazing place! It's one of those things where you don't have anything to do but be close to nature. When you are in the wilderness, you can't hide from yourself. You have to deal with them, I mean your problems, because nobody else cares. You can always keep secrets from other people, but your soul always knows. For some reason, the fresh air, the beavers, the lake, and the tricks of nature seem to pull it all out of you, and put you at peace with yourself. Even when you go back to the city and all of your daily stresses return. A true woodsman has a confidence and a knowledge that everybody respects. It's a wisdom that comes with experience. So if you want it, go after it. And if you have it, don't lose it. You would miss it.

Krista N.

July 7, 1993

A few random thoughts before I sign off:

- Why can't life be like this—simple. Does it really have to be so complicated?
- A rainy day in the woods beats a sunny day at work.
- I want to live right here.
- I love thunder, lightening, and rain.
- I am myself only ten days out of the year.
- Read all of this log book. Read it out loud to someone.
- Never underestimate the value of friendship.

Marc

August 23, 1993

God help us! We have a four year old boy!

Jim, Theressa, & Jerik

September 15, 1994

It was a dark and stormy night on the Lake of the Clouds. This was my second night at the peaceful cabin site. I came here alone...from the big city to get away from it all. The storm started brewing around dinner time, and when I went to bed about 11:00, it was still going strong! The wind was blowing so hard you could hear the leaves and branches falling from the trees. The wind would swirl around the cabin in gusts.

Then it happened. A knock at the door. "Who is it?" I said in a startled voice. But no one answered me. I sat quiet and waited, and then a knock again. This time my voice was shaking. "Who is it?!" I cried, but still no answer. At this point I was frantic—who could it be way out here, in this storm? A lost hiker perhaps? I was sleeping on a mattress thrown on the floor in front of a cozy fire. I crawled on my hands and knees over to the window to peer out and see if I could see anyone. As I peeked out the north window, my eyes met with another set of eyes looking straight at me in the dark!!! I screamed, "Leave me alone!!" The wind was howling all around me. I heard scraping noises, but I couldn't tell where it was coming from! Then it happened! A rock came through the north window! It was him, or should I say, "it."

I screamed and ran to the door to try to escape, as I watched it crawl through the broken window. I had locked the door and was fumbling to get it open for what seemed like an eternity. Just as it was inside, the door was free! I ran in the dark and rain and wind, tripping and stumbling over my own feet! I tried to calm myself down. Did I imagine what I saw? Or was it real? Better yet, what was it? It had to be at least seven feet tall and really hairy. It had bright, yellow eyes and breath that smelled like a sewer. Could it have been a bear? I didn't think so. Bears don't know how to throw rocks, besides it was covered with seaweed as if it swam from the lake!

As I ran through the rain, I feared it was behind—following me—tracking me— hunting me! I missed the turn on the trail that would take me to my car at the overlook. Next thing I knew, I was on the bridge to north Mirror Lake. I ran across the bridge without thinking. As I turned to look behind me, I saw the "yellow eyes" staring at me from across the bridge. Or was it my imagination? Was it stalking me? Searching me out? I reached for something, anything on the ground that I could use for a weapon. I found a large branch about four inches in diameter. I was ready to stand my ground! I couldn't run anymore! It moved towards me across the bridge, slowly. When it was no more than a few feet away I started swinging! I couldn't see that well because of the storm, but I must have struck it in the face. It cried and stepped away! Then, all of a sudden, I heard it jump over the edge of the bridge and into the swampy, foggy water. I waited for what seemed like hours before I proceeded back across the bridge. Then from nowhere, I felt a hand grab at my ankle, trying to pull me down below! I screamed and kicked as hard as I could. I struggled free and ran on as fast as I could. When I got to my car on Lookout Point, I finally stopped to rest. Luckily, a ranger pulled up, checking on things when he saw me crying and waving my hands at him. I told the ranger my story, as he listened very carefully. When I finished, he told me about three or four years ago, a woman and her husband were staying in the Lake of the Clouds Cabin on their honeymoon. Her husband had gone across the lake to fetch water at the spring, but never returned. They believe he fell into the lake and drowned. All they ever found was the boat that drifted to the edge. No sign of her husband. He went on to say, that every year on the anniversary of his accident, people have seen and reported strange things that happened around the Lake of the Clouds Cabin site. It is believed it is her husband, searching to find his bride.

Kristi

April 19, 1995

Leslie is reading True Bear Tales. Kellen and Kerrin are nervous about bears getting in the cabin. I open one of the windows and everybody starts to scream (except Hannah, the four year old)! We have four bunks and all three kids and wife, Leslie, are cuddled into one bunk. Chicken!

All of a sudden, we hear a scratching noise outside the cabin. I'm thinking "what could that be?" Probably the wind blowing a branch against the cabin. A few minutes later we hear it again—this time a thump and a bang. Wow, I'm a bit nervous! And then it happens—BANG, SLAM—the door bursts open and in comes a huge black bear, teeth snarling bright, claws stretched over his gigantic head!! He lets out a ferocious, ear-screeching howl, so loud the windows rattle in their frames! Well, there is no time to think. The kids and wife are screaming, all huddled together in one bunk. I immediately swing into action. First, I grab a slab of salami and throw it at his feet. When he bends to grab it, I jump on his back wrestling him down to the cabin floor (two points take down). I then proceed to put a figure-four around his massive trunk and lock his head and neck in a sleeper hold. In about thirty seconds he passes out. I then pick him up over my shoulders (he weighs about 250 pounds) and I carry him outside, walk him down to the lake where I toss him in head first. He comes to at this point looking pretty angry. So I shake my finger at him warning him he'll get more of the same if he comes back up. He then gets a sheepish look on his face and decides he'd better just get the heck out of here. So he turns around, dives into the lake, and actually swims away.

Needless to say the kids and the wife are ever so grateful and think their Dad is something else!

Steve

April 29, 1995

"A man only finds himself in nature," said Thoreau in the 1880's, and the feeling holds today. Man has spent his entire history working for immediate comfort and yet we are most at peace in our first element (nature). Schedules, TV, school, etc., all consume our lives, but leave us empty. So I hope that all those who visit the Lake of the Clouds sit back and reflect.

John

April 29, 1995

The weather is too perfect in a place such as this; where the mind can get caught up in fantasy. A mystified image of dreams, pasts brought to life in such vibrant realism. Where laughter with friends and silent solitude blend together as the same water image. I'm remembering everything as a picture, rather than an event, as if not I, but another sat in for me as I watched.... So wonderfully, tragically surreal—maybe someday I'll return, when my mind can understand it's brilliance.

Unknown Author

May 11, 1995

What a fine day—my birthday, thirty-one. Can you think of a better place to be?...We have prepared the ultimate five-course meal. Yes, living off the land! It's like this: Appetizer—toasted wood chips served on a bed of cedar greens and drizzled with worm juice! No less. Sharon prepared an incredible Hot Fungus soup with Acorn pieces, finely chopped....

Peter

September 19, 1995

Dave won so much playing cards we are wondering where to dump the body. I think we will throw him off the escarpment or make him swim with the fishes. Got to get the car keys from him before the dirty deed is done.

Unknown Author

June 2, 1996

Twenty years ago this was our honeymoon cabin. We are back again for the first time in twenty years with our children Clinton (twelve) and Taylor (ten). Back then we could not have imagined it would be such a long absence. We'll not make that mistake again. Where else could you go on your honeymoon, come back twenty years later, and have the place look exactly the same. This park, this lake, and this cabin are a treasure.

Jhan & Colleen

June 11, 1996

I've always wanted to see a bear...until I actually saw one. My family was out in the canoe (row boat) fishing, but I decided to stay at the cabin. I was reading a book, looked out the back window, and I saw a bear right outside my window. It was huge! I wanted to take a picture, but I was too scared to take one. It didn't break in or anything, so I guess bears aren't that bad after all! Besides that, I'm usually not big on camping, but I'm actually enjoying my stay. The fish were biting great over by the gravel side. The scenery is just beautiful. Linda saw a deer drinking out of the lake right in front of the cabin. I love staying at Lake of the Clouds!

Sarah

Late Summer 1996

Tuesday. Got out late—7:30 A.M., sun was clouding up. Still caught three, three-quarter pound bass. Made lunch—pancakes! Sure are good over a campfire with hot chocolate. Need to do dishes before going fishing again. Even out here I still have to do my own dishes. There's no justice in the world. 3:30 P.M.—just got back from the second fishing trip of the day—very productive! Ten to fifteen bass, some small, a lot from fourteen to eighteen inches. One of these times I'm going to have to take my camera along to verify these fish. As you can see, I came here to soak up the wondrous beauty God provided for us in L.O.C. and also to fish! And I mean to do a lot of both....

Wednesday. Good morning, it's 9:00 A.M. and I am making breakfast—pancakes, strawberries and cream oatmeal, and hot chocolate—delightful. As you can see by the time, I did not go fishing this morning. I woke up and it was a little windy and the lake was all misty telling me that it was just a little cold outside—stay in bed? Which was exactly what I did. I picked up the book my wife wanted me to read while I was here and read a couple chapters of that. I like it so much that I will probably leave it here when I go, so that others may enjoy it. My wife says that I remind her of the boy in the story - go figure. Out here on my own, cooking my own food, catching fish—well, read the book and you will see. I'll talk more later after I have eaten my breakfast and fished a little. Bye....

Thursday. 12:04 P.M.—best day of fishing yet. It started out slow with only two small fish in two hours. But all of a sudden—BAM! A five plus pounder and twenty-one inches. Three or four fish later, another five pounder, this one twenty-two inches. A total of nine fish in all, and yes, I finally got my fish story. The next cast after the first five pounder, I tied into something huge. Top water Zara Spook of course, that made my last fish look small. I only had him on for about fifteen seconds, but it was the best fifteen seconds of my fishing life. I had cast directly into the sun so when it hit, I could see him jump perfectly. Ecstasy—and then nothing. My line had broken. "Damn!" Just then the fish jumped completely out of the water showing his unbelievable size and flashing my Zara Spook at me to know where it was if I ever wanted to come looking for it. And so, to any fisherman or fisherwoman who reads this and by shear luck happen to tie into that fish, please leave the lure and a note as to how big it was in the cabin. I will be back next year, and the year after, and so on. Moral of this story—always re-tie your lures after every catch!

Friday. My first cast netted me a fifteen inch bass, but that was it for the rest of the morning....The good thing that did come out of the morning was that I finally got to see a bear. It was walking around the woods at the northeast part of the lake, where I could safely watch it from the boat. As far as I could tell, it was a big bear, weighing 300 to 400 pounds. After four years of coming to Lake of the Clouds, I finally see a bear. That made my whole week....

This place is my second home....No matter what happens in my life, I can always walk down the path to this cabin and know I'm home. In keeping with tradition, I have left behind my copy of My Side of the Mountain. If you can, please take the time to enjoy it as I have. And please leave it here. I plan on reading it again next year.

Chad

October 13, 1996

First Time Pack the Porkies Pledge

I pledge to always love and protect the Porkies. I will try to never do anything to make Mother Nature mad at me. I will also be kind to things great and small, like stopping my lawn mower to save a toad or snake. I will pack out what I pack in and leave only footprints (the candidate will then receive a Porkies patch and a swig of Pepsi Cola).

Gary

October 27-29, 1996

Jim and I used to live like this when we were younger. I was undecided whether I really wanted to come on this trip. But now that I'm here, I realize that it truly was a good life. Everyday you prepare for the next day. To me, it's like living day by day and living it to the fullest. I look back and things were a lot more time consuming, but you felt good about what you had done for the day.

Sue

April 4-5, 1997

Joel, Jason, and possibly Jay (if he makes it) hiked from the ski hill about five miles. Only took four hours. Jay coming up later tonight and has to hike in during the dark. He's going to kill Joel.... It is now 1:47 A.M. Saturday morning. Jay has still not shown up. Joel has walked out to meet him. Me (Jason) on the other hand has been working on the fire. I need water. I'm so thirsty!...Jay finally arrived around 2:30 A.M., a little pissed. But he brought the chili so we're eating good now.

I (Jay — see above) arrived at the ski area at 10:00 P.M. last night after driving eight hours from Chicago. I was concerned about arriving so late considering the five mile snowshoe hike in, but my S.O.B. brother (Joel) assured me that "everything would be golden." The hike in was long, rainy, and very, very dark. I finally made it to the lookout about 2:30 A.M. and had no idea how to get to the cabin. I had no choice but to yell and scream until someone answered. After I saw flashlights from the cabin I realized I still had quite a hike ahead of me. By the time I finally got to the cabin, all I wanted to do was drink about a gallon of water and go to bed.

*Advice to others: If anyone tries to talk you into doing something using the phrase "Everything is golden," stop, turn around, and run like hell!
P.S. The next day was much better.

Joel, Jason, & Jay

April 11-13, 1997
Joel and Jason from last week decided to make the trip again - but this time Jay stayed in Chicago, and they brought me.... The morning started out slow. We all just kind of hung out, cut some wood, and the guys did a little tree climbing. Jason even decided to take a little ride in the boat. This was difficult since the lake was still frozen over. But hey, he just grabbed a beer and sat in the boat on top of the ice. It didn't matter to him if he didn't go anywhere....From the lookout, we examined the stream that the footbridge crossed and decided to take the rowboat for a trip down it. We started the hike back to the cabin and figured we'd engineer some way to get the rowboat across the frozen lake and into the open water. Don't ask me how, but the boat was dragged across the ice and then some fancy run, jump, hop track-thing, but the guys propelled us into open water. Well, almost. We landed on top of an ice sheet and had to do some fancy maneuvering to cut through. This was only the beginning. The stream was clogged many a place by fallen trees and grass. The rowboat isn't too agile, but the guys managed to get us unstuck no matter how bad the hang-up. Going downstream wasn't too bad, but the trip back upstream was a different story. Spring is great to be on the water. Everything is just starting to melt and there were some cool ice formations. Ice was formed on the trees in the shape of champagne glasses stacked on top of one

another. Living on a prayer, we somehow got the boat back onto the ice from the water and walked back to the cabin.

Tammy

June 3, 1997

It was about 3:30 P.M. Heard footsteps in the brush outside the north window, which was open, and both of us looked over immediately. I expected to see a person looking in, but instead, a black bear stands up and peers through the window. Neither one of us said a thing and after he looked in for several seconds, he dropped down and meandered off. I grabbed my camera, went outside, and followed him. He walked away right on the trail you use to get to the cabin, just sauntering along. I snapped a couple of shots then returned to the cabin.

Just discovered damage caused by the bear. He clawed or bit our Super H_2O Sun Shower hanging from the pine tree between the cabin and the lake. Tore it right open, left teeth or claw marks in the bag. Must have happened right before we saw him because the bag is still dripping water.

Dan

July 17, 1997

Alison thinks bears are in the woods singing the song:
"We think human lungs are tasty,
We're tired of nuts and berries...."

The C. Bunch

August 28, 1997

An attractive woman or a red, classic Corvette are not beautiful in themselves, but rather trigger feelings in us which we already possess.

A gently stepping doe, grand cliffs and forests, water trapped by mountains, or the fish that swim in this water are also not beautiful in themselves, but inspire a sense of awe in each of us which would have lain dormant indefinitely if we would not have found this place to pry out this pleasure.

When our days are done and our possessions are garage-saled out, perhaps the most important things remaining are the pleasures which we have unlocked for others to enjoy after our passing.

Farmer Bob

October, 1997

THE END

This is the last page
It really puts me in a rage

Rangers gonna take this book
I think that's a big fat rook
No one will read my words
Laid out like little turds
Extolling the virtues of wilderness
Ah, but no, I must confess
When I have trod upon the path
At the end of the day I do the math
Add up the miles having walked
My body says that I have chalked
Up twice the distance on the map
Then on the door I hear a tap
And mister black bear walking by
Looks at me with studied eye
A hungry gaze upon me lays
He's in a mood for lotsa food
So down to the lake in a flash
I scare him away with a big splash
Then all the birds about me flit
They really made it worth the trip
Up to the overlook I gaze
At scurrying people all in a daze
They live too fast to sit and brood
Upon the throne in deep dark wood
So here I sit far from the crowds
In the outhouse at Lake of the Clouds
And meditate the Porcupines
The places I love they are so fine
And so as I lay down my pen
I say to all you women and men
See you yonder 'round the next bend
Cause that's all there is
This is THE END.

Rageman

Recipes to Die From... er, For

August 29, 1955
Lake of the Clouds Cabin
RECIPE FOR CHOWDER BASS OR PERCH:

1. Brown one-quarter pound of bacon—small pieces
2. Add one medium onion, chopped fine, to cook together until tender
3. Add three cups of hot water, four raw potatoes, peeled and dried
4. Add diced, good-sized lumps of two good bass, filleted and boneless; fish should be liberally sprinkled with one and-a-half teaspoons salt and one-half teaspoon pepper
5. Simmer all in uncovered kettle for twenty-five minutes
6. Add two cups of milk (powdered OK), bring to boiling point, but do not boil!
7. Serve! Will feed four hungires!

J.C.

May 17, 1986
Big Carp 6-Bunk Cabin

BLACK FLY PIE

- Take one good-sized window
- Open screen door while holding window
- Squash black flies into paste on glass panes
- Mix with diced raisins and cover pie shell
- Bake as you would for apple pie

While hot, glaze with brown sugar and one-and-a-half cups of water.

Very excellent campers treat!
Also helps build up an anti-toxin to their bites, and so stops itching!
*Twenty-five cents worth makes entire pie!

Unknown Author

June 28, 1997
Lake Superior Cabin

Unknown Artist

August 8, 1971
Lake Superior Cabin

OUR MENU

DATE	BREAKFAST	LUNCH	DINNER
August 5th Thursday		Lipton Rice Soup Candy Bars Kool-Aid	Hot Dogs Biscuits Beans Pudding
August 6th Friday	Eggs Hash Browns Bacon Coffee & Tang	Ham Salad on Rye Krisps Bullion Kool-Aid	Chicken Casserole 3-Bean Salad Butterscotch Pudding
August 7th Saturday	Eggs Hash Browns Sausage Hot Choc. & Tang	Rye Krisps Lipton Soup Kool-Aid	Ham Scalloped Spinach Pudding S mores
August 8th Sunday	Eggs Corn-Beef Hash Coffee & Tang	Lipton Soup Kool-Aid	Beef Stroganoff Corn Choc. Pudding
August 9th Monday	Cream of Wheat Fruit Bacon Tang	Sloppy Joes Biscuits Kool-Aid	Beef Strew Noodles Ice Tea Lemon Pudding
August 10th Tuesday	Pancakes Bacon Coffee & Tang	Egg Salad Bullion Kool-Aid	Spaghetti Pop Corn
August 11th Wednesday	LEAVE	AFTER	LUNCH

The S. Family

213

July 11, 1997
Buckshot Cabin

Newly discovered Recipe - BLACK FLY STEAK

Take two T-bones—cook over open pit—when done to your perfection, place on bench, go back and flip the kid's hamburgers—let kid use fly swatter—tell him to keep flies from steak—eventually, he will kill flies on steak—make sure he squishes them good—serve with favorite steak sauce and enjoy!

The C. Family

January 17, 1993
Union River Cabin

CAMP STYLE FRUIT SOUP

Place in a pot: one package dried apples, one package prunes, one package dried apricots, and one package dried peaches. Add water and simmer. Add more water when needed until very tender. Optional spices: cinnamon and nutmeg.

Kathy

June 28, 1970
Lily Pond Cabin

We topped off dinner with Girl Scout S'mores, which is a toasted marshmallow between two graham crackers, and a piece of Hershey's chocolate inside. Yummy!

The P. Family

May 24, 1972
Lily Pond Cabin

We got up at 8:00 this morning. Since we had forgotten to bring sugar for our Cream of Wheat, we used Tang. Jay plans on getting a patent on the idea. Tasted pretty good.

Mary, Shirley, Fox, Jay, & Deb

September 13, 1989
Lily Pond Cabin

My "Mystery Pudding" was a success! For those of you who would like to try it, you need the following:

Pecans and crumbled up Heath Bars on the bottom, chocolate pudding, and a splash of rum on the top. Yum! Try it and you'll like it!

Fran

April 19, 1991
Speaker's Cabin
To all you granola-eating, Ule Gibbons types:
    We understand how you want to lower your cholesterol and sugar intake 'cuz you are all out of shape and have desk jobs and all that yuppie stuff, but could you leave us some decent scraps behind? You know: FATS, SWEETS, saturated and hydrogenated oils, etc. That health food will kill us. I have a cousin who works in a testing lab and she says health food kills hundreds of rodents every year. So please, leave us some junk food!

Ed, the chipmunk

October 22, 1970
Big Carp 4-Bunk Cabin
    SHACK HAPPY FISHERMAN'S RECIPE FOR WHISTLE TROUT:
Ingredients:
    Twenty-seven whistle trout
    One bucket of river mud
    One large packet of rice
    One-half pound butter
    Twenty-seven pinches of pepper
    One-quarter pound of salt
Clean whistle trout. Soak for three hours in a solution of one-quarter pound salt in five gallons of hot water. Drain and stuff with a mixture of rice, butter, and pepper. Coat fish with a one-half inch layer of river mud. Bury in a bed of coals and leave for one hour and twenty-five minutes. Peel off layer of baked river mud. Skin should come off easily with mud, leaving fish's flesh clean and baked. Then feed the cooked fish flesh to the bear and eat the mud.

It's real good! Too bad about the bear!

Unknown Author & Artist

October 12, 1982
Lily Pond Cabin
    Australian Recipe for Making Coffee Without the Insert:
1) Bring water to boil in coffee pot
2) Put coffee grounds (three-quarter measure fill cup) into boiling water
3) Stir and take off fire
4) Let steep for a few minutes
5) Pour dash of cold water in; this will make the grounds go to the bottom
Unknown Author

June 29, 1995
Section 17 Cabin

The C. Family

September 9, 1987
Greenstone Falls Cabin
    In reading through the log, there appears to be a lot of hot dog dinners going on. Aaargh! You may as well roast Fred (the mouse)! Here's a few tips for quick, easy, light dinners that backpack well:
- MexiFiesta Fantastic Frijoles—boxed, dehydrated beans, MexiVelveeta, flour tortillas, salsa, and white rice.
- Potato Melt—real potatoes fried in oil with onion chunks, green peppers, and seasoning, topped with melted cheese; a great breakfast.
- Veggie Souffle'—steamed broccoli, zucchini, cauliflower, mushrooms, and onions in a skillet; top with one egg and mix; serve over a warm corn tortilla; a treat!

- Potato Pancakes—panni bread is best!
- Spaghetti in Mushroom Sauce—fry real mushrooms.

This was our menu for the trip. Add wine to dinners, fresh oranges to breakfasts.

Carmel & Rich

May 11, 1986
Big Carp 6-Bunk Cabin

MICE SOUP OR DIP RECIPE:

1,118 parts mice
One cup sour cream
One-quarter teaspoon full paprika
Pinch of basil (optional)
One-half cup spider food
One pound diced mushrooms
Two pounds viscera
Five egg shells
Two pounds shredded cheese
Four adults regurgitating
* for dip, add Metamucil

Pre-heat oven to 375 degrees. Place mixture of above ingredients in casserole dish in hot oven. Cook forty minutes. Serves seven to eight.

Unknown Author

May 18, 1987
Buckshot Cabin

Deidre B.

August 8, 1988
Greenstone Falls Cabin
> Recipe for light packers: FETTUCINE 'AL FREDERICO

Ingredients:

> One medium onion
> One clove garlic
> One pound noodles
> Handful of wild mushrooms (amanita muscaria)
> *Editor's note: amanita muscaria are HIGHLY POISONOUS!*
> One Fred (mouse)
> One-quarter cup Parmesan cheese
> One cup dried milk (mix well)
> Salt and pepper to taste
> Flour
> Butter

Skin and gut Fred. Saute' fillet of Fred with onion, garlic, and mushrooms. Cool pasta 'al dente. Bring milk to a simmer, add flour and butter to make hot roux. One tablespoon will do. Add to noodles. Add remaining ingredients.

Be sure to serve with a medium Chardonnay. YUM! YUM!

> Dave

July 19, 1998
Buckshot Cabin

Kev, Dan, Jason, Mike, Jeff, & "Stinky," the Scared Toad
When we arrived at the site we were bright-eyed and bushy-tailed, a group of happy-go-lucky guys ready for peace and quiet, and mad-cap adventure...

...we enjoyed the pleasantries of nature...
...AND THEN...
...we became hungry and left the beach...
...we arrived at the cabin and realized we forgot the food...

...we survive on a peanut, a cigarette butt, and a gum wrapper we found
between the rocks on the beach...
...NOTE: a peanut, a gum wrapper, and a cigarette butt is not enough food for
five growing boys...

...Stinky now has a reason to be scared, for hunger plays tricks on the mind...

...PREPARING
THE
FEAST...

...we forgot about the fire ban...
MORAL: Don't try to eat Stinky!
Kev, Dan, Jason, Mike, Jeff, & Stinky

Recipes to Die From...er, For

Wonders
of
Winter

September 22, 1995
Mirror Lake 8-Bunk Cabin

We had the first snow of the season last night. I thought I was coming here to welcome fall to the Midwest. It seems winter came instead. I was in a tent two nights ago. I am glad I opted for the cabin on this night.

It's a very heavy snow. I awoke last night to the sound of clumps of it falling on the roof. At first, I thought I was being invaded by some critters, but when I investigated, I saw the snow outside. Lots of branches have fallen, too. There is a huge one outside of the front door. I can't help but wonder what that would have done to my tent, if the branch had fallen on it?

The reflection is more beautiful than reality. I watched the stars glitter in the lake last night. I was surrounded by a deafening silence, and only heard a faint noise come from several minutes away. Liebnig wrote that all things mirror the universe in their own unique way. Mirror Lake reflects the universe in a most wondrous way.

Greg F.

May 3, 1997
Whitetail Cabin

You know what they call summer in the UP? Two weeks of bad snowmobiling.

Les V.

March 4, 1995
Gitchee Gumee Cabin

Skiing morning
Two tracks of powder pure snow
Deer sign everywhere

Kids skiing slopes
Mom in the cabin
Waiting for old friends to arrive

Fresh brewed coffee
For the soon to appear guests
Snow flurries drift and swirl

Susan C.

November 26, 1985
Mirror Lake 4-Bunk

It is the morning of the 26, year 1985, three days after we were to have left. Our problems seem to have started to occur sometime between the night of November 22 and the morning of the 23. This is when a bone-chilling arctic cold front moved in, dropping temperatures well below the zero mark. Accompanying these sub-zero temperatures was a low pressure system bringing in moist air from the south, which in essence turned into about eighteen inches of a fluffy white snow.

So that morning, we got up and decided that we had better eat a good breakfast because we knew we would need all the energy we could get, plus we also wanted our already burdened backpacks to be as light as possible so that we could make our way up the three mile South Mirror Lake Trail, to where we would reach our trusty, four-wheel drive Jeep, which would take us out of this God-forsaken country.

So after much deliberation, we finally decided that if we were to make it out of the woods before dark, we would have to be on our way.

As Bob checked the cabin to make sure that everything was picked up and in its place, I was outside, standing almost waist deep in snow, wondering how in the hell we were going to make it out of here alive. I stood there gazing out over Mirror Lake, which now looked like the Siberian wastelands of Russia. I heard the sound of Bob putting the padlock on the door and I knew our journey was about to begin.

As we started down the trail, weather conditions started to go from bad to worse. The wind started to blow so strong that it created white outs, and at times, it was hard to even see Bob, who was six feet in front of me breaking trail. As we got about one mile, or two hours, from the cabin, we realized that we had lost the trail and didn't know where we were headed. So we decided to turn around and try to find our way back to the cabin. As we got to the footbridge, I heard Bob yelling and screaming for help. Bob had lost his footing and slipped off the bridge into the freezing water and ice. When I got there, just his head and arms were above the ice, and his backpack was stuck underneath. I told him to undo his pack and grab my arm. As he did, his pack with all his clothes and food went out of sight.

As I got Bob onto safe ground, we almost started to jog, so we could get Bob back to the cabin and give him some of my clothes. As we got back to the cabin, we realized we had put the key to the cabin door in Bob's pack, so we had to break one of the windows to get in.

It is now nightfall, and the wind is just whistling through the broken window. We are sitting here wondering if we will ever be found by a rescue party. It is really getting unbearable with no food, and we are freezing our butts off. It is now getting very late, as we are losing hope we will ever make it out of here, as we struggle to keep our cabin warm and our fire lit.

Unknown Author

March 10, 1989
Speaker's Cabin
  Ice blocks, the size of rooms, thrust at various angles, dripping frosting of snowy white—the work of some Artist of wild magic skillful in his craft. Blue that pierces the soul—silent blue, frosted blue, wet blue frozen in time and space, content to await release and again merge with current and wind and wave until called again to serve as sentinel in the frozen expanse.

Brian

Winter, Unknown Year
Union River Cabin

S. & M.

April 15, 1978
Mirror Lake 8-Bunk Cabin

We arrived early this morning, about 1:00 A.M. The roads were not plowed yet so we had an eight mile hike in, most of it on snowshoes. Still can't believe there is three feet of snow in the middle of April! It was a real treat hiking in under the stars and a half-moon. For a while. Then it got cloudy. We could hardly see our hands in front of our faces, let alone the many snowshoe-grabbing snags. Many members of our party (six members in all and a dog) took nasty spills, and one snowshoe we are now using for tooth-picks. I guess Gary can hop out tomorrow. It was a real bitch seeing the orange trail markers after the clouds came out and our advance party, Paul and Dave, who were going to get a fire and dinner going, ended up hopelessly "turned around" as their lone flashlight had failed. We caught up to them about one and-a-half miles from the cabin. Aided by a strong flashlight and blind luck, we managed to drag ourselves in. It was extremely touch and go at times, and several people had wet feet from the many streams hidden under the snow.

When at last we arrived, we devoured a loaf of bread and a package of bologna. Then we all crashed and slept until one this afternoon. We awoke to a lovely spring morning and sat out front and absorbed much sun. To top the day off, we saw a butterfly which was kind of strange with all of the snow.

It is the last night. We really did not arrive early enough last night to appreciate it. Tonight there are no clouds and only an occasional wisp of water vapor. There is a half-moon, maybe a little more, but it is extremely bright. We tried to do star gazing, but it is too bright out with the moon. Tomorrow morning, at about 4:00 A.M., we will try again. The moon should have set by then.

The sunset was fantastic. The sunrise tomorrow will, we hope, be exquis-ite! And the birds will no doubt give a concert as worthy in tone and harmony as a symphony orchestra. They performed as good tonight.

You are probably wondering what kind of strange people we are, that arrive in the middle of the night, and yet awake to watch stars and get up before the sun. Well, we are considered very normal in the outside world. The six of us are students who have spent too much time in academia. Could we not learn as much, if not more, by spending the four years here? It did not hurt Thoreau and would do us all good.

We also should not, I hope, disappoint the readers if we do not make claims on how much alcohol we needed to have a good time. We needed none. There is a perfect high to be had by meeting nature, its sounds, views, and feelings on its ground. It has also helped that there is no one else out here as of yet. There is an abundance of solitude about, and it takes almost no looking to find it.

When you are deprived of this feeling of being a part of nature as much as we are in today's cities, you make the most of it. Even if it means losing a little sleep. Sleep I can always catch up on.

Jerry

November 11, 1986
Greenstone Falls Cabin

In spite of the fact that we didn't get any deer, this has been very well worth the effort. Just a quiet walking through the pristine, snow-covered terrain was exhilarating enough. The rustling water appeared to be so inviting that we drank it straight out of the river. That impressed me because I had never had that opportunity before. Our main water supply is melted snow. The feeling of isolation creates the notion of total freedom which is very appealing at this stage in life. I hope that I may experience it again.

Pete C.

January 30, 1988
Buckshot Cabin

A trip outside
and the trees
are complaining
and crying under
the icy weight
coating the branches
from earlier rain

"The Two Happy Lemmings"

February 7, 1996
Whitetail Cabin

Bushwhacked on snowshoes straight north from the Lake of the Clouds area to the big lake they call Gitchee Gumee's shore. Then east across the dunes and ice shelves back to the cabin. 'Shoed a good portion of the trek, guided by the downward twists and turns of the Cayahoga Creek Ravine. Some fantastic stands of hemlock towering over spacious openings on the forest floor. Very nice. Some very pleasant moments were spent in close encounters with a dozen and-a-half whitetail as I descended in elevation, meandering with the Cayahoga Creek bed. The deer stubbornly held their ground until the space between us had shortened to less than thirty feet, many times. The deep, extremely wet snow forced the deer to jump away slowly in high bounds. It was easy to empathize with their plight as heavy snow piled atop the snowshoes. Above normal temperatures, in the thirties range, has the snow in perfect packing conditions. Excellent time for a snowperson in the yard. Made the thighs burn on the trek, however. All in all, a great day. Hate to think of leaving tomorrow, so I won't. I will look at the spectacular, star-studded sky, instead.

K.R.M.

May 8, 1996
Lily Pond Cabin

SOLO TO LILY POND:

As a supervisor of an outdoor adventure program, I always tell my staff, often in a haranguing tone, "Don't forget to take your snowshoes!"

"But it's April," they usually protested. "There couldn't be anything but a few patches of snow left."

By May 1st, most people had already mowed their lawn and played three rounds of golf, snowshoes and skis tucked away in the corner of the garage where the lawn chairs had been. Madison, Wisconsin may only be a five hour drive, but it's another reality away from the Porkies.

So I traveled east as far as the county line on South Boundary Road. Ontonagon County does not budget this road for plowing. I eased off the road next to a Blazer (Ohio plates). Fresh tracks, perhaps three to four people, leading up the left side of the road where the sun has melted most of the snow. In the woods, only patches remain. There are four sets of tracks. One person is pulling a sled. No snowshoes.

A last minute check of the pack. Still too heavy. I took some obligatory pictures of snow drifts and a still frozen Lake of the Clouds yesterday. The camera stays. Extra pants? Who needs them. One candle is enough. Too much food. Leave some behind. Cigars and the flask of scotch? There are certain pleasures one must never be without, especially when traveling alone. Pack it.

Still the pack seems heavy. Snowshoes? I look at the patchy snow in the woods and think how tedious it will be to put them on, take them off, put them on, take them off...I hear a voice, my voice, from the past, scolding, "Don't forget to take your snowshoes!"

From where I started, the most direct route to Lily Pond seemed to be way off the Little Carp River Trail, less than one-half mile north of the South Boundary Road. I would have to cross the river. And from the look and sound of the melt water around me, the stepping stones of summer were probably far below the surface of a cold spring torrent.

I decided to follow the people from Ohio. As much as I hate to hike along roads, I knew that I would have a solid surface to take me within three miles of Lily Pond. I was soon rewarded by the sighting of a Pine Warbler, listed as a rare sighting, this one posed on a willow barely fifteen feet away, long enough for me to check and recheck my field guide. The camera would have been worth the extra weight. I could have left the scotch.

Continuing up the road, the bare patches were less frequent. It looked like the people form Ohio were beginning to struggle. They seemed to be searching for solid footing on different parts of the road. Every third step or so broke through up to ten inches.

By the time I reached the Little Carp River Road, there were no more bare spots. Time to put on the snowshoes.

With the increased shade from the hills and trees, the snow depth increased to twenty inches in places. The Ohio people were post-holing on every other step. I was feeling quite smug shuffling across the surface on my snowshoes. Ahead I could see the last Buckeye plomping forward, near the bridge over the Little Carp River, where he stopped to read a signpost, chest heaving. He was a magnificently obese man, over three hundred pounds, and much of the poundage seemed to settle in his broad rump. He wore blue jeans, wet to above the knees from the snow, perspiration spreading from the top, a long gap of flesh between the smiling blue jeans and the jacket.

We talked briefly and I went on. The Ohio people were going to the Greenstone Falls Cabin. He was almost home.

5:00 P.M.: Trackless snow. The trail left by an outlaw snowmobile turned back at the last stream crossing. No more human tracks, only faint rumors of ancient skis. The snow depth is over three feet at times. Even the deer have wisely avoided this area. The temperature is perhaps sixty degrees and I can hear running water nearly everywhere. Occasionally I would break through, even with snowshoes, and water would spill over the tops of my boots.

I came across another photo opportunity, an old pine snag sculptured by pileated woodpeckers into some strange totem worshipped by who or what? It is a work-in-progress, a huge mound of wood chips at the base of the trunk.

Later, coyote tracks. What do they eat here? No signs of rabbits or mice. Later, coyote scat, perhaps three days old. Probably female, as urine and feces were mixed together.

6:30 P.M.: Very tired. Frequent stops. I reached the point where the trail met the Little Carp River. The home stretch was just on the other side. But the main channel of the river was at least three feet deep. The typical crossing, large rocks and fallen trees, were either hidden under the strong current or washed away.

I searched for a crossing downstream. Nothing. Upstream? Nothing. I realize that if I was going to cross the stream, I'll have to do it barefoot or get my boots hopelessly soaked. Either way, I'd have to build a fire on the other side to warm up my feet. The valley was now shaded from the sun and the temperature was dropping.

Time to have looked at the map. In an instant, the solution was evident. There was no need to cross the river! Follow the west bank of the river up to Lily Pond and cross on the bridge there. It was longer and off the trail, but I hadn't been following the trail anyway, I had just been following marks on the trees. The snow had covered rocks, blowdowns, small streams, nearly everything, including the footpath of the summer people.

7:30 P.M.: I reached the bridge at Lily Pond in a near state of exhaustion. The cabin was a wondrous sight. It was evident from the snow drifted against the door, that I was the first to use it this year. My last great physical effort was to dig enough snow away from the door to open it.

8:30 P.M.: Rested. A hot fire in the stove. Two cups of tea.

9:30 P.M.: After dinner, I sat on the bench on the bridge. A beaver worked on his dam. A lone, common merganser drifted on a black patch of open water. I took a couple of pulls on the flask of scotch, puffing peacefully on a cigar.

10:30 P.M.: Soon to sleep, I decided not to leave the snowshoes out in the cold. I brought them in, leaned gently against the wall next to my bed.

Unknown Author

January 15, 1970
Mirror Lake 4-Bunk Cabin

We are quite cozy now, and enjoying the great peace. How beautiful the pines are blanketed with snow. I ventured out through giant drifts of snow— four inches of snow carpet the floor. This morning it's beautiful. The sun is shining making the snow appear sprinkled with diamonds. The ice on the cabin hangs to the ground. It's probably ten below zero. Cozy inside. We were very warm sleeping due to the fact we had two in one sleeping bag. Kind of "survival of the fitted." We fitted!

Sally

March 25-26, 1988
Mirror Lake 8-Bunk

Wardicus, Mikeules, Daveomedes, & Bradysseus
(Spartan names for a Spartan adventure!)

PORKIES X-COUNTRY SKI ODDESSY — 1988!!!!!

It all began on a dark and stormy night in March. Our goal, Mirror Lake, and the warmth of a cabin fire. Little did we know that the stretch of trail ahead would test the very fiber of our being.

As Wardicus was heat waxing the skis, the ranger's 4x4 pulled up. He stepped out and asked our destination.

Bradysseus said, "Mirror Lake Cabin!" in a gung-ho voice.

The ranger just shook his head saying, "That's an awful long and hard trail. We just like to know where you're headed in case we have to come and get you out."

Wardicus sneered, angry at being underestimated.

Mikeules replied that we were well prepared and he shouldn't worry about us hardy men.

Wardicus, Mikeules, and Bradysseus hefted their packs and slapped on their skis. Wardicus, hitched to the large sled, led the way. He was the strongest skier of the three.

Daveomedes, after working all day, would stay at the truck 'til 8;00 A.M. when he could register our party and get a cabin key. Then he would set out with a sled to catch up with us at Mirror Lake. The other three...were too anxious about the expedition, having driven twelve hours, to rest or stop.

We started skiing where the snowplow had stopped. Wardicus had a head lamp to show us the way. We settled into a nice pace. After several hours we stopped and collected water running down the rocks from rain and melted snow. We dropped in purification tablets and headed out again. After a half-hour, we took a water break to evaluate our position. We thought for sure we should have been there by now. "There" meaning the M-107 loop. After another hour or so, Wardicus, with the big sled, arrived first at the loop. He put on water (melted snow) to make up some Exceed energy drink to refuel us. While the snow melted, Wardicus and Bradysseus skied three hundred feet to the escarpment lookout and stood in awe at the majesty of God's country, with Lake of the Clouds two hundred feet below. Then the two of us skied back to the loop, fueled up, and reconnoitered the first part of the trail to Mirror Lake. We found one area, a large saddle-and-draw down hill that might be tough with the sled.

We skied back to the loop, packed up the gear, and set out about 9:30 A.M. for the cabin, four miles away, as the crow flies. As soon as we hit the deep snow, we knew we were in for an endurance test. Wardicus couldn't pull the sled with skis on. Bradysseus tried to push but wasn't effective with his skis on. As soon as he stepped out of his skis, he sank to mid-thigh. Wardicus switched to snowshoes and was able to move the sled with brute strength and determination. Tempers were starting to flare as we got deeper into the bush. Then the sled pole connections broke. We pulled a MacGyver and were able to fix it. We decided to just enjoy being out in the woods and whatever happened, happened. We eased the sled down the draw on foot, sinking once in awhile in the two or three feet of snow. Once we made it to Lake of the Clouds, a half-mile from the loop, it was an hour later. From here on, it had to be better. Little did we know the hell was just beginning.

Bradysseus was chosen to break trail, Wardicus would pull the sled, and Mikeules would push when needed.

Bradysseus reached the bridge first and found a two by two row of snow over two-thirds of the bridge. He began kicking it into the water to be able to carry the sled over. Then we drove on into the wilderness.

Forty-five minutes later we arrived at Scott Creek. Bradysseus was first across the narrow bridge of snow, then Wardicus with the big sled. The sled started to slide into the creek. That was it. We'd had it with that *!*$#%@ sled. We unloaded all the gear and attached it to our packs and bodies. Mikeules pulled out his twenty-two caliber handgun and each of us pumped nine rounds into it. Then we knife and axed it and left the hacked up, shot up hulk at Scott Creek.

Suddenly Daveomedes came over the hill in snowshoes, sled in tow with food and a gung-ho yell. He had the cabin key. Two or three more miles and we'd be there.

Disaster struck. The last man across that narrow bridge of snow was Mikeules. Wardicus just said, "I wonder whose pack is heavier?" We heard a splash of water and a monotone, "Mine." It was Mikeules, up to his nuts is Scott Creek. Daveomedes tossed the cabin key to Bradysseus and told him to break trail and get a fire started. He took off while Daveomedes and Wardicus pulled Mikeules out of the creek. He already had purple legs by the time he got his soaked, freezing pants off. He was putting on dry clothes when I, Bradysseus, left their sight. I had no idea what lay ahead, but I knew I had to conquer it. We all did.

Our first obstacle was a six hundred foot climb within a half-mile. It took an hour-and-a-half and much of our energy. Bradysseus had to crawl up the steepest part. If he skied, he slid backward or fell. If he walked, he sank. He reached the top thinking the cabin had to be close by. He was dead wrong. The others, a half-hour behind, were going through the hell he had been through.

Halfway up, Mikeules broke a snowshoe and had to drop his pack and come back for it later. After all, we all thought the cabin was just ahead.

It took two more hours of zigzag trails and falling into three feet of snow before Wardicus caught up with Bradysseus. Mikeules was right behind him. All were dehydrating and in need of a good meal. Where the hell was the cabin?

We skied on 'til finally Bradysseus stopped for water, packed deep in his pack. Wardicus and Mikeules trekked on. After a rest and some water, Daveomedes was in sight. Bradysseus packed up and followed behind Daveomedes and his food sled.

Daveomedes in snowshoes was faster and pulled ahead, out of sight.

I could hear the yells from Wardicus. It must mean they've found the cabin. I trekked on with new confidence.

Then I fell. It took so much energy to get up in three feet of snow with a sixty pound pack on my back and skis on my feet. I strained and was up again skiing. Before Wardicus was in sight, I would fall four more times. Finally I reached Wardicus and the cabin. We had conquered this damn trail and were all well rewarded by the fully equipped cabin and dry firewood. We gorged ourselves on tuna helper, potatoes, and chocolate pudding, drank water, and slept like rocks in our bunks.

Bradysseus

January 30, 1978
Little Carp Cabin

It snowed yesterday until sunset when it cleared up. Pure colors-blue sky, white snow, red sunset-like you seldom see in nature. The lake in winter is completely overwhelming....

I have the whole place pretty much to myself all winter...solitude is a scarce commodity these days. True solitude, easily acquired and gracefully accepted, makes us conscious of what an enjoyable and valuable thing human companionship is.... I have found magnificent solitude and peace here all winter. I feel almost selfish hoarding it all for myself and the few friends who come with me.

John

March 20, 1989
Buckshot Cabin

From reading the July/August entries in this book, I think I prefer this place in the dead of winter. The solitude and silence are absolute. There is one long lane of clear water in an otherwise unbroken whiteness. The weather for the past three days has been perfect, cloudless skies and a gentle north wind to remind you of how it might be should the miles-per-hour increase.

We are to be here for five days. Our greatest asset, equipment-wise, has been the snowshoes. Breaking a new trail through the woods would have been impossible without them. There is no way to describe the stillness of these woods and shores after this record season of snow. There is clearly in excess of four to five feet of snow, even at this late date. The huge snow sculptures are ten to fifteen feet tall out from the beach. There seems to be a lot of animal shapes sculpted by the wind. Very common is a perfect cone with one side scooped out from it to make a folded cape effect.

The light is brilliant and we are wearing sunglasses as a precaution. We have seen animal trails (canine type) heading out onto the ice. We have looked hard but seen no trace of movement out there. But there is movement. When the wind changes there is the heart-chilling crash and grumble of the floes moving into each other. The most empty and northern sound imaginable.

Unknown Author

April 13, 1980
Section 17 Cabin

This cabin nestles along white drifts. Thin, gray smoke, pungent of cooking and warm memories, wafts from the chimney. The soft whoosh of the saw sounds rhythmically, a descant to the steady rustle of the river, interrupted by the heavier sounds of splitting wood. The screen door opens, sounds rush up, and a muffled silence reasserts itself with its slam, for one indoors. Voices sound outside, and steps on the sill. Indoors, the fire crackles gently. Icicles, dripping now from the indoor warmth, hang from the rafters above windows vertically and irregularly striped with vapor, turned once more to water.

Unknown Author

October 2, 1993
Lily Pond Cabin

I arrived here Saturday afternoon to spend a night in the Porkies and to enjoy the beauty of nature. I sat on a beach and glanced over at the pond and wrote this poem:

I carry my pack
On my back
And trudge through the trail
Looking at crimson
Yellow and red leaves
On the path
And watch the snow
Flakes gently brush
The forest floor
I see the changing of
The season before me
I feel the cold brisk
Air around me
And listen to the flow
Of the water
As it rushes by a

Beaver dam
I watch as the sun set
The temperature dropping
And the promise of
Frost outlining
My cabin windows

Cindy T.

November 3, 1993
Speakers Cabin

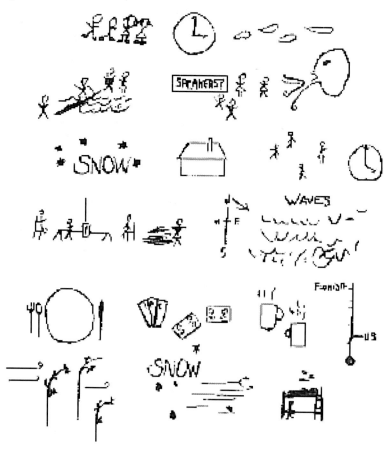

Unknown Artist

December 24, 1991
Gitchee Gumee Cabin
    This is our final evening after four days of winter backpacking. We are in this cabin for only one night, Christmas Eve, to dry our sleeping bags, our tent, and our skin. Day One found us situated beneath a south-facing slope along Lake Superior Trail. We managed to cover seven miles on our first day, although we had a late start. A wilderness trail sled, North Face accessories (tents, pants, backpacks, you name it-no, we're not dealers who get their gear at a discount; instead we'd rather invest our money in reliable equipment than in a house), and snowshoes made our traveling easy. Finding level areas away from the trail can be difficult, but we did manage to construct an area suitable for our seemingly gigantic winter tent. Darkness had already begun to fall, however, and we were forced to prepare our supper in the dark. Hurray for candle lanterns. Later in the evening, though, the full moon of the Winter Solstice illuminated our surroundings. We snowshoed a few hundred yards in the night to the top of the ridge that protected our tent from the winds. What a sight to behold! The giant, burning orb of the moon was bright enough to light the whitecaps on Superior, and all the snow around us was aglow. Sunglasses were almost in order to witness the spectacle (this is why we winter backpack). Our sleeping was easy the first night, as were all nights. Our weather has been so mild, ranging from ten degrees at night to forty degrees on Sunday. The freeze/thaw cycle, however, can play tricks with one's safety; staying warm and dry became our priorities. Days Two and Three found us two miles closer to the lake, on the north slope of a ridge facing Superior. Our goal was to set a base camp along the shoreline, but exposed trails and difficult terrain made it a wiser choice to remain further inland (shortest day of the year has a bearing on the distance to travel as well). A day hike on our third day led us to Buckshot Landing, where Superior was pounding against the existing ice shelf. Volcano-like openings in the shelf were observed. Water could be seen gushing out of the holes with a mighty force. Only a fool would venture out onto the shelf. Alas, the next day, portions of the shelf were seen afloat and crashing together on the rough lake. Our second and third nights were colder, not far above the temperatures we had prepared for. Sure is fun not having to feel cold at night! And now, our journey ends with a one night stay at this warm and cozy cabin. The stove is a true workhorse; the BTU's are tremendous. And thank you to all that have worked to construct and furnish this home away from home. No mice, no drafts, no uncomfortable bunks! After four days of winter camping, this cabin is truly a treat. And whatever dampness we had in our stuff has quickly evaporated in the toasty little oven of a home. Tomorrow is Christmas Day and we travel home to Minnesota.

Matt

February 13, 1992
Union River Cabin

> the man by the river lay on the snow
> beneath the hemlock long after sunset,
> the overcast sky still lit by an opaque
> first-quarter moon overhead reflecting
> evening light, and he listened
> to the gurgling of the stream beneath
> ice, and embraced with his eyes
> and soul the light against dark, dark
> against light of the snow and the
> tree trunks, and he missed his lover
> but felt privileged to have such a
> lover, and this fixed in his brain,
> he returned to the warm darkened
> cabin, lit four candles about his
> bedside, rested his aching muscles
> in between trips to the stove to stir supper
> and read long into the night.

J.H.

January 2, 1986
Lily Pond Cabin

Damn, it's cold. Many thanks to Team Four from November 20, 1985, for not latching the window. We are guessing it's about minus twenty degrees, but we aren't sure because the thermometer froze. We snowshoed through the park the last three days and haven't seen a single mosquito or person. The last person we saw was a ranger at the road, and he laughed and told us to "have a good time." We haven't checked out the spring because the waist-deep snow prohibits any unnecessary travel. This cabin is not well insulated, but it is definitely warmer than our tent. Everyone we know thinks we're crazy, and we're beginning to believe them. Mice are not a problem (found a frozen one) and neither are the bears (didn't find any of those frozen)...Haven't tried fishing and have no intention of doing so. Couldn't find any worms, possibly due to the snow. Didn't see the sign on the door about that "unlawful" stuff (considered using it for firewood, however) and have absolutely no guilty feelings about it either. Everybody writing in here, previously, has left their own set of directions and advice. Here is ours:

- Wear snowshoes to outhouse and bring newspaper...to prevent frost-bitten cheeks (not on face) and becoming a permanent fixture in the outhouse (kind of like licking a flagpole).

- Carry bench out window and stand it on its end in order to get on the roof to dig out the chimney. We recommend the broom in the corner to aid in this digging. Move the bench away from the edge of the roof to prevent the falling pseudo chimney sweep from breaking any bones.
- Do not sunbathe either nude or otherwise.
- Leave the bench used for getting on the roof outside the window as a step for getting in and out. Close the window immediately after entering or exiting to keep out the frigid wind.

Hope you had a merry Christmas and a happy New Year! If we survive this trip, we'll probably return to the Porkies sometime in the future. This is some of the most beautiful country in the world.

Marc O., Josh P., John G., & Paul T.

November 8-9, 1992
Greenstone Falls Cabin

Greetings, hikers. I am one in a party of three. We came from Lake Superior Cabin via Little Carp River Trail. Here we are back in the snow belt. There was hardly any snow on the shores of Gitchee Gumee. Two nights previous, however, we hiked in to Mirror Lake and overnighted at South Mirror Lake Cabin. That day hike was in calf-deep snow during a gentle snowfall. It was an invigorating first encounter with winter. The packing has been very pleasant. The cold temperatures have not been a factor at all. Much of this has to do with the knowledge of warmth that awaits us at the end of the day. The cabins, I find, are top-notch; authentic, cozy, and even reminiscent of more austere days. The cold nights become friendly, almost fascinating, from a cabin warmed by an old, cast-iron stove. And it throws some nice heat, eh?

Tim H.

November 29, 1984
Lake Superior Cabin

Bitter cold, low leaden skies threaten snow.
We struggle through miles of half-frozen mud.
Trees loom over us, dark against the sky,
streaked with gray-green moss.
We wade across clear, fast-running streams,
our feet aching from numbing cold.

For each beauty, a thousand perils, a thousand deaths,
though, mostly of beings so inconspicuous
that we are allowed to ignore them.
Life and beauty, feeding on pain and death.
Indeed, beauty created by death;

> dead boughs draped with glittering icicles.
> The blind, unconscious life force struggling against
> the cold indifference of the universe.
>
> Jim

December 31, 1978
Speaker's Cabin

An early start the next morning to scout a trail to Big Carp. We decided to travel light so we could make good time. We left with what we considered to be the bare essentials for what we expected to be a day's trip. Little did we know of what we were to encounter. We started off down Superior Trail and got lost in "the silence of the forest." The terrain was quite rough and our progress was slow. Snow began to fall as the silence grew thick around us. The silence was so thick we could hardly move. It was so thick that we couldn't even hear each other's voices. All you could hear was your own heartbeat. We laid in the snow and fell into a peaceful trance as the falling snow slowly covered us up. The next thing I remember is waking to the sound of many voices. We got up and brushed the snow off and headed in the direction of the voices. As we got closer, the voices grew louder. It sounded like thousands of people laughing. We traveled on in silence, all wondering what it was. Then we saw it. Lake Superior. Ice mountains on the shore, breaking up, forming ice islands under the force of the waves smashing against them. We decided to ski along the shoreline the rest of the way to Big Carp. The going was much easier as the silence was much thinner and the terrain was much flatter. We soon became aware that it was getting late in the day and we still hadn't found Big Carp or Little Carp. We decided that we must have passed it, so we doubled back along the shore. A fog lingered over Superior, big hunks of ice sloshing around. Some of the ice mountains had round holes in their peaks like volcanoes. We expected next to be seeing polar bears walking around on this tundra. The wind came up as the sun went down and we began to worry about getting back here in the approaching storm. We felt our way back with the wind in our faces, always hoping to see the cabin around the next point on the shoreline.

> David, Peter, & Bill

January 15, 1997
Gitchee Gumee Cabin

It is snowing again and I'm writing while the rest of the crew is getting one last ski in before packing up to go. The deep snow is so beautiful and peaceful.

We had so much fun the last few nights making music, dancing, playing cards and games, and exchanging massages. You totally forget to worry about what time it is, what's on TV, who you should call, etc....and tune into your surroundings.

Food tastes better after being outside all day. There is something magical about a meal with friends around a candlelit table in a cozy cabin.

I played with a little, short-tailed shrew as he made his way through the snow. He probably didn't think it was so fun to have something so big stalking him. He had on such a soft-looking, plush, fur coat. I wonder if he is the one who put the little pile of feathers in the back corner of the outhouse. Munch, munch...shrews are voracious eaters.

Make sure to look at the lake at many different times of day. The lighting changes and it is quite a show.

Tami D.

April 5, 1972
Little Carp Cabin

On the way back, took some pictures of the birds on the ice blocks. Beautiful scenery. Probably not unlike the arctic. When we got back here, Jen and I went out on the blocks at the mouth of the Little Carp. The sun had been behind the clouds near the horizon and made a beautiful picture. A ribbon of clear blue sky stretched across the horizon and just before the sun set it came into full view. The wind had all but stopped and was starting a gentle breeze out of the south. Not a sound could be heard. It was not hard to imagine that all that existed was God, the Earth, and us. Sometimes I think I get closer to Him on these wilderness trips than at any other time....

It's fantastically beautiful. The special winter silence; no insect noise or even the breeze in the trees. We were touched and thrilled to experience it.

Jen & Charlie A.

November 11, 1995
Little Carp Cabin

The excitement of the day came at sunset. We were across the river down by the lake. There are huge pieces of driftwood over there. Their silhouettes of gnarled and twisted wood stood out hauntingly against the bright reds and oranges of an unforgettable sunset. Closer to the lake, the water sprays on driftwood and creates hundreds of icy fangs hanging under the logs. The spray catches the last hues of sunlight and casts droplets of gold onto the frozen shore. The view warms our hearts as it freezes our fingers to the camera. Our faces are also frozen, but in grins of delight and wonder. Ah, these moments are so short, but carry us through the days and weeks of stress and heartache.

RJ, Linda, & John

November, 22-23, 1990's
Section 17 Cabin

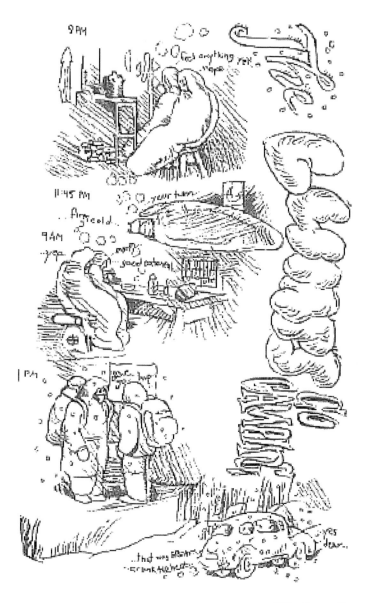

"The Lumps"

January 1, 1986
Speaker's Cabin

I yawn long, loud poems to the sky and snow. No lonely leaves of grass, Father Walt, only songs of frozen ice. Sheaves of glass. The new year has sprung here and with myriad bottles spring myriad memories. The date is up, Mad Hatter, and we must hurry, hurry, hurry into the garden hole to re-enter the idiot's croquet game. Look out Izod, Copezio, Klein, and Poppogullo, our identity shall be reaffirmed as we return to confirm with Mastercard and Visa, our affinity with all forms significant. Notre raison d'être? To be, to be, to be. Dear Hamlet never knew the ice floes of Superior. Dear Shakespeare, dear, dear, dear. I am affirmed. The unspoken voice speaks loudly from Speaker's and I am ready to return.

Unknown Author

November 3, 1985
Lake Superior Cabin

This time of year shows such a contrast between the cycle of the tree and the cycles of the ground cover, that its opposition leaves you shaking in wonder. The trees were stark naked, dead by all appearances, yet the ground was covered with the vibrant green of ferns and moss, and dancing all about were delicate white moths. Hundreds of them. The very visible "burial mounds" of long dead trees gave an even more powerful image to the contrasting cycles. Breathtaking!

The horizon was clear and we got to see the great lake swallow the sun.... I leave the Porkies a changed person.

Lisa S.

Bears, Oh My!

June 7, 1983
Mirror Lake 4-Bunk Cabin

Our first father and son camping trip concludes with two days and two nights in the Porkies—the last night here. Well, a time we had—blue skies, cool nights, wonderful talks, and close memories—fishing, walking, and a hummingbird next to the window near this table. And flies and fear. Let me tell you about fear. Not just being afraid but the kind of fear that makes one sit bolt upright for four hours with Bowie knife in white-knuckled hand ready to strike at the first hint of red-gleaming eyes. The kind of fear that makes one's heart beat so loud that a rational perspective on one's environment is simply inconceivable.

Last night...was fear. Sleeping in a nylon tent, father and son one-quarter mile from here, like the directions say, and we could have been mashed like the bugs on a window. 11:00 P.M. last night, they came in from nowhere or who knows where. First, the teasing swish of leaves and sticks moved by something soft and heavy. There was rhythm to it. The birds stopped singing. Then the tent walls moved. Just a brushing curiosity, I supposed, so "shut up" says I to myself. Maybe they will go away. For one-half hour to forty-five minutes there was this vibrating tenseness separated by ten millimeter nylon, six inches if a foot away. I felt warm breath. It could have been my own. A mental tug-of-war. Curiosity on one side of the nylon and unrelenting, incomprehensible fear on the other side.

The questions were mostly speculations. My child? Why here? Protect? How?

The "first wave" stopped and for another half-an-hour I waited, trying to decide whether we should run for this cabin. I waited too long. The next wave started, only this time with more resoluteness. Pushing the doorway and screen. I used the knife, pushing the doorway back and squawking, "Beat it." Matches—life saver—they hate light—maybe. I decided to prepare Gabriel for a run to the cabin. At 12:30 to 1:00 A.M., I told him to put his pants on. I wasn't prepared for his response. "What for?" I said, "We might have to leave the tent and run." Sure. No light, pitch dark, haven't been to the cabin. Makes sense at 1:00 A.M. though. Silence. Relief. Gabriel's sleeping. After a box of matches the tent smells like sulfur. It comes again. Too late to leave. Maybe it's not a bear. Anything that does not do us in three tries can't be too swift, or else just over-confident. Speculations. The wind, small creature, imagination. Always came back to "the black teaser." Now 3:00 A.M. Only a couple of hours until sunrise. Then safety.

James Thurber wasn't camping when he talked about "something going thump in the nighttime." Collapse—fear, collapse—sleep.

At 5:00 A.M., the birds are back. We made it. At 6:30 Gabriel is awake. "Why did you want me to put my pants on last night?"

"I was scared, Gabriel."

"Of what?"

"Creatures. Mostly bears."

"Dad, there weren't any bears here last night."

Gabe & Lee

Summer 1975

Buckshot Cabin

To Whom It May Concern,

These may be my last words on this planet, so please don't disregard them. I feel no malice towards any man, but as for that perverted bear outside my door, well, he's no man. He's been trying to eat my meat all day, but I'd rather keep it on my bones. Since these may be my last words, I will tell you to watch out for this bear and also to tell you that there is really only one type of food that will get rid of him. It is *ihosaduhftoaiwh*.....................................

Please disregard all above. The man is demented!

Yours truly,

Joe E. Bear

Unknown Author

August 11, 1966

Big Carp 4-Bunk Cabin

By the way, a small black bear came up to camp this afternoon and even looked into the windows at one time. We didn't see the mother, however, if she's still around we may run into her on the trail to 17 (heaven forbid, with only a hunting knife for protection). To whomever visits this place next, my advice is don't go outside if a bear comes around. No matter how small they seem, they still can do tremendous destruction to human flesh. Don't feed them! Whatever you do! For they will only want more and could very well tear that door down if they are hungry enough.

J.R. & R.J.

June 17-18, 1971

Lily Pond Cabin

In all of our hiking we hadn't even run across one bear. We were just in the process of screaming, "Where are all the bears!?" when right out of the woods came a big, black bear. He came right into camp, walked around the cabin several times, then we made the mistake of feeding him some biscuits and fish. Don't feed them! They will hang around forever! Our bear returned several times and kept us hanging pretty close to the cabin.

Ken E., Bob & Rob G.

Bears, Oh My!

September 1976
Big Carp 4-Bunk Cabin
Final Note to the Bear:

Sorry that we didn't see you this time. We would have loved to take some pictures of you. But then again, we would not have liked to be eaten by you. I would also like to apologize to you for not leaving any food around the outside of the cabin for you, but we were afraid that you would mistake the next camper for your dinner. My friends and I like bears, and belong to the "Bears are People Too Society." So if you see a tall guy with a moustache, a short guy with a beard, and a medium-sized guy with a potbelly, don't eat us because we are your friends. Peace, Mr. Bear.

J.B.

September 1976
Big Carp 4-Bunk Cabin

> Had three people in for lunch
> My they were a tasty bunch
> The jawbone of one still remains
> Please forgive me for the stains

"Smokey"

September 1976
Big Carp 4-Bunk Cabin
Hello,

I'm Fred, a backpacker who happened by. Naturally, I looked in the cabin window. I saw a terrible mess.

The previous party here must have had quite a bash. The place was a shambles with blood all over the floor and walls. I found a crumpled body in the corner with a potbelly, and his head bitten off. Also a moustache stuck to some flypaper and a chipmunk nest, which on closer inspection, appeared to resemble a beard. Various parts of bodies were scattered around the grounds, except for three noses neatly arranged into a fairly nice candle holder grouping.

As there were still two days paid rental on the cabin, I decided to stay (one of the noses hummed the message to me on the rental situation as I rammed a candle up its left nostril). First, I cleaned up the mess, dumped the bodies in the outhouse; boy, the outhouse was a little bit rank. DIARRHEA! Then I exercised my prerogative to rifle the personal effects:

1. Three backpacks, one with a bite out of the frame
2. One-half bottle of Mohawk vodka—very cheap
3. One bag of chocolate chip cookies
4. A large pile of bear chips

5. A Polaroid camera with a thumb print on the lens
6. $3.85 cash—I kept the cash

Well, I have to split before Ranger Rick shows up!

PS. Where in the hell are all the bears that people are talking about? People exaggerate. Bears are not dangerous! If I see one, I will be firm, stand my ground, and drive him away. The bears around here have been getting their way for too long anyway, and I, for one, intend to stop cow-towing to them! So bears, beware!

Fred the Backpacker

September 1976
Big Carp 4-Bunk Cabin

I was hungry as a horse
So I came back for a second course
Nuts and berries wear me down
When there are better things around
Lo and behold, before my eyes
Stood F the B, hands on his thighs
Shouting, making noises like a seal
I always like an easy meal
It's just that his three eighty five cash
Gave me the runs and a terrible rash
I bloated up just like a tanker
So now the outhouse is quite a bit ranker

President: "Ranger Rick is a Person Too Society"

"Smokey"

September 1976
Big Carp 4-Bunk Cabin
Checked cabin, buried bodies, replaced door.

Ranger Rick

September 19, 1976
Big Carp 4-Bunk Cabin
Greetings,

I was just tooling down the Big Carp River Trail, when I smelled a foul odor coming from an outhouse. I had walked a long way, and the pack frame was hurting my gazumbies, so I decided to rest in the cabin. When I walked around to the front of the building, I noticed the door was broken, as if some-one had eaten his or her way through it.

I climbed through the door and found a man with his hands on his hips, and his upper body bitten off at the waist. Curiously enough, there was a trail of gooey bear chips leading to the outhouse. It's just my luck that the only guy that I find after three weeks in the woods is so helpless he can't carry his own pack, let alone mine. I asked him what happened but he didn't under-stand. Finally, I realized what the problem was. After a quick search of the cabin, I found his ear under the table and put it in his back pocket. Now he could hear me. He relayed a terrible story by gesturing wildly with his right leg. It took quite a while to get the whole tale told, because every time he raised his leg, he fell down. This had to come to a stop, so I helped him to a chair, placed a pen between his toes, and paper on the floor under it. I don't understand what he wrote. "F the B. I didn't run. F the B."

Now I was in a quandary. Should I dump this weirdo, or give him a break. After weighing the pros and cons, I decided to stay. After all, eighty-five good men are hard to find, especially men who don't talk or eat a lot. Also, Mother wants me to settle down, and she likes short men.

So getting down to work. I started cleaning the cabin after lighting a can-dle that was shoved in a realistic looking nose, and I saw a gleam in the bear chip streak. Lo and behold, it was $3.85. How about that! A bear with bread! I wonder if he has to pay the buck and a half a day for camping too.... I'll talk to you after dinner.

Sheila the Backpacker

September 1976
Big Carp 4-Bunk Cabin

I stopped by the cabin for dessert
And the sight of Sheila made my stomach hurt!
She winked at me and offered dinner
But I, myself, would prefer to grow thinner!

"Smokey"

August 1994
Lake Superior Cabin

"Bear"

When I saw
Your wild form,
I stopped still,
My heart clenched—
My nerves froze—

My soul danced!
You looked into my eyes,
Recognized me,
And ran.
You know,
Better than I,
We were not meant
To meet.

Beth

October 22, 1986
Mirror Lake 4-Bunk Cabin

I am convinced the bears and grouse work together to create a little "nature humor."

A grouse and a bear get up early and set out together looking for a muddy spot in the middle of one of the hiking trails. Once they find the ideal spot, the bear selects his largest foot and places it in the center of the mud, producing a nice, clear print. Now the bear ambles up the hill and finds a spot with a good view of the trail. The grouse, meanwhile, conceals himself in a dense bush a few feet from the paw print.

Eventually, an unsuspecting hiker ambles down the trail and spots the print. Crouching, he examines it closely and an image of a snarling, five hundred pound bear with a mouthful of foam appears in his mind. At this precise moment, the grouse explodes out of the bush.

Uproariously funny, if you're a grouse or a bear.

Steve

July 4, 1991
Lake Superior Cabin

We were just walking up the other side of the river and with no warning (we couldn't hear because of the rapids) came the bear, and me, the wannabe wildlife photographer, what do you think I did? I fled the scene immediately at a high rate of speed, camera in hand.

Cheri W.

August 21-22, 1978
Lily Pond Cabin

I'm a pretty skeptical person when people tell me of all the situations that involves a bear. If you read this log, a bear is mentioned quite a lot...it's all a bunch of bullshit! You might be wondering then why I'm expressing such a strong viewpoint then, right? Well, you see, a couple of years ago I really did get involved and also got very hurt from an attack by a bear.

If I had one wish, it would be never to have gone on that hiking trip that lasted from July 23-27 in 1975. I was only seventeen then, and at that time I thought I knew everything about camping. I guess I was really ignorant of the fact that I had so much to learn.... I was always the kind of guy who would do crazy things just to get a laugh, to get accepted. But now, and ever since the accident, I've learned to be myself and face any problems that confront me without resorting to some artificial games to maintain friendships.... For our last day, as a treat for us, we were going to have hamburgers. After I ate my first one, I decided to walk on the path with the second hamburger in my hand. I didn't want to eat it immediately. I wanted to find some remote spot where I could be by myself.

As I was walking I heard something. I didn't know what it was, but I knew it was an animal. As I turned around I saw two baby cubs following me. They were so small that I didn't think they would harm me. Then I realized they were after my hamburger. At this point I wasn't really scared because they seemed so small. Then they started running after me and for some strange reason I thought it was humorous. I thought I was performing for my friends, but I wasn't performing and it wasn't any joke. But I was so young and I did something so foolish that I'll always regret for the rest of my life. I picked up a rock and I hit one of the cubs in the face. I don't know why I did it, but it was so spontaneous that I couldn't control myself. The other cub then ran off in the other direction as I started to approach this poor baby cub that I so ignorantly hurt.

When I was about five feet from it, I heard some thumping that instantly made my heart beat faster. I turned around and a big bear started charging me. I didn't know what to do and I started to panic. I couldn't even run and my eyes seemed fixated on the bear's eyes. I started to run and tripped on this log that was protruding from the brush. I just didn't know what to do, so I picked up a long stick, hoping to scare the bear off. As I stood there brandishing my stick, the bear swiped at my stick and knocked it completely out of my hands. I tried to pick it up again and he clawed me in the right hand, which made it numb almost instantly. I looked at it and all my fingers were still intact, but the outermost palm of my hand was gone. My hand was covered with blood and I think I started to cry. I started running again, but the bear kept charging me and swiped me across the right side of my face.

I don't remember what happened next, but my friends told me later I was screaming and screaming. They said that the screaming brought them running towards me and it scared the bear off. But at the time I was laying on the ground crying with half of my face gone and blood still oozing out of it. I really thought I was going to die, but God was on my side. Two locals who lived here heard my cries and also came running. I finally passed out and when I woke up I was in their cabin with a bandage wrapped around my entire face and my right eye. I ended up losing that eye and had a huge scar that will remain on my face and hand for the rest of my life.

You wonder why I am on this camping trip. Well, it is my first one in two years and I realize that it was ignorance that made me look so pitifully ugly. So please act rationally when you confront any bear. It might save your life.

David W.

Unknown Date
Lake of the Clouds Cabin

DON'T FORGET TO WEAR YOUR BEAR BELLS!
Unknown Artist

August 25, 1956
Big Carp 4-Bunk Cabin

Following are the "bear" facts about our unusual but certainly enjoyable stay here on the Carp.

We arrived via the Big Carp River Trail...at 5:00 P.M. The cabin had been left in nice shape, but when Bob visited the house out back soon after arriving, he found it was already occupied by a mother bruin who was evidently trying to house break the half-grown cub she had with her. We finally "shooed" our visitors away and Bob took over the house by himself.

The next incident didn't occur until nearly two hours later—we had had fair luck fishing; Bob brought in a couple of fourteen inch rainbows and I had

five nice rainbows all over sixteen inches. Bob had gotten back to the cabin
first and had his fish in the frying pan when I got in. We left his fish on the
stove and both went down to the creek to clean mine. We had our back to the
cabin door which we had left open and all of a sudden we heard a grunt
behind us. Bob was so startled that he fell over into the Big Carp River-he had
reason to be startled since the mother bear we had gotten rid of a short time
earlier was back to call on us again. This time she wasn't after our toilet paper
but after our supper-she was beating it out of the door with our frying pan and
fish in one hand and our coffee pot in the other hand. The cub came running
out behind his mom with Bob's pipe stuck in his mouth (these last items
might be stretched a little).

Anyway, we had more fish so we didn't begrudge the bear family a good
square meal at our expense.

"The Old Fishermen," R.H., H.S., & C.S.

July 28, 1984
Greenstone Falls Cabin
The Man in the Black Fur Coat

He lumbered in to the campsite without a sound
Wearing a black fur coat that hung tightly to his body
With his nose so black and shiny, he sniffed the
Aroma that escaped from the cabin's wall
Appearing awkward he slowly moved toward the
Majestic hemlock
Stretching upwards, his razor sharp claws carved his
Mark into the virgin bark
His large powerful paws enveloped the young
Unsuspecting hemlock
Yawning, rubbing his eyes, he lowered his massive body
To the solid ground below
Peering through the screen enclosed opening, he sought for
A way to enter the rustic abode
Pressing his nose against the screen and leaving a
Pool of white milky liquid hanging from the fine
Wire fabric, he groaned and stretched as if to
Invite himself to dinner
Scraping his knife like claws against the wire mesh
Which stood as the only barrier between him and
The inviting odor that permeated the walls of the cabin,
He circled the cabin like a tiger caged in a zoo
Ideas of how to penetrate the fortress that stood in his way

Raced through his cunning and creative head
As a last resort, the mammoth animal rapped at the door,
He banged the screen
But the cabin's inhabitants moved not an inch
Or made a sound
Dusk grew near
The sun began to slowly withdraw behind
The giant hemlocks
The vibrant colors of red and orange
Streaked the horizon
Slowly, with disappointment, the gentleman of the forest
Returned to the darkness which swallowed up the earth

Dr. Nicholas S.

June 1986
Speaker's Cabin

The Porkies have been a fine place to unwind. However, the grossly exaggerated stories in "the journals" found in most of the cabins do not really give a "true" picture of the Porkies! My first trip to the Porkies, years ago, more accurately tells the true story:

The black bears of the Porkies have always had a reputation for their mischief. A few friends and I "packed in" with a tent and a few supplies. Before we got halfway to Shining Cloud Falls, two black bears started following us, at a distance. Before long, they caught up! It was a male and a female black bear. The male bear seemed hungry, so I dropped my backpack and ran for my life to the nearest tree, with the male bear right behind me. As I looked up at the tree, I noticed the nearest limb was fifteen feet from the ground. I lunged for this limb with all my might and missed it. But fortunately, I caught it on the way down. I watched helplessly as the male black bear unzipped my Jansport pack and meticulously sorted everything out on the ground. He finally got to my two-man, Northface tent. Within ten minutes, he set up the tent on the ground and beckoned his female partner to come in. She walked right in, but came out in about five seconds. Apparently the two-man tent was "too small" for the two bears. At that moment, my partners had fired two shots from a twenty-two caliber pistol. The bullets hit the dirt between the bears. Only this time, they ran for "their lives!" Just as the bears were leaving the scene, the male bear stooped over and grabbed my wallet that he had sorted out earlier.

I reported this incident to the park rangers who were not surprised. It was 6 months later that I got a phone call from the Ontonagon Police Department.

Bears, Oh My!

They had finally apprehended that male bear trying to use my Visa charge card to purchase a four-man tent at a sporting goods store in Ontonagon!

The last I heard, the bear was sentenced to life imprisonment at the Milwaukee county zoo. I recently visited him there and he seemed to be doing quite well! He has a two room flat, and he was entertaining several female, black bears when I dropped in.

Several of my friends will testify that the above account is true. If I have learned anything from this account, it is, "Always carry your wallet in your pocket!"

Gary L.

August 30, 1993
Mirror Lake 2-Bunk Cabin
Patrick and I are now in this cozy, warm cabin, happy not to be outside with "'Ole Smokey." Phil and his son, Phillip, invited us to spend the night with them after we were scared, really scared by a black bear who visited our tent looking for a snack. We were reading, and Patrick looked out of the tent window and told me that a bear was coming toward us. I didn't believe him but he desperately nodded in the affirmative. We didn't know whether to stay in the tent or run away. Quickly we got our shoes on. He ambled on past us, sniffing the air, and just about as we were breathing a sigh of relief, he turned around (at this point he was maybe fifteen feet away) and started coming towards us again. This time he approached us (by this time we were out of the tent, behind it—must be noted that our tent is tiny, basically a one-man tent that sleeps two) walking toward us slowly and stopped within only about ten feet of us. The feeling inside we cannot describe. I was absolutely terrified. The reality of the situation was now sinking in. We were croaking sounds from our mouths. He was holding back due to the sound of our voices, because he hesitated each time we made a noise. So be loud if you meet them. He was at that point, no different than a raccoon, just scavenging. But he had the power to hurt us very badly and we were terrified.

Now being warm in the cabin, it seems farther and farther away. I can't imagine what it would be like, spending the night out there tonight. Beware to backpackers/campers. If you have a run in with such a bear, it's hard to get the spook out of you.

Sabrina

July 3, 1957
Big Carp 4-Bunk Cabin
We arrived at noon, having been at Buckshot Camp since June 30. Came by boat—rough water—wind on the nose—so the camp sure looked good! Packed our gear up from the landing and got set at camp. So, Non went out to

the toilet—next I knew she was calling frantically for me. Recalling the old familiar saying of "falling in," I tore out of the camp to see Non framed in the doorway of the outhouse, her mouth open, eyes wide, pants down, and a black bear parked half way up the ridge with the damndest surprised look on his face that a bear can generate. Seems he looked in the door and found himself face to face with Non! Sure was funny!

Milt S.

May 25, 1985
Big Carp 4-Bunk Cabin

We took our time and enjoyed the sights...During one of our many rest stops, a porcupine came waddling by, not a bit concerned about us, and not knowing that these beautiful mountains were named for him.

Later on, about one half-mile before we came to Little Carp Cabin, Georgiana spotted two bear cubs in a tree which was seventy-five yards off the trail. She pointed and gasped, "Look! Bears!" Wayne and I peered through the trees to get a look at them. We turned to see Ellen hustling down the trail. She no more than heard the word "bear" and made tracks. We laughed at her bravery, then sang songs and whistled while we hiked so as not to surprise any momma bears.

Julie

May 13-14, 1997
Whitetail Cabin

Grrrr,

Bear sleepy. Just woke up. Want to sleep but can't because HUNGRY! Bear hungry! Want food. Smell food. Smell food in cabin. People in cabin. People scared. People run. Bear not chase them. Bear could catch them if wanted to. Bear want food. Smell food. Smell bacon. Bear likes bacon. Smell peanut butter. Bear likes peanut butter. Smell candy. Bear likes candy. Smell honey. Bear loves honey! Bear not like plastic bags. Get stuck in teeth. Bother! Bear must hurry. People tell Ranger. Bear not like Ranger. Ranger shoot bear in ass with dart and Bear wake up some place strange. Bear like campers. Campers bring food to woods. Bear go find some more. Bear go.

Bear (a.k.a. Jim)

Bears, Oh My!

Here and There,
Then and Now

October 29, 1997
Little Carp Cabin
PORCUPINE MOUNTAIN TRIVIA FACTS:

The Great Flood: 1983 was the year of the great flood. On June 20, at 11:45 P.M., a torrential thunderstorm stalled over Summit Peak. For over four hours the heavy rain fell! Beaver ponds began to burst and added their volume to the flood. Worst hit were Pinkerton Creek and the portion of the Little Carp below Lily Pond, where water rose to depths approaching thirty feet! Some backpackers, flooded out of their tents, had to climb to safety in trees. Entire hillsides were denuded and eroded. Log jams caused rivers to change course in several locations. And in Lake Superior, their roots weighted down by rocks and dirt, huge trees bobbed upright on the swells! A one-quarter mile stretch of South Boundary Road was washed out and backpackers lost thousands of dollars worth of gear. Rangers found that the rowboat at Lily Pond had collected rainwater. The water in the boat was thirteen inches deep.

The Buckshot Boot: Late Sunday afternoon, November 17, 1968, a mile east of Buckshot Cabin, a deer hunter discovers a laced boot. Protruding from the top of the boot are the remains of a human leg bone. In an extensive search the next day, the matching left boot was discovered about fifty feet away. No clue as to the person's identity has ever come to light.

Fred's Buck: In 1933, Fred Bear, a famous bow hunter and manufacturer, bagged a buck while hunting in the Porkies. The animal dressed out at 285 pounds. The ease with which he made his kill, however, prompted him to switch to bow hunting exclusively.

How Big Is That Bear: Judging a bear's size can be a tricky business. The following tips may help.

> Body Shape: If the animal appears squat and round, it is a smaller bear. A big male will appear long.
>
> Head Size: The ears of all bears are about the same size. If they appear large and close together, it is a smaller bear. A big bear has a big skull and the ears look small and wide set.
>
> Foot Size: If the foot or track appears wide, four inches or more, it is a good size bear. Run!

Albert, Jill, & Kathy

1978
Lily Pond Cabin
I think I am probably one of the youngest people to have entered the park. The first time I came to Lily Pond I was only four months old! I was very upset when I learned that the rangers are planning on phasing out these cabins. I think that if people care enough to clean up after themselves and have respect for the cabin and its grounds, maybe they would not be torn

down. We are doing our best to save the cabin, but it won't make any difference if others don't care, too. My father spent the day fixing the stove and we hope people will take care of it. Don't make a fire in the right compartment; that is for storing the wood. The fire is made on the left side in the top.

Monica D.

May 22, 1989
Speaker's Cabin

Eighteen years ago I passed through this very spot as an unseasoned, but very gung-ho camper on the outpost trip, sponsored by the state YMCA, Camp Hayo-Went-Ha at Touch Lake, Michigan. I remember it well. Vietnam was still going on and I was in Junior High, itching for my first date and dance. The "outposters" were a mighty crew at that. Bearing packs made by Himalayan, old canvas Eureka tents, stiff leather boots, and Seidels freeze-dried food (or whatever that was), we hauled up here in the back of a 1966 GMC Stakebead and dropped us off at the Union Mine Trail. Slowly but surely, we made our way through Trap Falls, the Escarpment, Mirror Lake, Greenstone Falls, Speakers Cabin to Presque Isle, on to Black River on the Lumber Trails and about 10 miles further to the "Outpost," a rustic bunkhouse built by the YMCA as a rendezvous point. To a young kid like me it was a real test of courage, stamina, strength, skill, patience, not to mention a humbling and truly enlightening experience. Memories have a way, over time, of filtering out all the pains of a trip like the incessant bugs, the awkward, uncomfortable packs, the stiff, blistering boots, and the heat. But at the same time, the memories, when sparked, if you sit still and quietly meditate, can reproduce the very peak pleasures and experiences that make life so rich. Things like half-baked brownies, the views, a fish on your line, a religiously invigorating dive into Lake Superior, shaving the counselor in his sleep, ghost stories, bear stories, stories to top stories—all too numerous to state, but you get the idea. What an experience! I wasn't sure when I'd be back, or whether I could ever try to top that experience again. Life was all so up-in-the-air then.

Now here I am, eighteen years past, back to see my old friend, the mountains. I have to chuckle a little—things sure are different. Now we sport hi-tech shoe-boots, Coleman flex-frame packs, a nylon dome tent, a first need water purifier, and herbal bug repellent, amongst others. I guess comfort is a pleasure that time and payment of dues will render.

Eighteen years have seen a lot of pain and pleasure go through this body, mind, and spirit of mine. The relationships, the breakups, graduation, foundering through college and wondering what to do with the rest of my life. Graduation from college found an eager, young cabinetmaker living out of a 1974 Oldsmobile in Traverse City plying the trade. Tiring of the city, I moved around—Central Lake, Marquette, among others. But the recession hit hard and wouldn't allow me to stay up here and "live off the land." I was too independent, naïve, and headstrong to settle down.

Then along comes this lady, who follows after me, and longs for me for five years. But I was looking for the perfect, idyllic setting, mate, and lifestyle, all the time not paying attention to what the Great Spirit was handing me on a silver platter.

Tonight, past the light of candles, my French-Canadian wife lies asleep with the dog at her feet. That's special enough, but tonight it's extra special. Only three months along, she's carrying our (hopefully) daughter, Hannah. And what did she want to do on our last big vacation together alone before the family comes along? Come to the Porkies of course! I wanted to relive those steps of youth gone by, but at the same time, allow for my wife to enjoy the trip. The long trails proved a bit too much, even for my hardy girl. At first disappointed about tackling the whole park, I conceded in relief to do shorter hikes and live the Thoreauian lifestyle, cabin to cabin. I guess that's God's way of enlightening us to the wisdom already within each of us. In an earlier time, I had to conquer the Porkies....But now I enjoy the fact that I no longer have to conquer anything other than myself.

Being here, at peace, with my home on my back, in my extended home, with the kindred spirits I cherish most five feet away, I couldn't feel any more complete than if I were in the Master's care right now.

Good night, all, and may your dreams ride on fragrant mountain winds to faraway places.

Tim & Michelle W.

July 11, 1972
Big Carp 4-Bunk Cabin

Five of us arrived here yesterday afternoon. We had hiked in with others of the party to Mirror Lake from the south late Sunday. Monday we hiked out, saw Lake of the Clouds again, had a picnic, and while some had stayed at Mirror Lake and the others that drove us went to Ontonagon, we began the nine mile Lake Superior Trail about noon. We made good time and the trail was dry except in a few swampy places.

Workmen had been here by boat and buried the garbage pit and dropped a huge hemlock on it, in back of the toilet. All garbage not burnable must be packed out. The toilet is quite full so they'll need to dig a new one.

We made a fine meal and rustled up firewood. The boys had real fun netting about twenty suckers and put them in a pond. We are having two for breakfast along with fried potatoes and the rest of the pork chops. We let the rest of the suckers go back into the main river.

It is thundering and has rained a little so I guess we will have a wet six and-a-half miles returning to Mirror Lake today. Last year, when packing across there with heavy packs, we were in steady rain all day.

This is a most beautiful spot for the cabin to be and we appreciated it as on previous occasions. It is a sad thing that a bureaucracy would decide to get rid of the cabins which have given such pleasure to thousands of hikers, many of whom were family types with children. The cabins gave hikers a goal to hike to. Please write to the Department of Natural Resources, Parks Division, Lansing, Michigan, or to Governor Milliken to help save the cabins!!!

Last year we had a awful time fighting Senator Mack of Ironwood and Gogebic and Ontonagon boards of supervisors via hearings at Bessemer and Ontonagon, letters to Lansing, articles in papers, etc. Those people wanted to open the park with roads, logging, mining, and build tourist facilities. Wilderness lovers saved the park, but now for some unknown reason, they would tear down the cabins. An act like this would give people less security and enjoyment, and surely there would be more ground fires and pollution all over the park, for it would add to the burden of tent campers, which there are many.

Yesterday, two young men were fishing here and cooking the fish on a stick over a fire. They were so poor they had nothing else to eat and no tent. We told them about the half-shelter about four miles east of here on the Lake Superior Trail, and that there were a few odd items of food left there. They were so happy and took off like mad even though the sun had nearly set!!! Imagine camping and hiking in the Porkies without food? Yesterday morning, we had them use our boat at Mirror Lake, but they didn't catch fish there.

There are hordes of flies down by the beach at the lake. I would say it is because so many suckers died or were killed and rotted since spring.

We have had a good breakfast and are getting dishes done. Also, water is heating to mop the floor. We hauled up wood. The long drift log is cedar and is dry, so it will make good firewood, especially to start a fire and for quick heat.

The lamp was broken so we have kerosene in rocks for the wick and kerosene in the bottle by it, marked "K" on the cover.

Suckers here are easily netted, and due to the cold water of the large, late snow melt, they are sound and good to fry—can fillet them. We only kept or killed what we could eat.

There is a can with a plastic bag on top —it has grease from pork chops to fry fish or potatoes in.

We will be so sorry to leave this scenic area and to leave Mirror Lake on Saturday morning, not knowing if the cabins will exist in future years. We have been in these Porcupine Mountains about a dozen times, in various cabins, and on most trails, so we would feel a deep loss if the rugged areas were ruined so a few could get rich. If they "develop" it, it will be like any other area man has ruined, so why come to see it then?

The V.H. Family

October 7, 1979
Section 17 Cabin

There was a time in the '50's and '60's when the cabins were mostly unknown and little used, as was the park. But all that changed. In the late '60's, Senator Mack and the Gogebic and Ontonagon boards of supervisors fully intended to break up the park and mine, log, and build roads through here. A large amount of people got up in arms about that and managed to save the park. Then the environmentalists got goofy and decided every man-made thing had to be destroyed to call this a wilderness area. That meant another fight for they and commercial interests wanted the cabins destroyed! So you see, what you enjoy and appreciate now has been fought for via letters, taped statements, political debates, hearings, and expressed feeling. It didn't all just happen, and if we don't care enough to care for the cabins, trails, and forest, we will lose their use or be restricted far more. Any nature lover will not litter, nor start a forest fire, or vandalize a cabin or a sign. Like with our liberty, this wilderness will be done away with if we don't appreciate it enough to care for it and fight for it.

Joe V.H.

Unknown Date
Lake of the Clouds Cabin

All of the rocks exposed in the Porkies are Pre-Cambrian in age—that means what geologists believe are somewhere between 800 million to 1.2 billion years old.

1. The great escarpment you came over or undoubtedly will cross consists of ancient lava that once issued forth from cracks over much of the Lake Superior region. If you look closely at the lava on the lookout to the northwest you

will see tubular and round, white spots in the rocks. These mark gas bubbles in the lava that later filled with calcite and other minerals. These bubbles or vesicles were also filled with native copper later on, which explains the number of old mines in the park. If you find any agates on the Lake Superior shoreline, these too originated in the vesicular lava, only to later weather out to be tossed in the waves and washed on the beach. The tubular vesicles (or white-filled bubbles) in the lava mark the bottom of a lava flow—the round vesicles become more common near the top of the flow. Using this criteria, one can count the several lava flows just at the Lake of the Clouds lookout.

2. If this park reminds you of Isle Royale, it's because the rocks there are almost the same as here. Sometime after the last pool of lava cooled, mountain-building forces indented the flows downward, causing the lava to stick up....

3. These volcanic forces were not constant. There apparently were periods of quiescence where Mother Nature was allowed to erode the lava and deposit various forms of sandstone and conglomerate (a rock consisting of rounded pebbles). These sedimentary rocks were pushed down and folded along with the lava. Since the sandstones and conglomerates are less resistant to weathering, a valley was carved out and Lake of the Clouds filled it part way.

4. After all these rocks were deposited and formed, a great molten body of rock pushed its way upward at a point just south of here. All the rocks in the Porkies were affected by this upwelling—in many places the topography was accented by the new uplift, such as at the escarpment. The molten rock moved slowly as it rose, and as it got near to the surface, it began to slowly cool. It cooled so slowly that crystals formed in the rock—crystals big enough to see with the naked eye. Thus the rock that was part of this molten upwelling is today called a porphyry by geologists (porphyry is a rock with crystals big enough to see in it, surrounded by a fine-grained or smaller crystallized material). This rock is now exposed at the surface at the pinkish road-cuts along the highway between Silver City and White Pine. Most recently, glaciers covered this area, the ice moving southwest along the basin formed by the indented lava and scouring on Lake Superior. The cliffs and valleys of the Porkies were also carved out by the glacier, but most of the relief in the park is due to the ancient Pre-Cambrian rocks beneath.

B.H.

April 13, 1993
Big Carp 6-Bunk Cabin
It says in my book...the park includes exposures of Copper Harbor conglomerate which is 1.1 billion years old and up to five thousand feet thick. The Copper Harbor conglomerate consists of sandstone with minor amounts of conglomerate material.

I wonder if the outcropping the bridge is attached to is Copper Harbor conglomerate? Maybe a geologist who reads this would make a comment.

Unknown Author

May 19, 1985
Big Carp 6-Bunk Cabin

By walking to the Lone Rock by way of beach, one must have strong, secure ankles capable of walking on forty-five degree inclines of rock, probably bound up from the Superior basin by the forces of plate tectonics, etc. One must note the fossilized mud-cracks and sand bottoms which were near shore millions of years ago. You should also note the forces of wind and waves upon the tilted fortresses of rock and enjoy the powerful forces of nature which occupy this planet. By the way, the rocks bordering the bridge on both sides are conglomerate and were probably at the bottom of the ancient seas, exposed, eroded, back to the bottom, exposed, and are now being eroded. The number of times of this is not exact. Note the power of the waves, being capable of throwing boulders of a different type onto a flat rock of another. Take advantage of what nature has to offer.

Wiffle

September 16-20, 1974
Mirror Lake 4-Bunk Cabin

Four days of hiking as a prelude to a meeting this weekend of The Wilderness and Natural Areas Advisory Board, on which I serve. It is advising the DNR on the stated matters and is mainly responsible for implementing Michigan's Act 241 of 1971—The Wilderness and National Forest Act. It was the first such state law in the US and was patterned somewhat after the Federal Wilderness Bill of 1964. Dedication of portion of this park will be up for consideration in the near future, so I want to have a first hand look at the interior.

In 1972, I botanized the Lake Superior shoreline with Dr. Edward Voss of the U of M, hiking the whole shore from Presque Isle to headquarters. From this point of view, the park's uniqueness is mainly in its mature forests, rather than any particular rare plants

The master plan for this park was adopted by the DNR Commission in about 1971, and calls for phasing out the cabins when they reach the end of their life span. As the pages of this diary indicates, this is a point of some controversy! Some people suggest more be built; others decry the deterioration of the area from overuse. The general trend in state and national parks is now away from the developed campground, and back to tent camping. In the end, economics will doubtlessly win out. These facilities are expensive to construct and maintain, considering the meager income they generate, and it is the legislature that funds all DNR expenditures, item by item.

On the protectionist side, Ian McHarg, the Scottish landscape architect, has noted in Design With Nature, that poverty and inaccessibility are the two great protectors of the landscape. Neither operates here – as the US population and affluence grows, these areas will come under greater pressure, and use will have to be controlled or they will go down hill. Sections of the Appalachian Trail and some National Parks are already on a permit basis. There are two basic ways to control use:

A) Permits, with limited entry
B) Decrease accessibility by longer hikes in or let cabins go out of use

Which do you prefer? If neither, then in the long run (and probably short, too), Americans have some fundamental decisions to make on how large our population should get and how much material goods we're to produce. Too many people will overrun the place; too many goods may make it impossible to resist the loggers and miners who still have their eyes on the area's resources (the mineral rights are still, to a considerable extent, owned by mining companies and they have the right to come in and work these claims, with all that entails). We're in the process of learning, once again, that we can't have both guns and butter, and we also have to learn that the survival of places such as this does not fit with the perpetual growth of people and the Gross National Product.

John & Mary Lou T.

May 22, 1983
Buckshot Cabin

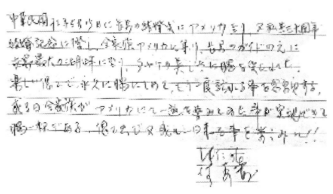

The C. Family

October 16, 1965
Little Carp Cabin

   I stayed in this cabin for two nights. I am from Ethiopia. I came by boat and by plane. I've passed through many places in Africa and Europe, and I have not seen such a beautiful and most naturally rich place in my life. I am very sorry, because I may never come back. I love it and it makes me feel like America is my second home.

Zewdie H.

June 6, 1995
Buckshot Cabin

६ जून १९९५

[handwritten text in Marathi/Devanagari]

— जयदीप

Unknown Author

1968
Lily Pond Cabin

This has been the most dangerous and exciting vacation I will ever have. Yesterday, my mother, my cousin, and I ventured out about a quarter of a mile on our way to Summit Peak. I heard the tornado when it was still far away. I was awaiting my turn to crawl past a pile of fallen branches when I heard a roar, like a far off wave, blowing toward us so fast that it was on and over us before I could say anything. It was a huge wind that pitched swirls of steamy gray mist along with it...It appeared out of nowhere with terrible, murderous power, and just as terrifying, right after that, a huge wind swept through. My mother said, "It's a tornado! Get down!" We did. The mist was swept up beyond us, too, and the big wind didn't let up. Roaring through madly, tearing leaves through the air, pulling trees up by the roots, as my mother and I lay flat with her hands over her head. I kept down in a half-crouch, ready to run because of dead trees nearby. My cousin had a Walkie-Talkie, and he called the cabin with it, so that we could hear my sister's hysterical voice. It was hard to hear her in the steady rush of terrible wind, but we heard her say, "There's a forest fire! It's got to be! There's smoke all over the place!"

Greg

Because my brother refused to finish this, I will have to. I really don't know what happened to them, because I was at the cabin. Here it wasn't quite so drastic, but I panicked anyway, seeing misty film, thinking it was smoke. Greg, Mom, and Mike came back to the cabin and we all ran past the garbage pit and down to a ditch close by. Once the storm had passed, we walked three miles back to the car. We asked the ranger to tell us what happened. He said it was a squall! Worst one in fourteen years! And the smoke was clouds!

Unknown Author

October 30, 1992
Big Carp 6-Bunk Cabin

Shortly after we arrived here, two rangers motored to shore in their boat. They unloaded some wood and cut down some trees—all in preparation for the moving project being done this winter. The plan is to shift this cabin to the east one cabin length and raise it off the ground to a new foundation. This will help with the erosion problems along the stream bank and remove the lump under the floor by the table (it's an old wood stove). We hope the cabin can be moved without falling apart as it's one of our favorites. The rangers cut some of the wood into stove lengths and told us that if we put one of the chunks of wet maple in our stove, it would sizzle and keep us warm all night.

Gail, Brad, Cathi, & Joanne

1997

Mirror Lake 4-Bunk Cabin

Porkies Trivia Game:
1. What is the highest point in the park?
2. How high is it?
3. When was the big flood?
4. How much rain fell?
5. What type of airplane crashed in the Porkies?
6. When did it crash?
7. Were there any survivors?
8. What was the first ranger cabin built in the park? HINT: rangers call it the honeymoon suite.
9. What was the first rental cabin built in the park?
10. How many cabins are in the park?
11. How many are log construction?
12. How many cabins are available year round?
13. Who owned the land at the mouth of the Big Carp River?
14. How many miles of foot trails are there in the park?
15. When was the South Boundary Road constructed?
16. What is the height above sea level of Lake Superior?
17. What is the height above sea level of Mirror Lake?
18. When was the park born?

Answers:
1. Summit Peak
2. 1958 feet
3. June 21, 1983
4. Thirteen inches in four hours; water rose in the Little Carp River, below Lily Pond, to a depth of thirty feet. Some backpackers had to climb trees to escape the flood.
5. US Army Air Corps, B17 Bomber
6. April 18, 1944
7. All ten survived; only one had to be rescued (He parachuted into a tree and was knocked out. He came to hanging from the tree by his ankle).
8. Mirror Lake 2-bunk
9. Mirror Lake 8-bunk
10. Sixteen
11. Five; Mirror Lake 8-bunk, 4-bunk, and 2-bunk, as well as Whitetail and Union River
12. Three; Gitchee Gumee, Whitetail, and Union River
13. Raymond Dick and Walter Speaker, both of whom were members of the "Save the Porcupine Mountains Association"

14. Ninety miles
15. Fall of 1964, the first vehicles were able to drive across the newly constructed South Boundary Road
16. 601 feet
17. 1532 feet; highest Lake in the state of Michigan
18. Since 1945, the Porcupine Mountains have been managed as a state park by the Michigan DNR

Unknown Author

October 5-17, 1975
Mirror Lake 8-Bunk Cabin

DNR forest fire personnel from Wakefield, Baraga, and Porkies Park field offices labored on a large fire north of the river. Size about thirty acres or more, started Sunday, October 5. On Tuesday morning, a second fire was started on the big, rock bluff from another campfire. This was around fifteen acres in size. Porkies park rangers assisted greatly in the mop-up work involved. Also, two crews of inmates from Ojibway Camp, Marenisco worked in extinguishing all the burning stumps, logs, etc. Fire Division personnel spent nights in the 8-bunk cabin after working from morning until night, plus some nights on the fire. Portable pumps plus hundreds of feet of hose were used on the fire, plus shovels, axes, and pump cans. On the 13th of October, a third fire was observed across the lake burning out of control in two large hemlock trees. This also was started from a campfire left unattended. Today is the 14th of October and fire people are still putting out numerous ground fires and stumps burning. This fire will never be completely out unless we get a lot of runoff snow to cover the ground.

These campfires left unattended to cause forest fires are sure a waste of natural resources, a waste of taxpayers money, and a waste of time and energy. Time better spent improving roads, bridges, and natural resources. This area sure wouldn't look very scenic burned to the ground. If these wildfires continue, maybe fires will have to be banned. On October 17, the fire was declared to be completely out.

Unknown Author

May 23, 1989
Speaker's Cabin

What a place this must have been for the inhabitants of the old shacks up the hill. All the seasons, the quiet, the experiences, seeing the years go by in a place as close to heaven as anything else. And there they pass on, leaving passersby to wonder, how did they get all that stuff back here? How did they manage, at times, the intense solitude? Who were they and what were their lives like? It's kind of sad to see things like that go by the wayside. Like the many homesteads that lay abandoned and in ruin all over this UP, with their stories known only by the land, the Master, the deceased spirits who once thrived there, and save only a few left alive who remember them. But it's a treat to sit next to a toppled over, South Bend cook stove and imagine the venison stews and doughy biscuits, rich dark coffee and fried lake trout, that graced its top. And the old wrought bed frame that cradled a nature-loving spirit with his dog at his feet. The axe by the door, the oil lamp on the table, the few rag tag books on a dusty shelf that made the last evening hours seem like fine wine. What were their thoughts, their feelings? Their trials and tribulations? Go on up, sit amidst the ruins (with a bug net of course), and take some time to have a cup of that coffee, a bowl of that stew, and swap some stories with the spirits of that place. It's a memory you'll never soon regret.

Tom & Michelle W.

September 16-19, 1976
Section 17 Cabin

Just today I read a short article by F.L. Olmsted in 1865. He was primarily responsible for establishing Central Park in New York, and also shared responsibility for establishing Yosemite National Park. He believed we need natural scenery to inspire and rest our minds. That our minds get bogged down with our planning, our attention to small and petty details, which have bearing on some general and of more importance. Probably everyone who comes here enjoys a renewed peace, as the mind is relieved of other pressures while we enjoy the natural beauty which surrounds us.

Kathy, Bob, & Anna

April 20, 1986
Little Carp Cabin

Some of the small creeks around here have interesting Indian names. Wabeno Creek is named after the Ojibwa sorcerers and magicians who got their supernatural powers from the morning star. Kenabeek Creek is named for the big serpent or snake-like creatures which the Ojibwa believed were in the lake. Memengwa Creek, the first one which flows onto the Little Carp upstream, is named for the fairies (like little people who inhabit rocky places, especially caves and overhanging rocks), who play tricks on people and make rock pictographs, usually with a reddish paint. You supposedly can hear them talking and laughing near rapids. They supposedly looked like monkeys with no noses and liked moonlit nights for cavorting around. The Indians called the Porkies Kaug-Wudju and were fearful of a powerful spirit which lived on the high cliffs above Lake of the Clouds.

B.K.

November 11-13, 1977
Lily Pond Cabin

It has been quite windy here before it snowed. As the radio announcer mentioned last night, it has been two years to the day since the Edmund Fitzgerald sank. We remember that well since we were vacationing in Grand Marais, Minnesota when it happened. The storm that sank it was also the first one of the season.

Lynne & Chuck B.

October 18, 1991
Whitetail Cabin

The entire area from Lake Superior to the Whitetail Cabin parking lot was completely cut over between sixty and eighty years ago. The only virgin area that remains is the dense stands of hemlock. They are probably over two hundred years old. If you get off the road and walk cross country, you'll notice old stumps everywhere in the woods. These are mostly hemlock stumps with some white pine. There were probably yellow birch stumps also, but these must have all decayed. The area around the cabin is predominantly paper birch and aspen. In the next thirty years or so, most of these trees will die of "old age" (insects, diseases, decreased vigor, etc.). The sugar maple and occasional yellow birch will then take over. These are longer lived species that get established under the paper birch and big-tooth aspen. When I come back here at age one hundred, there won't be any white birch or aspen, only a hardwood stand of sugar maple, yellow birch, and some red maple. At that point in time, the hemlock will start seeding in from the original virgin stands. As a big, old maple falls over, it will release a hemlock that has been growing in it's shadow. Give this tree another hundred years, and it will look like the hemlock we see out there now. Therefore, in about two hundred years or so, more or less, this will all be a hemlock stand again!

Doug

June 15, 1982
Section 17 Cabin

If you take the time to study a log on the trail that has been sawed through, you'll discover that a great deal of the hemlocks and white pines are over four hundred years old in this park. Also, the black birch and sugar maple are significant because of their size. This place is one of the few remaining areas of virgin timber in the Midwest. For this reason, and reasons of uniqueness concerning wildlife, all of us should concentrate on preserving this park, as well as all others, for the enjoyment of future generations. What we have left, if abused, will be a loss for all of us.

J.F.

July 27-31, 1966
Section 17 Cabin

Had two V.I.P.'s drop by today. State troopers looking for the walkaways from Marquette prison—walkaways were spotted up by Little Carp beach. They came in and had tea, date bread, and summer sausage, and then settled near the Ranger Cabin because the walkaways were figured to come by here. Then about a half-hour later, the troopers came back down and stated that the walkaways were caught three miles from here....

I found a prisoner's cap about thirty feet away and I'm taking it home.

Author Unknown

June 6, 1994
Mirror Lake 4-Bunk Cabin

Today is the fiftieth anniversary of the D-Day invasion of Normandy. As the four of us, Chuck, my brother-in-law, Matt, his fifteen year old son, Richard, Chuck's father, and I, Paul left on the South Mirror Lake Trail, we remarked how it was odd that we were setting off with heavy packs upon our backs in a far away place. And we talked about how scary it must have been for all of the brave soldiers who stormed the beach so long ago, not knowing whether or not they would even go home.

This is my first trip to the Porcupines and in all honesty, I am not sure what to make of it. I have never camped in such an out of the way place where there are bears in the wild. The environment is very beautiful, but it seems a little overwhelming to me. I don't know very much about getting along in a remote place, so I am following the lead of Chuck, Matt, and Richard, all of whom are very experienced at this. But I have come to this place with an open heart and mind, and I will try to savor the time I have to spend here because my life is at all other times so focused on things of the material world- mortgages, career, and car payments.

Paul R.

May 15, 1991
Speaker's Cabin

On the shores of the Gitchee Gumee, reminds one of "Hiawatha," Longfellow's poem. Seems there was no Hiawatha around here, the only historical one being out east, a holy man among the Iroquois. Some say Longfellow was influenced by a legend among the Ojibwa about a man named Manabozo (the name of the first waterfall on the Presque Isle River). Manabozo was to have lived on Madeline Island, west of here in the Apostle Islands. He had a very close companion, some say his brother, others say a pet wolf. While he was away hunting one day his companion died. Upon hearing the news, Manabozo felt complete agony and vowed to follow his friend. He died and was dead for four days but on the fourth day he came back to life. He related how his friend was doing well in the land of the dead, but he had returned to teach men the way he had died and returned. Later on, the medicine men of the Ojibwa formed a society to preserve the knowledge of Manabozo's way. They called it the Midiwewin, in English, the Grand Medicine Society.

Unknown Author

August 7-14, 1988
Speaker's Cabin

We had a welcome visitor today. An old lady who is the granddaughter of William Speaker, after whom this cabin is named. She gave some history of the area. He had a cabin across the stream, the foundations of which can still be seen. He had dug out the stream and built a dock for small boats. Parts of the pier can be seen in the lake still. On the trail going down to the lake is the opening to the old fruit cellar. The ruins of three cabins behind the outhouse were for relatives of his. The old man is ninety and living in Black River Harbor.

J.B.

August 2, 1989
Lily Pond Cabin

We counted the growth rings of a large hemlock that fell in a windstorm on the Little Carp, near Greenstone Falls. It was a sapling in 1754! The massive white pine just as you enter this cabin area from the trail is at least that old. I would estimate 1700 when its seed first touched the ground. Consider this, friends, as you enjoy this rare place.

John, Laura, & Sara A.

September 28, 1981
Section 17 Cabin

The Porkies represent a truly unique feature in the world. As a botanist, I was pleased to learn that the Porkies are the second largest virgin forest in the entire Eastern U.S. and the largest virgin, northern, hardwood forest in the world! The Boundary Waters virgin, Pine-Spruce forest in the largest virgin forest in the East and Midwest.

Only one-half mile upstream is the largest white pine in the world and the largest quaking aspen in the world is along South Boundary Road.

What makes virgin forest like this so wonderful is that it has existed here in such splendor for so long without man's manipulation or help. The forest around you here has three to four hundred year old trees and the forest itself has probably been in this form for up to six thousand years! Before that, the land was recuperating from the Ice Age glaciers that left ten thousand years ago.

It is in special places like this that I feel closest to God. Nature is in its purest form here. Whether man existed or not, this forest would still be here. This forest needs no help from man to reach this exquisite state of beauty and tranquility. I hope this park is allowed to exist and evolve for several thousand more years without the interference or exploitation by man. We need special places like this!

Please, help defend this park from future, short-sighted legislators, greedy loggers and developers, and others who would break up and do away with parks like this. The only reason the Porkies are so special and unique is because logging, mining, road building, subdivisions, and other activities have been prevented here. These are fine elsewhere, as we need wood, roads, and places to build permanent homes. But the Porkies should remain, virtually, "forever wild."

Bruce, Helen, & Josh K.

October 8-9, 1980
Lily Pond Cabin

I'm wondering what the newly elected "moral majority" will do to our American wilderness areas. I just don't trust the likes of Ronald Reagan, Robert Dole, Strom Thurmond, Jesse Helms, etc., to be sensitive to the Porcupine Mountains or our beloved Boundary Waters Canoe Area. Those of "our kind" who depend on the holy sanctuaries of the wilderness have a tough battle ahead. Sad. We will have to be our nation's conscience, and pray that these areas can be left untouched. May my son and his brother/sister-soon-to-be also find their peace in the woods.

Rick, Julie, Jesse, and babe on the way

September 28, 1985
Mirror Lake 4-Bunk Cabin

I think this park can offer most any kind of challenge that a packer could want: cedar swamps, river crossings on narrow trees, mud, rocks, and wash out trails. It causes great awe to see the tremendous changes to the park by the "One Hundred Year Flood." AWESOME! It makes one realize how truly insignificant one really might be.

B.M.C.

August 13, 1974
Mirror Lake 4-Bunk Cabin

Somehow, here in the wilderness, even the Nixon news seems remote and in some ways insignificant. Closeness to the earth seems to make affairs of the world less important than they otherwise are. However, I have been thinking about this event at odd moments. It is a tragic thing for a man to reach a position of the greatest power, that any man has ever reached, only to overreach and trample on individual liberties. Thanks to the free press—I never realized before how important that is—he was exposed to the world.

We are hopeful for the Ford administration. He seems an open, honest man and will give the Republican Party another chance.

Ken

June 20, 1984
Lily Pond Cabin

If you sit real still for just a few moments, you will enter a time warp. Back to the first eyes of man. You can see the woods as they were twelve hundred or more years back. The animals are doing much of the same now, as then. The trees watch their domain as they have since times past. So sit still, breathe the air of past life, hear the sounds, and experience the true woods. Feel the history.

Steve R.

July 23, 1969
Mirror Lake 4-Bunk Cabin

Met a very interesting man next door who claims he was the first person to use the 8-bunk cabin when it was made.... Years ago, he claimed, this used to be a nice bass lake but the conservation department redid the lake and planted trout. If you're a little tired, Donnelly says he used to hike in here in the '20's and '30's for pleasure and guiding. There were no trails, no cabins, the road ended at the Union River from where they would start their hike and then compass all the way in. Sometimes they would make an error and end up on the other side of the lake which he didn't care for since they had their tent frames, benches and such set up on this side. When they camped at Lake of the Clouds, they would use the Carp Lake Mine as a refrigerator, but many years ago a land slide closed it. He got eleven echoes at the Vatican in Rome, and some one told him he could get thirteen here, so he's going to shoot his pistol tonight to test this. We found an old bed spring a little ways down from the eight bunk and a little ways off the trail. He claims this was an old trapper cabin.

Dr. & Mrs. P.

August 17, 1987
Section 17 Cabin

It's our third day in the "wild" and I have ceased straining my ears for the sound of traffic and airplanes. As Anthony and I walked the Lily Pond Trail yesterday, I couldn't help but to allow my imagination wander back to when the first settlers came through. I felt I could share their amazement at the vast richness of our country with its abundance of foliage and winding, gurgling brooks. As my pulse quickened as I approached each twist in the path and the unknown lurked around the corner, I felt like a pioneer battling fear and curiosity. I can only hope that two hundred years down the road, places like the Porkies will still exist.

Unknown Author

April 20, 1976
Little Carp Cabin
HOW THE PORKIES GOT THEIR NAME:
The Indian name means, literally, "Porcupine Mountains," and they were called this because from the main Ojibwa village at Ontonagon, the profile of the range looks like a crouching porcupine. An early French map from the 1670's shows the Ontonagon River, and down the Superior coast to the west, "Montagnes de Porc-Pic," so the name has been used for the landmark range for a long, long time.

B.K.

Youthful Insight

May 18, 1980
Greenstone Falls Cabin

Gabriel S. (age seven)

June 6, 1997
Speaker's Cabin
I think I am going to like it here.

Laura R. (age seven)

September 1-2, 1971
Section 17, Cabin
Hello,
This is Rodney. I'm from California. This is a good cabin except for the beds and the mouse. They both squeak.

Rodney

October 6, 1995
Whitetail Cabin

I really enjoyed our stay here just as much as Stacy. Although we may have had our grumpy days, we were grumpy as a family. That to me is very important. This trip would have meant nothing to me if I was not with my family.

Keith J. S. (age eleven)

September 21, 1992
Section 17 Cabin

We want to write this nature poem
Because we're in the nature home
From the sun to the river
To the hot to the shiver
It's a real nice place to be

From the tallest tree
To the bumble bee
To the shortest tree
To the feet of me
The Porcupine Mountains are the place for me

Julie B. (age eight)

July 1986
Speaker's Cabin

I made a boat. I put pretty rocks in it and I sent it out to sea.

Unknown Author

May 2, 1987
Lake of the Clouds Cabin

Trillium

Paula

October 30, 1994
Big Carp 6-Bunk Cabin

Ten years have passed since I swore to my parents that they would never force me to come here again. Now I begged to go, to bring my own daughter to experience the Porkies (so kind of them not to bring up my earlier protests until halfway in). At nine and-a-half months, Emma has really enjoyed her time here. Caked with dirt and intrigued by the big bath under the bridge, she has begun her lifelong bonding with the U.P. (Grandma and Grandpa raised here, Mommy dragged here and loved it). She's once again provided us with great joy and the world from the eyes of a child!

A closing word—this area is wonderful. It has changed much over the years, as has family. We've lost a few and gained a few, but all souls reunite in these beloved Porcupine Mountains.

Tamilyn

July 2, 1979
Lily Pond Cabin

Hi, boy this place sure makes you appreciate your shower, telephone, curling iron, radio, etc. But I'm not complaining. The weather's great, a little chillier here than Illinois. I wonder what's happening back home. I miss my friends and relatives, but love the scenery. God's world has so much beauty, all you've got to do is look around and find it. I thank Him for all the people in my life. I'm fifteen and don't want to grow up. I look at the hills, trees, and the lakes and think of how young I am compared to these.

Pattie

August 25, 1967
Mirror Lake 4-Bunk Cabin

When we went fishing, my dad caught a clam. I got to sleep on the top bunk, and that was the first time I ever got to sleep on the top.

Unknown Author

June 23-27, 1976
Little Carp Cabin

This is a good forest and this is a good day.

Brent F. (age five)

October 6, 1967
Speaker's Cabin

The cabin has bad breath.

Timmy (age six)

September 30, 1992
Big Carp 6-Bunk Cabin

LIKE A WAVE

Deep inside we're like a wave
Trying to act so tough and brave
And like a wave we all can break
With every little step we take.
When waves are cold in a storm
The sun comes up and they are warm
And just like waves we can cry
And a friend comes to dry our eye.
So when you see a friend that's glum
Think of waves and be their sun.

Sarah C. (age thirteen)

September 4, 1965
Lake of the Clouds Cabin

Suzy (age nine)

June 15, 1972
Buckshot Cabin

My name is Sarah and I'm thirteen years old (almost). We arrived here about 11:30 A.M. after a beautiful hike. I was amazed at the clean cabin and the sparkling lake, but my dad got a tick on him and I wasn't sure if I was going to like this place. Many hikers have passed here and said hello. We (my brother, Josh, myself, and my mom) took a great hike along the beach. My youngest brother, Josh, said he had three ticks on him, but maybe his imagination is just a little too big.

Sarah K.

July 30, 1997
Big Carp 4-Bunk Cabin

Hi! I'm Skye. I'm ten years old. I'm having a great time. The rapids are awesome when you have time to explore them!!! Before this cabin we were at Presque Isle Campground. Before that, Lily Pond, which is fun. And before that, Union Bay. I highly recommend Lily Pond. It's a blast! Gotta go!

Skye H.

July 1, 1996
Gitchee Gumee Cabin

We are now on our second day at the cabin. The boys, four years and soon to be two years old, are having more fun than they could ever imagine. They say things like, "Look at the lake, dad," "Boy we sure got dirty," and "Do we have to wash up?" They were wild boys before they got up here. All clues of being civilized again are fading with the sun.

Lamont, Julie, Christopher, & Tyler

October 12, 1975
Big Carp 4-Bunk Cabin

On our last night here, our dog Josie got sprayed by a skunk. He always sleeps inside. It was terrible. It smelled a lot.

Annie P. (age nine)

June 23, 1997
Section 17 Cabin

If you think about it, TV is not as good as people like to think. If you are not careful, it can damage your eyesight. Many shows shown to the public audiences can give children bad or unhealthy ideas or frighten or disgust some. Actually, little of the TV that children watch is helpful or educational in any way. Either it makes you want to buy something, or gives you a bad influence. I should know, because I'm only a twelve year old kid myself. I watch such shows as I am criticizing right now because often, even as I watch something, I show disgust at the sick or cheesy humor. I find few children's shows that are meant to be funny in some way or another, are not, so often violence is added, no matter how little of it is realistic. Falling off cliffs is a favorite. So are giant hammers, TNT explosives, and anvils. WHAT IS THIS WORLD COMING TO???!!!

Caitlin L.

September 24, 1989
Lake of the Clouds Cabin

Interpretation of the Mountains

Colin

July 1975
Section 17 Cabin

The Magic Berry

Once there was a berry on a tree and it fell—KABOOM—onto the ground. It split apart and a bear came out of the berry. The bear turned into a new berry on the tree in the same spot. It was a regular berry again and somebody ate it. And it was good.

Eric M. (age six)

May 28, 1985
Big Carp 4-Bunk Cabin

My dad got a sucker. It was gross. Lydia cried because she was hungry. She always eats. We swept the house. We did not bring pillows because it is too heavy. I think I am going to like it here.

Lucy S. (age seven)

February 21, 1997
Gitchee Gumee Cabin

Hello, again! We are leaving tomorrow. I'm going to miss this place. I'm going to leave behind some big giggles. I've learned a lot in these four days, including a lot about my family. My family is like four roses in a field of daisies. We have our varieties. I've been very relaxed over the days. I've had time to think about these people, my relatives, my friends, my cousins, and my world. I hope I come to enjoy this relaxation again sometime. I love this place. I wake up to the smell of eggs and pancakes. The silver, towering trees against the shimmering snow. The birds chirping. The ice crashing together afloat on the never ending body of water. The fire crackling in the wood stove. I hope (whoever you are) that you have a relaxing time.

Al

October 6-10, 1995
Speaker's Cabin

Emily's Message: I enjoyed Jiffy popcorn, being with Daddy, and keeping up with him on the hard trails. We even found weird tracks. I think it was a mountain lion. My most fun part of the whole trip was having a special time with Daddy.

Maggie's Message: I love Jiffy popcorn and I like the outhouse. I like collecting rocks and I love to sing lullabies to Penny, our dog. It was lots of fun having as many marshmallows as I want. My most special part of the whole trip was Mom and Dad reading me a big kid book.

Emily (age six) & Maggie (age four)

July 21-25, 1968
Lily Pond Cabin

Lily Pond is nice with flowers and trees. Lots of lilies. Lots of frogs. Pretty things are everywhere. Especially at Lily Pond.

Julia J. (age seven)

June 4, 1984
Greenstone Falls Cabin

I am on summer vacation. I'm going into the fourth grade. For the fourth grade teachers there is Mrs. Lind and Mrs. Webber. We have some nice fish to fry. The bugs are bad some time. I found a caterpillar, Mom found two frogs, and Uncle Joe and I found a frog too. With the frogs mom found, I put them into a cup. One was small and the other was bigger. Then with the two frogs in a cup, I put it on a tree. After a while, the cup dumped over and the frogs got out. I slept in the top bunk last night. I'm going to sleep on the other top bunk tonight. We are from Ontonagon. Dad caught his limit of fish. Dad, Mom, and Uncle Joe are eating fish right now. Uncle Joe likes fish, Dad likes fish, and Mom likes fish.

Julie L.

August 19, 1981
Lake of the Clouds Cabin

Amanda

October 9, 1995
Big Carp 4-Bunk Cabin
　　Well, I've been coming here nine years and I'm only nine years old. And in all that time, I've never seen someone make paint out of rocks and water. And we did! Yes, real drying, colored paint! We even painted our faces!

Unknown Author

August 22, 1996
Big Carp 6-Bunk Cabin
　　This is our last full day here. As with previous trips here, we have over-packed and are eating like mad. This is Michelle's first time here with us and her first packing adventure. She had tread the trails like a pro, until the dark, and then it takes an army of defenders to escort her. Nerves come with understanding and we are working on that. The pack in on Pinkerton became eventful when Bobbi needed a little first aid while still practicing her new found Olympic skills. Needs more practice on wet, slippery, stream rocks. Yesterday morning while the wife and I were trying to get those very few quiet moments together, our daughter Angie wanted to show off her river log-crossing skills. After watching her take an unexpected morning bath, she looked at mom and said, "Why did you push me?" No one was within ten feet of her. No first aid required.

Dave H.

August 1, 1988
Little Carp Cabin

We hiked in the trail,
Now my feet are frail,
I took off my pack,
It really saved my back.

Jennifer (age eleven)

July 7, 1992
Greenstone Falls Cabin
　　Matt (almost thirteen) told of a funny experience he had the first night when the shutters were all closed and the lantern turned out. It was so dark that he couldn't tell if he was sleeping with his eyes open or closed!

Michael, Marlene, Matt, & Laura

June 17, 1972
Buckshot Cabin
　　GUESS WHAT?! I saw him. I saw the "Buckshot Bear." My dad got up early and he was making breakfast. We were all just opening our eyes when

my dad said, "Everyone be very quiet, get out of bed, and come over here near the window." We did. There he was. Right on the path. It was very exciting.

Sarah K. (age thirteen)

August 10, 1994
Little Carp Cabin
This is the best time of my life.

Brock S. (age four)

June 29, 1989
Lake Superior Cabin
Jason and I went up the hill next to the cabin practically all day long. We also went to the beach and went out onto the rocks in the lake and pretended that they were boats and used sticks as paddles. When we came out of the water we were numb from the waist down, and we forgot our towels.

Julanne E. (age nine)

October 13, 1976
Big Carp 4-Bunk Cabin

Fall in the Porcupine Mountains

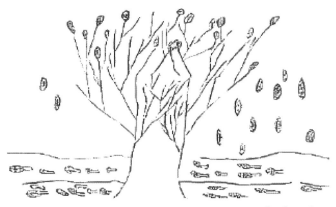

Jordana (age seven)

May 6-8, 1982
Big Carp 4-Bunk Cabin

Fresh from Algebra, Physics, and too much pressure, twenty-one Madisonians from Memorial High School greet the Michigan North Woods. How can we fathom and understand the forest in three days? Our first day was rainy and cold. However, with a good positive attitude and lots of camaraderie, the five mile hike to Big Carp Cabin was accomplished. With frame packs stuffed to the brim, rain ponchos covering everything but our bodies (we looked like an army of hunch backs), we managed to cross our first river on a two inch wide log. Like the initiations of a sorority or fraternity, every one of us crossed the river (even though we were afraid) and passed into a relationship with each other and the forest we never could have imagined two days earlier in Chemistry.

Sleeping on the floor like slaves in the bottom of a ship, we spent our first night warm and dry. Our group spent the next day discovering the sun (the clouds moved out), the hemlock trees, and the club mosses.

Mrs. Cary, one of our "adult" leaders, knew more than the Peterson's guide about plants, birds, and animals. We hit her with questions like "How do the red cup fungi reproduce?" and "What kind of bird is small, brown, and likes to twerp?"

With a slight aversion to crossing rivers on very thin logs, we thank God we never had to cross the Little Carp. However, swamp crossing, tree jumping, moss squashing, and tree hugging became like second nature to us.

The forest became a personal friend. And yet, the fascinating thing was that it was so complex we couldn't begin to get to know it. Our senses were overloaded, we couldn't grasp the complexities!!

On our second full day, we took it easy and had breakfast at about 10:00. Still, the pancakes made by two of our "manly men" tasted great! We split up into two groups, some going out to Buckshot Cabin and the others to Shining Cloud Falls. Mentally, a small group was easier to handle, and running up and down the trail chasing each other with mud and snow was fun.

Another interesting part of our trip was getting to know a girl named Kilsa from Brazil that came in our group. Cross-cultural communication next to a sunset on Lake Superior is somehow unique. She taught us a song in Portuguese about the sunset and sunrise. It wasn't a stupid children's song but a complex song with real meaning and thought. It took a lot of effort to understand her and the meaning of her song, but when the beauty of the words shown through, the effort became worthwhile. The forest, with its complex beauty and unique animal and plant life was like her song. It was hard for some of us to understand, and it was easy to just let the foreign words, or strange birds, just pass on by. But if one takes the time and the effort to understand the forest, it is worth it. Sometimes it doesn't make sense. Sometimes it's raining and your feet are cold, the river is flowing too fast, and the log is too skinny, but if you've got the guts to cross it, you can do it!

Everyone crossed that river on the first day, and everyone saw the red and orange sunset, but whether we understood what we were seeing was the question. It matters only that we appreciated what we saw, respected it, and treated it like a good friend.

Memorial High

June 6, 1996
Whitetail Cabin

The Sea Shore

It was the most beautiful night of my life.
I was sitting on a rock near the shore.
That night the waves got higher than ever.

Lindsey (age nine)

August 8, 1989
Lake Superior Cabin

My parents say we are real campers. Camping wouldn't be too great without parents.

Jessica B.

Helpful Hints

September 22, 1991
Gitchee Gumee Cabin

I'm here to relax from work and "to be." For one "to be," it is important not to do anything, such as sitting quietly and listening to the wind and watching the trees and clouds across the sky. It is a form of meditation that is easy to do, and when one is relaxed enough, you'd be surprised what you can think of in a short period of time. Solutions to problems come easy and creative juices flow.

Unknown Author

June 18, 1986
Section 17 Cabin

Earlier in the afternoon I put my creative juices to flow and what did I create, but a "candlestone." Use and enjoy this light source and please replenish it as needed. It is serving us well tonight and I hope it does likewise for you.

If by chance someone fails to honor the sanctity of others that is gained on such exercises into "nothing to do," and by creating things such as candlestones, and the one I created no longer exists, please feel free to make your own. They are much more decorative and enjoyable to look at than a tin cup or bottle. Simply find an eight to twelve inch, interestingly shaped, flat rock and mount two or more candles to it with wax. Set on table and light candles. Best effect is achieved after darkness has arrived.

John & Cindy A.

August 21, 1986
Section 17 Cabin

Techniques to endure a mega-mile hike through a downpour with forty to fifty pounds on your back, weighing, yourself, less than a hundred pounds:

1) Think about your mother. How would she feel under the circumstances?
2) Turn the trek into an opera, using the tune of the famous Italian opera, "The ants go marching one by one, hurrah, hurrah...." Change the tune at mile intervals.
3) Be thankful it's not snowing.
4) List all the ways in which the trek could be more difficult. For example:

    a) You could have no destination.
    b) You could have brought your kid sister or brother.
    c) You could be carrying a cooler.
    d) You could be carrying your partner.
    e) You could have a broken leg.
    f) It could be dark out.
    g) Et cetera.

5) Convince yourself that you're almost there.

Connie & David

May 14, 1995
Buckshot Cabin
Helpful Hiking "Moves" for Doing the Lake Superior Trail
(Buckshot to Carp River)

Peter Y.

August 25, 1996
Mirror Lake 4-Bunk Cabin

How to start a fire with ONE MATCH! One, count them, one match (according to my boyfriend, Steve, ex-Eagle Scout from Minneapolis):

- Find really, really, tiny, baby branches and twigs
- Find kind of really, tiny, baby branches and twigs
- Find not as tiny branches and twigs
- Find teenage-sized branches and twigs
- Find momma-sized branches and twigs
  ...and you guessed it...
- Find daddy-sized branches and twigs

STEP A: Place a handful of the baby twigs over a bit of a hole in the fire pit (hole is necessary for the ONE MATCH to be placed in).

STEP B: Line up your wood, ascending size away from the fire pit. Be ready!

STEP C: Get really, really close to the hole under the baby twigs.

STEP D: Light match and place it in the hole under the baby twigs.

STEP E: Cross your fingers (I made that part up. He never said that.)!

STEP F: Then add wood as per your best judgement, being ever mindful not
to blow out the match!

Now, if you were a Boy Scout in Steven's troop, and you didn't start a fire with your one match, the bigger Scouts would kick around your tinder (baby twigs) and make you start again.

Good luck!

Michelle C.

September 23, 1981
Buckshot Cabin

The stove does work when it is full of wood. That is to say it will boil water within about twenty minutes if you pack it with wood to the top. Starting the fire is easy if you put two or three large birch bark pieces in the bottom of the stove with half-a-dozen or so pieces of six inch kindling on top. Set a match to it and watch it burn. Be sure the damper is open to give you a good draft. Otherwise you'll end up clearing smoke out of the cabin for an hour or so.

Suzanne & George C.

May 21, 1971
Mirror Lake 4-Bunk Cabin

HOW TO BUILD A FIRE FOR COOKING! Learn by yourself (and take two days doing it) or follow these simple directions:

1. Chop your wood into very small chips or splints—dry wood helps.

2.   Stack alternately and parallel- wood for support, paper, twigs, then the chips and splints from Step One.
3.   Light and keep feeding with splints.

By the way, keep the side air draft half open. Also keep the top flue regulator (that's the lever on the top of the stove at the back) half open (in the middle).

Unknown Author

September 10, 1977
Lake of the Clouds Cabin

If you have trouble getting a fire going in the stove, it's really no different than building a campfire. Try this:

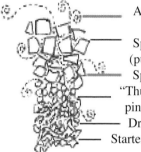

Air circulation

Split hardwood: birch, oak, hickory, etc.
(put in only after fire is blazing good)
Split softwood: pine, poplar
"Thumb" wood layer, preferably softwood like pine and poplar
Dry twigs, chips, shavings
Starter base of crumpled paper, birch bark

Don't cut down live trees. That's a terrible injustice. To the tree and they won't burn worth a damn anyway. Also, don't strip bark from any tree, especially birch. It's really harmful, and can kill them or allow disease or bugs to get in the bloodstream. It shocks the tree's system, too. How would you like to have your skin peeled off?

Unknown Author & Artist

September 13, 1983
Mirror Lake 4-Bunk Cabin

MOUSE TORTURES:

* Take away all delectable munchies from the cabin and feed him solely on Spam and Lipton Cup-a-Soup. This is slow, but will eventually kill any living creature.
* Trap him in a stove kettle and play "Wipeout" on the lid with spoons until long after he has squealed for mousy mercy.
* Tie him to the rowboat and whip him with seaweed as he tows you around Mirror Lake.

- Suspend him by his tail from your clothesline, just downwind from "the Mighty Hunter's" hiking socks.
- Make the rogue cook your supper on this incredible stove under threat of being immersed in a cold cup of blackstrap molasses if he fails.

J.R.

May 27-30, 1986
Lily Pond Cabin

Being scientifically inclined, I've decided to drink the spring water before boiling it to put an end to the long lasting controversy over whether or not the water is safe to drink. Outcome:

Amount ingested: One cup

Time—11:00 A.M.: Ingestion of water

Time—7:14 P.M.: No adverse effects.

Time—9:20 P.M.: No intestinal disturbances or any other discomfort (I rather doubt that any bacterium could live in the pipe with constantly running water).

Time—9:30 A.M.: No sign of abnormalities due to drinking spring water. I hereby declare it safe to drink without boiling.

Now keep in mind that some people are sensitive to the mineral content in spring water and may get intestinal disorders due to this content, but the disorders are not due to bacteria....

Just back from Greenstone Falls. Beautiful! One change and a big one. Seems there's been a landslide that wiped out part of the trail (Little Carp River) just after the Cross Trail Junction. DNR is working on a new trail, which now crosses the Little Carp River and travels along the southwest bank....

I leave in case of emergency an Armour Potted Meat Food Product. Do not open unless dying of starvation, and then only if nothing else is available. This stuff is made from the scraps that the janitor sweeps up at a slaughter house. If you don't believe me, read the label carefully but not before dinner for you will lose your appetite. What is "partially defatted beef fatty tissue??"

Judy & Tom E.

August 26, 1973
Lily Pond Cabin

We went to the spring for more fresh water and on the way back across the pond, we made an earth-shattering discovery. This is especially great if you get lonesome and need someone to talk to. Stop the boat in the middle of the pond and shout, "Hi!" You will be amazed to hear someone shout "Hi!" right back to you.

Charlotte R.

Unknown Date
Mirror Lake 8-Bunk Cabin
    These are some wild flowers that grow nearby:

Wild Lily of the Valley:
(Maianthemum canadense)
- Also know as Canada Mayflower
- Small, starry flowers in the month of May
- Two heart-shaped leaves

Boneberry:
- Small, white spray of tiny
  flowers
- Three branches, each with three leaves

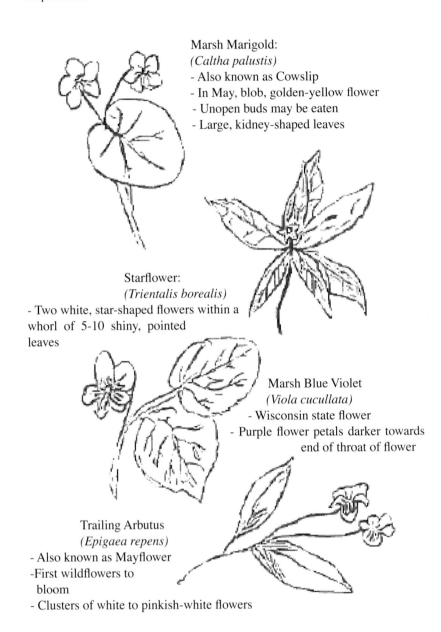

Marsh Marigold:
(Caltha palustis)
- Also known as Cowslip
- In May, blob, golden-yellow flower
- Unopen buds may be eaten
- Large, kidney-shaped leaves

Starflower:
(Trientalis borealis)
- Two white, star-shaped flowers within a whorl of 5-10 shiny, pointed leaves

Marsh Blue Violet
(Viola cucullata)
- Wisconsin state flower
- Purple flower petals darker towards end of throat of flower

Trailing Arbutus
(Epigaea repens)
- Also known as Mayflower
-First wildflowers to bloom
- Clusters of white to pinkish-white flowers

Dawn M.

June 14, 1991
Greenstone Falls Cabin

THE TEN BIGGEST LIES AT THE PORKIES:

10) You don't need to take a shower. Really.
9) Eat a tuna and mayo sandwich while hiking. Don't worry, the mayo won't get sour.
8) You don't need to take a canteen of water with you while hiking.
7) Hikers don't use the cabin outhouses.
6) The river water tastes good.
5) The water's not cold. Jump in! Trust me!!
4) Flies? What flies?
3) Mosquitoes? What mosquitoes?
2) Ticks? What ticks?
1) Bringing three coolers, one hundred pounds of food, and ten pound dog bowls isn't a problem. Really!

Gene H.

November 15-18, 1990
Lily Pond Cabin

We found a downed tree of some kind of hardwood three hundred yards yonder, up the trail. We hauled by the "mule method." This is not recommended for the weak of heart or the weak of legs.

Brentwood, Jimmy, & Matt

July 18, 1971
Lily Pond Cabin

We've been up here several times over the years. I will give you fishermen some advice about this lake. We always seemed to have the best luck about one hundred yards out in front of the outlet from Lily Pond. Just let about five feet of line drop over the side of the boat. The trout and other fish seem to stay closer to the top than the bottom. Don't use sinkers. You'll catch suckers and chubs and trout (more suckers and chubs the closer to the lily pads you get). I hope this will save some of you people who come in here to fish a little time, so you can spend your trip catching fish, not trying to locate them.

Gary M.

September 21, 1969
Mirror Lake 4-Bunk Cabin

While here, our group caught a total of fourteen trout—ten rainbow and four brook. Two were caught on home-tied red and yellow streamer flies, two on a blue and silver wobbling spoon, and the rest on worms. The best spots seem to be the deep area between the big rocks, the pine-covered point, and the west end.

James K.

Unknown Date
Mirror Lake 8-Bunk Cabin

About one-third of the trout caught are native Brookies. Mid-morning to early afternoon seems to be the most active feeding time. A French spinner with a small piece of nitecrawler works best. Unfortunately, suckers and chubs like them, too. A Panther Martin spinner works good, too.

Unknown Author

July 2, 1987
Greenstone Falls Cabin

D's Recipe for a New/Better Candle:
1) Mop strand, twisted and coated with wax from existing candle (that's the catch; you need a candle to make a candle)
2) A vessel (salmon can or other heatable container)
3) Wax (from an existing candle)
4) Heat source
5) Undying patience and a true love for the trade

D.A.G.

May 19, 1974
Buckshot Cabin

As we are sitting here on the rocks watching the sunset, we think of all the situations that have arisen that Ann Landers and Amy Vanderbilt would not approve of, or even know what to do about. So we have decided to write our own Camper's Etiquette:

1) Number One, and most important: Toilet Manners! What is the proper thing to do when caught reading on the "john" with the door open? Does one stand up and expose himself while slamming the door, or does one say, "It's taken," and strategically place his newspaper.

2) How to remove leeches if strategically placed: Pee on them. If they are not strategically placed, have someone else pee on them.

3) When sitting at a campfire eating, the only proper way to wipe your mouth is to cross your legs, put your mouth to your knee, and wipe it.

4) What to do about enhancing the flavor of instant banana cream pudding? A little spicy spaghetti sauce adds just the right zing, while a few wood ashes provide your daily carbon requirement. Wild ginger leaves add just the right poisonous touch. The outhouse enjoys this delectable treat any day or night.

5) At Girl Scout Camps, they tell you that ticks don't come out until the middle of June. This is not true, but a complete fallacy they fed into our not-so-innocent minds. Ticks are out in abundance by the middle of May. Our fearless leader saved us many-a-time from loss of blood by removing the parasites. When asked about his most exciting operation, he told, in detail, about removing ticks from the lower, right hips of the twins, Mony and Marianne. He also removed a tick on the rampage, ascending Jean's right leg.

6) The twins also experienced hazardous difficulties with the spider. While having a rousing game of spoons, a shriek was heard from the table, as Mony leaped back with terror from the table, abruptly arresting the game. While everyone asked what was wrong, Mony described a huge spider that had crawled down her arm. Momentarily, Marianne, the other half, felt a small tickling on her hand and reached to itch. Finding the same spider clutching her hand, she also leapt back with a look of terror, trying to dislodge the spider. After that, Steve, with his high-power beam, continually plied the area underneath the table in search of the feared spider.

7) So far, we haven't said much about the only two, halfway normal people in our group, Steve and Phil, our fearless men.

8) First, let us mention the proper spring fashions for backpacking (these fashions almost made the cover of Vogue, but they had just done an article on backpacking, so they said maybe next month). First, roll a pair of crummy jeans up as high as possible, depending on how loose they are. Since Mony had a pair of overalls on, she rolled hers all the way up to her knees (what raw sex). Then roll the two pairs of socks down almost to boot level giving a layered effect. Be sure the long underwear is showing if you have it on. Be sure to roll the sleeves of your shirt up, and if you have a T-shirt on, roll or push the sleeves up to give a greaser effect. Proper arrangement of the long braid, as modeled by one of our top models, Mollie, is to bring the braid around over the red bandana and tuck the end in front. Then adorn with old blueberries and wintergreen. Another attempt to achieve the proper temperature was vetoed by a certain relative of those involved...an anonymous member tried to wear her overalls with no shirt, but it was considered quite revealing and too daring for a mixed group.

Nicki S.

July 19-20, 1989
Big Carp 4-Bunk Cabin

To All Concerned Squatters (anyone using the outhouse):
ATTENTION: Watch out for rattlesnakes, coral snakes, whip snakes, vinegaroons, centipedes, millipedes, ticks, mites, black widows, cone-nosed kissing bugs, solpuigios, tarantulas, horned toads, gila monsters, red ants, fire ants,

Jerusalem crickets, chinch bugs, giant hairy desert scorpions, and ex-wives before being seated.

E.A.

Unknown Date
Mirror Lake 8-Bunk Cabin
BACKPACKING HINTS NOTEBOOK

#1: Don't buy boots that are heavier than you really need.

#2: Don't carry too heavy a load. A half-barrel is OK, a full keg is too much.

#3: Watch where you are going. Any experienced hiker will tell you that falling off a cliff hurts.

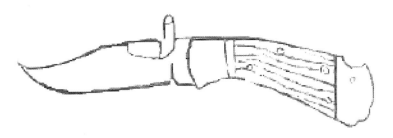

#4: For those of us too lazy to grip a knife blade, there is a flipper available for lock blades. The makes the arduous chore of opening your knife much simpler.

#5: If you're deer hunting and want a good scent to mask your human odor, try shitting your pants. I discovered this effective trick by accident while hunting in Montana.

Umbrella Hat
(available at finer back-
packers outlets)

Snorkel

Rubber Underwear
(can be sold to any
bed-wetter when you're
done with them)

#6: It's wet walking along the Correction Line Trail. The Backpacking Hints Notebook has a solution, of course. Happy Correction Line hiking!

...The Unknown Backpacker...
#7: To avoid startling game along the trail, you might try making yourself look less like a man, the natural enemy of all wild animals.

#8: A post maul can be handy for driving tent pegs on hard ground.

#9: If you're lost in the wilderness, remember that following a stream will eventually lead you to help.

#10: Boil water, even in the wilderness. This stuff is fertile, boys.

Unknown Author & Artist

July 2-3, 1970
Mirror Lake 4-Bunk Cabin
Fish sure do taste good when fried over a wood fire and eaten by candlelight.

Mr. & Mrs. R.W.

June 5, 1985
Greenstone Falls Cabin
The floor has been swept and mopped, but I would still recommend eating off the table.

Ed N.

November 21, 1992
Little Carp Cabin
I learned many simplicities on this trip, but this one is the best:
Sometimes we need to step into "another woods" to get out of our "own woods," the one we live in, to glance back and view where we're at in life, how good we've got it, and where we're headed.

Keith K.

July 23, 1996
Lily Pond Cabin
We have left you a weather rock. The instructions are as follows:
- If it's dry, it's nice out
- If it casts a shadow, it's sunny
- If it's wet, it's raining
- If it's white, it's snowing
- If you can't see it, it's foggy or night time
For hot weather, place the weather rock over the fire.

Bob, Ellen, John, & Shirley

July 15-19, 1997
Lily Pond Cabin
The B. Family Discoveries at Lily Pond:
- Fish bait: worms can be found by rotten stumps near fire pit and beetles under logs and stones.
- Four year old discovery: Leeches are not worms. They clamp on skin. Ouch! Blood!
- Canoe can be converted to swimming pool/washing machine. Place dirty clothes with youngsters in canoe. They provide washing services by stomping them clean.

- Do not place worms on seating area on bridge. They might be knocked into creek.
- Nature sounds throughout the night are awesome. If only we could hear them over the "big guy" snoring.
- The bear claw marks on the cabin make a great "ghost" story theme for campfire entertainment.
- Life is at its loudest when the world is quiet.
- Good-byes are always hard. So instead we'll say, "See you next year, Lily Pond." Happy trails to you!

The B. Family

May 15, 1981
Buckshot Cabin
The following plants are common within a few feet of the cabin:

Asarum canadense, Wild Ginger
Albus balsama, Balsam Fir
Artium minor, Burdock
Alnus incana, Tag Elder
Allium tricoccum, Wild Leek
*Aster macrophyllu*s, Large-leaf Aster
Acer rubium, Red Maple
*Betula alleghaniensi*s, Yellow Buck
Betula papyrifira, White Buck
Caltha palustus, Cowslip
*Carex pensylvanic*a, Early Wood Sedge
*Callieigonella schuber*i, a Moss
Clintonia borealis, Bluebead
*Cornus canadense*s, Dwarf Dogwood
*Cornus stolenifi*na, Red-osier Dogwood
Dicranum scoparium, a Moss
Erythronium americanum, Yellow Trout Lily
Galium (aparine), Bedstraw
Lonicera dioeca, Honeysuckle
Maianthemum canadense, Canada Mayflower
Mnium affine, a Moss
Morchella (escufenta), Morel
Populus tremulordes, Quaking Aspen
Viola pallens, small white Violet
Viola papallionacea, small blue Violet
*Viola pubescen*s, hairy yellow Violet

Unknown Author

Unknown Date
Mirror Lake 8-Bunk Cabin
The B-J Ceiling Lamp: A simple way to increase your candle power and aid you in playing poker, reading, or writing in the log.

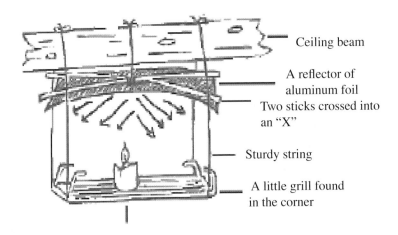

Ceiling beam

A reflector of aluminum foil

Two sticks crossed into an "X"

Sturdy string

A little grill found in the corner

A candle of suitable size (not too big or you will burn through the reflector)

The B. & J. Families

June 23, 1988
Little Carp Cabin

Now I sit
In my stinky vapor,
'Cause someone stole
My toilet paper.

Elizabeth B.

June 6-8, 1997
Little Carp Cabin
The four of us came in along the Pinkerton Trail. Along the way it became more and more apparent how unorganized we were. For three days, we each packed for a week, and still had nothing that we really needed. As the

days went by, dreams of huge trout were replaced with wonderful sunsets and companionship to boot. We tried to follow the advice of those who wrote before us and found that there was some good and some bad. Most of the fishing tips did no good and I guess we should have paid more attention to the dates on the swimming tips. I guess that means we should leave some advice of our own. This enormous place is too much to be taken in on one visit. Enjoy the things in front of you and come back again.

Chad F.

August 2, 1975
Section 17 Cabin

We highly recommend sitting on the mossy rocks where the water is the fastest. It makes you feel as smooth and soft and super-clean as after a sauna. The coolness of the water is very refreshing.

Elaine & Kevin H.

March 19, 1996
Gitchee Gumee Cabin

Old Indian Trick #36:

Do not go to the outhouse in your underwear and boots and leave the camera with someone else. Same goes for firewood.

Greg & Carol

Memorial Day, 1985
Section 17 Cabin

REMEMBER!!! Adventure is not in the guidebook! Beauty is not on the map! Seek and 'ye shall find!

Kevin

Tales
and
Legends

October 22, 1979
Mirror Lake 4-Bunk Cabin

All the good fortune and ill fortune associated with outdoor living (hiking, backpacking, and fishing) can be attributed to an Indian spirit named Um-wah. Um-wah is the spirit of lakes, mountains, and forests. His children are the fish, animals, and birds that inhabit these regions. Um-wah guards his children carefully and makes life particularly difficult for human beings that attempt to take his children. Um-wah can generally be considered responsible for lost fishing lures, backlashes, snags, stubborn motors, prevailing winds, and rain. Um-wah only rewards proven fisherman with any of his children. However, sacrifices can enhance a mediocre outdoorsman's chances for success. Um-wah particularly favors hats as items for sacrifice. Expensive cowboy hats are best. Good fishing can be assured by tossing your hat into the lake. Once Um-wah takes a fancy to your hat, he will go to any length to get that hat. The author lost a hat to Um-wah after offering to sacrifice his hat for several of Um-wah's children (twelve to seventeen pound Northern Pike in Northern Manitoba). After being rewarded by Um-wah, I mocked the Indian spirit and kept my hat. Um-wah apparently sent one of his children to take the hat from my car on the way home. Um-wah will have his sacrifice.

Um-wah also tests and rewards young backpackers in the Porcupine Mountains. We brought two rookie backpackers to the Porkies. Um-wah tested them on the hike from Lily Pond Cabin to Mirror Lake. They hiked with heavy packs through a downpour across rain-soaked trails without a hitch. Um-wah rewarded them (and their dads) with a cabin full of dry firewood. Um-wah tested the young backpackers. They met the test and were rewarded.

So, treat Um-wah, the spirit of lakes, mountains, and forests with respect. Take his children sparingly and remember his affinity for hats.

A Disciple of Um-wah

October 27, 1996
Whitetail Cabin

I come when no one is here, but most of the time I like to watch. I've lived in these woods for more than six years. Of course, no one's ever seen me. I come right up to the windows at night to get a closer look. A couple of times I came inside while people were sleeping. I also follow people when they go on their little hikes. My favorites are the young couples who do it in the woods. I also like the people who bring their pets. I hope they don't miss them too much. So if you're not afraid of the evil of the night, light the red candle and put it in the window. I'll be coming.

The Woodsman

October 16, 1997
Whitetail Cabin
Woodsman-

I've been watching you. You came to these woods six years ago, and in all of your wanderings and sneaking about, you have not yet chanced upon my palace. I have cast spells upon you. Two years from now I will catch you and make you give back the pets you have stolen. You are not as creepy as you think. You have holes in the socks you wear. You do not eat balanced meals. I know. I watch the watcher. I have watched you since your arrival. I am all powerful. I will see that you are found out. Watch your back, woodsman.

The Woodswoman

January 20, 1998
Whitetail Cabin

This day dawns cold. The sun looks like a pale candle in the haze of the memory of this sleepless night.

Yes, we laughed at the (Woodsman). We thought ourselves too civilized, too knowing, too sophisticated to fear the consequences of a red candle in a window in Whitetail Cabin.

This day marks the loss of innocence, the loss of hope. Dare I say it? The loss of faith.

The red candle! How we laughed! Our contemptuous giggles hid no fear. We were not whistling by the graveyard. We were secure, confident, solid.

This day we mourn our innocence. We grieve our hope. We sing the dirge for our faith.

Fear the Woodsman. Depend no more on the Woodswoman. Fear the darkness of the light of the red candle.

This day, pray for hope, pray for rescue.

Unknown Author

May 31, 1995
Lily Pond Cabin

Dan told an interesting story last night about the legend of Lily Pond. A young Indian girl (named Lily) was in love with a brave from the rival tribe which lived on the other side of the pond. They planned to swim to the middle of the lake and meet one night, so they could escape down the stream together. Well, Lily never arrived and nobody knows what happened to her. Her ghost is said to haunt this area and that is why the pond was named Lily Pond.

Karen D.

Unknown Date
Mirror Lake 8-Bunk

You say you've never heard of a jack-a-lope? Don't be ashamed. Few people have, except a very few of us experienced hunters. Many that have seen them never live to tell the tale. If you have seen one, ask the Park Ranger (he has a picture of one but doesn't say much about it for fear that it would scare off the park backpackers).

Author & Artist Unknown

Star Date 9.3.84
Section 17 Cabin
Captain's Log:

Found ourselves stranded on pre-historic planet. Were able to find small, wooden structure to shelter us from the rain. Kept warm by burning local plant life. Enjoyed the scenery. Local inhabitants are strange fellows; black, furry quadrapeds, curious, shy. Language unknown. Found their footprints in area but no sightings in vicinity. Did see one yesterday at the mouth of the river. Was unable to establish communication.

Hope to have transporters working soon. Then on to planet Zuras, third one in the Deltoid formation, Sector C.

Gary & Sara

1988
Lily Pond Cabin
Captain's Log: Stardate 2024

Sulu fell in the water on this Earth pond, swam for an hour before reaching shore. Scotty refused to beam him up until he is completely dry.

Unknown Author

October 1990
Speaker's Cabin
Captain's Log—Stardate 4623.2

Using the slingshot acceleration effect of the sun, the Enterprise has come back in time in search of something from Earth's past which is desperately needed in our time. Due to a gross miscalculation, the food chain has been disrupted with the extermination and extinction of the mosquito. Many species of fish, amphibians, and birds are suffering because of the loss of this food source. Consequently the entire 23rd Century ecological balance has been upset. Our mission is to locate and collect enough mosquitoes to repopulate the Earth.

Spock's research showed this particular area to have (historically) the biggest and most numerous mosquitoes on the entire planet. Therefore, he, McCoy and I have beamed down to obtain a few specimens. We hope to complete our mission shortly and return to our own time period.

Captain's Log—Stardate 4623.9

We have searched for hours and except for a few, common black houseflies, we have seen no insect life. The climate (at least today) does not seem conducive to mosquito life, but Spock insists the "UP" is the best place to find the little buggers, so we will continue searching.

Captain's Log—Stardate 4624.1

That idiot, Spock! He somehow misunderstood the old Earth calendar and had us show up in October instead of June. His mind just hasn't been the same since he underwent Fal-tor-pan. Anyway, passing through time warp is not a precise thing so it doesn't pay to try it again to come closer to a June arrival. I guess we will have to remain in orbit until next year when we can complete our mission. We will give your Aurora Borealis an extra boost now and then with our phasers as payment for the mosquitoes.

"James T. Kirk, Captain, USS Enterprise"

June 1988
Mirror Lake 4-Bunk Cabin

The Legend of Mirror Lake

Long ago, in an age when this land was pure and virgin, Indians were at one with nature and white men had not even crossed the great ocean leading to this continent. It was along the very shores of this lake that the ancient Vimacanju tribe dwelt. Like all primitive civilizations, the Vimacanju had their brief moment of glory, followed by a tumultuous downfall, and then silence…silence, and a closely kept memory of mystical exploits. Until tonight, the Vimacanju history and secret has been kept from the ears of white men. But the spirit of nature exerts an unrelenting force driving the secret into the open. Unlike the secrets of the past, revealed to man for his own good, but used for a destructive end instead, the legend of Mirror Lake can only be good. But there is one condition. It must fall on the ears of a noble traveler who knows the value of nature, and is so pure at heart, that only goodness can flow thereof. And so, the task has fallen into my hands. I am the last living man who knows the secret. Though my skin is red like the Indians, I learned to think like the white man in his schools. Since I became alienated from two worlds, I came to know the real world better. My lesson begins with this: forget your world and always search for better. I will proceed with the history, but it is done with a shaky hand. The only guidance I have is the enlightened vision of yesterday. Two travelers I saw: one with a lantern in hand and the other loyally following. This man with guiding light is the only pure-hearted member of the white race who has seen the truth in stony, rock caverns and jagged mountain peaks. This will be the next man to lay eyes on this text, and I have faith he will save my writings in secret.

When it began is not important to mention. It will suffice to say that countless generations have passed since then. The Vicamanjus started as a secret group chosen by the North Wind from the best members of each tribe. Every winter the wind would begin blowing and the local tribes would despair until the chosen hearkened to their destiny. This group of chosen started at an early age and grew up with the animals and elements. They were bare, but protected. Countless seasons passed before the chosen could converge for their purpose, but in time, they gained the wisdom to emerge. Yet, the more belligerent, local tribes did not realize the value of their message, and soon war began. The hosts of enemies assembled around this very lake and ruthlessly began to close in. It was on the ground beneath this cabin that a

316

handful of godly warriors made their stand. No enemy lived to witness the unprecedented engagement when thousands fell. In the end, only one Vicamanju lived. He escaped alone carrying the message of destiny. But wait! I hear a calling that beckons me to stop! But, alas, search for the lesson and you will find it within these pages. My moment in this spot has ended at last, and I may roam freely again in peace.

By firewater and smoke alone do you understand these words.

Unknown Author

May 21, 1994
Whitetail Cabin

The Twelfth Day

My name is Mike. Today is the twelfth day, the day I'm going to die. How do I know this? Let me explain....

I came to Whitetail twelve days ago with my wife, Julie, my brother, Steve, and his wife, Sally. The first two days Steve and I went fishing and hiking while Julie and Sal cooked us dinner over an open fire. On the morning of the third day, the four of us were at the visitor's center talking with some other campers. Then a park ranger approached us and asked if we were enjoying our stay so far.

We nodded, and he laughed and said, "They all seem to like the first two days fine, and then the flies come out."

"What flies?" Sal asked. She had always been afraid of everything.

The ranger, who was an old man, probably in his sixties, with white hair and a raspy voice, crouched closer to us and whispered, "You're the folks staying in ol' Whitetail Cabin, aren't you?"

"Yes," Steve answered. "Is there a problem?"

"Well, yes, son, there is," he said. "You see, every three days the big black flies come around by Whitetail. The whole swarm will attack you and eat you alive. Literally. The weird part is that they always leave a limb. You know, an arm, a leg, whatever they don't eat. I guess it's their way of leaving their mark. Someone always finds parts of the body. Sometimes they find it the next day, sometimes it's weeks later."

"Steve!" Sal exclaimed.

"It's alright," he assured her. "He's just trying to scare us."

When we turned our attention back to where the old man was standing, he was gone.

"Oh," said the family next to us, "that same old story again." The women smiled at us. "It's been going around this camp for years. Just a scary story to tell around the campfire."

We didn't think about the flies anymore. That is, until that night. It was our third night. We were already in bed; it was about 11:00. Sal announced she was going to the outhouse and that she would be right back.

We heard the door to the outhouse close and then we heard a scream.

"She probably saw a spider," Steve said. We all laughed and then fell asleep.

The next day, I was the first to wake up. I noticed that Sal wasn't in her bed. I thought that she had gotten up early to take a walk or something. It never occurred to me that she might not have come back to the cabin the night before. While walking to get firewood, I heard the outhouse door creaking as it swung open and closed. I looked inside and I still can't believe what I saw. Her clothes were strung out all over the walls and stained with blood. I opened my mouth to scream for Steve, but the words just wouldn't come out. I think that's when I fainted.

Steve and Julie found me about an hour later. The also found Sal's bloodied clothes and her foot. A limb. The flies mark. The next couple of days we all sat around wondering how this could have happened. I was the only one who seemed to consider the story of the flies.

On the sixth day, while we were all sitting around mourning Sal, Steve announced he was going to take a walk. I never thought it would be the last time I would see my brother.

When he didn't come back that day, Julie and I got worried and went out to look for him. We had only been looking for an hour when we saw it; his left leg was lying on the leaves in the woods.

For the next three days, Julie and I never left each other's side. We didn't even leave the cabin. I decided that mentioning my suspicion of the flies would only scare her and myself more. So on the ninth day, I didn't tell her what I feared would happen to one of us that night.

When I woke up on the tenth day and Julie wasn't there, I was terrified. Where would she go? Why would she go anywhere? My questions were answered that afternoon. I was on the rocks down by the lake and noticed that the water was discolored. It was red. My wife's arm was floating on the water. Her wedding ring was still on her finger.

Now it's the twelfth day. The day I'm going to die.

Mike R.

April 21, 1996
Gitchee Gumee Cabin

About the Glow-in-the-Dark Toilet Seat: I would like to clear this up for all of you since I know something about it. The psychopsuedophotoluminescent effect was first studied by the ahead-of-his-time naturalist, Derrick Liefenhaus. He lived at about the same time as Antony van Leewenhoek, the inventor of the microscope. The were friends. In letters Derrick Liefenhaus wrote to the Royal Society of Naturalists in the late 1600's, he described the "shining rings" of the outhouses of ancient Norsemen. Liefenhaus was the first to correctly postulate the cause of the glow. His work, however, like the careful elucidation of the patterns of inheritance by the equally brilliant Gregor Mendel, was not noticed by his contemporaries. The phenomenon was virtually forgotten until rediscovered by Benjamin Franklin in 1780. The glow of the toilet seat is caused by daylight, diffused after shining through the green corrugated fiberglass roofing material, falling upon the white toilet seat. Benjamin Franklin knew this effect from having seen it in the outhouses of the Mohican Indians of the era just preceding the arrival of Europeans to the eastern coast of North America. The effect only occurs during daylight hours with the door closed. The light, with all the visible wavelengths filtered out except for those responsible for the color of a glow-in-the-dark watch face or a glow-in-the-dark scary eyeball from a twenty-five cent 'toy-in-a-plastic-bubble' vending machine, strikes the toilet seat and gives it the glow-in-the-dark appearance. The reason the effect is sometimes present and sometimes not is that conditions must be just right! You can only see a glow-in-the-dark toilet seat when there is daylight! And you can't see it even in daylight if the door is propped open to let the smells out because the visible wavelengths other than the glow-in-the-dark eyeball color enter through the door and masks the phenomenon. There is a book about this seat and the psychopsuedophotoluminescent effect at the Visitor's Center ($12.85). Ask the helpful state park employee behind the desk for it.

The B. Family

January 8, 1978
Mirror Lake 8-Bunk Cabin
Hello there:

We are a group of fur trappers who have been chasing a downed Japanese Aviator for three months. We first encountered him near his wreck in the Aleutian Islands and have been trying to capture him ever since. But due to his oriental cunning, he has been able to elude us to this point. This chase has included almost two weeks in this fine park, after crossing Lake Superior on an ice floe. We have had the privilege of staying in no fewer than six, count 'em, six of these fine cabins, and are truly appreciative of the fine bases of operation that they provide.

Well, a few days ago we intercepted a coded transmission from the Aviator asking for an airlift back to the Land of the Rising Sun. After a day of decoding, we barely had time to throw our supplies together and charge on over here from Lily Pond and foil his plans. No sooner had we dropped our packs and organized a surveillance party, we heard the whirring of chopper blades. Without enough time to unpack the LAW rockets or heat-seeking missiles, we ran to the edge of the woods to observe the goings on. Yes, descending down to the ice was a big, two-motor copter and the Aviator was out waiting for them. Losing no time, all six of us charged out onto the ice with blazing automatic weapons in an effort to bring the bird down. After emptying a few clips in a brief volley, we succeeded in hitting the chopper's fuel tank, and KA-BOOM! Nothing was left of the chopper but spare parts. The Aviator was seen scurrying back into the woods, but an immediate search failed to uncover him. We are afraid it will be a long time before he surfaces again. So if, on one of those dark and windy nights, when that distant outhouse has beckoned, you hear a faint rustle in the bush and look to see only the pale reflection of a bottle-bottomed pair of spectacles, don't worry. It is not a bear or a wolf or a coyote or a leach or even a snowy owl. It is only a four and-a-half foot tall Aviator with only a samurai sword for protection, no match for a red-blooded US (or Canadian or French) citizen. Just grab the little beastie, put him in a stout footlocker with a dish of rice and send him UPS blue-label, collect to:

Her Majesty's Secret Service
Quebec, Canada

Your efforts will be generously rewarded. For the six of us, we are needed for a mission in Keewatin.

And in Memoriam: Marc E., who sacrificed himself so the rest of us could be free.

Inspector Cleausou, Chuck LeBurr,
Baron vonBalachiara du'Ranior,
Mickey the Courageous, LaRogue, & Janeen

August 22, 1997
Section 17 Cabin

The Board

Long ago he was left to rot—
Spiked to the ground, with a group of his friends.
The Board.
Trodden upon daily by his persecutors
He suffers so that their feet may stay clean.
But, unlike his brother boards
He alone has the power to wreak vengeance.
No, he cannot move,
But he need not.
For, if he wants, they will come.

Oh, yes, they will come.
So he waits
Silent
Sinister
Always watching for a weak knee,
Or a wobbly ankle.
Then, he transforms—into a limp noodle—and
Secure footing vanishes, like mist into the night
And he screams in silent laughter
As they pitch face first into the mucky mire.
And he watches in grim satisfaction
As they gather their soiled belongings
And drag themselves away, beaten and defeated.
And he steels himself once again,
To watch—and wait.

Note: The Board is not a fictional character. Look for him at the fifth step of the fourth boardwalk from the junction of the trail to the Carp River Road, on your way back to the parking lot.

Brian H.

August 25, 1982
Buckshot Cabin

To our "pleasant surprise," it was discovered that "Grizzly Mouse" (whatever number) does indeed live on. We were concerned after reading past entries that the original settler of Buckshot may have met permanent demise. However, at an undetermined hour of early morning, "Grizzly" made himself known by unintentionally landing on Jack's arm with his four slightly chilly, clammy feet. Both Jack and "Grizzly" were surprised, but it was "Grizzly" that scurried quickly off. However, "Grizzly," never once fazed by the encounter, continued about his business with no delay. We became rather jealous when we heard the clinking of ice cubes in a tall glass and munching of caviar on thin crackers perked our ears. "Grizzly" sure knows how to do things in a big way. I think the party broke about dawn.

Jean

June 25, 1985
Lake Superior Cabin

We, too, had an encounter with the notorious cabin mouse—he is a massive animal, weighing a full eight pounds if he's an ounce. He consumed four sticks of salami, one bag of gorp, and he downed one gallon of Tang. I suggest complete respect when dealing with this fellow-he is an awesome beast.

Sunburst Youth Homes Group

September 19, 1980
Buckshot Cabin

Larry & Judy K.

1978
Buckshot Cabin

My Turn

I've hiked these trails for thirty years
I've seen my share of trials and tears
I've heard the North Wood's loud lament
My days on earth have been well spent
This cabin's been my only home
The hikers here my ways have known
The crumbs and scraps they leave around
I take as rent to use these grounds
I let them use this cabin spare
It shelters them from storm and bear
They meet me with the trap and gun
I live in fear `til they move on
Go easy travelers on this road
We share a troubled heavy load
The forest creatures live here, too
Don't kill us to make room for you.

"Grizzly Mouse"

July 23, 1983
Buckshot Cabin

It all began back in '67! I had a peanut butter sandwich next to my bed. I woke up at 0300 hours to grab some quick grub. A dirty mouse had eaten my Jif sandwich! I knew from that moment on that my life would not be an average one. After months of training, I could set a trap without getting my thumb.

I, would be ready, for anything....

Sixteen years later, after getting contracts everywhere, from London to Bombay, my phone rings. I let it ring four times. I slowly reached to pick it off the tan cradle. "Is Joe Bendzinsky there." Wrong number. Six months later the phone rings again. "This is the Porcupine Mountain State Park." I knew in a second that this was the code name for the Porcupine Mountain State Park.

So they wanted a certain mouse, called "Grizzly Mouse," stopped. So once again, I had become, "Mousenary." I came in from the

west. Everything looks normal. I rechecked the Top Secret pictures of "Griz." I was sure I had seen that hideous face before. Then I figured it out. He was my roommate last night at the Little Carp. I should have known by the way he got into my pack and devoured my noodles, raw. He's probably got this place bugged...Yep, I knew it. Flies. Bugs alright, lots of them.

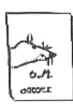

Well, I've got the traps set and my thumbs splinted. Now all I have to do is wait for him to make his move. I know he is a sucker for chewy granola bars, his favorite.

Next morning: "G.M." took all the bait from the traps and most of another package of dry noodles and shuffled off to Buffalo. The chase is on!

Dave H., "Mousenary at Large"

August 11, 1978
Section 17 Cabin

This cabin was built on the site where a clutch of black bears attacked and killed a group of Dominican monks in 1758. Some believe that the spirits of these mangled monks have inhabited bears and other forest animals of the upper peninsula ever since, and have given rise to the superstition of: "Pack a loose backpack and be carried off by the Wurdalek."

If we ignored the unearthly screams we heard all night as we huddled in the corner, a pleasant time was had by all.

Elizabeth, Gary, and dog, Oscar

October 29, 1994
Greenstone Falls Cabin

Today concludes our first day of searching for Dan M., known better as "Little Dan M." by those who know him better. We rose early this morning to look for him. He wasn't in the outhouse nor at the parking lot. We have become less experienced since last year. We forgot to bring candles and broke our lantern mantle. But the question remains, did Little Dan fall into the outhouse hole as he christened the Rodent Ranch Outhouse? Did he simply disappear into the trackless wilderness? As he is our friend, we thought a search was in order. Of course, it would be madness to start our search on an empty belly, so we ate a hearty breakfast. We set out at about 10:00 in tight formation, with our packs loaded with the necessary rescue gear, primarily gorp and "Wilbur's" chocolate pieces. Of course, those who don't know "Little Dan" would think us unfeeling to not search beginning at daybreak, but knowing Dan's love for leaning back in a chair and beginning a tale breezily:

"And no shit...there I was..." and concluding with, "It was an awesome experience, not to be repeated."

We decided that he must have gained from last night's experience, even if lost in the woods overnight. We tried to take our minds off our concern and chatted with forced lightheartedness on the trail; Chel mentioned a rare fern, John talked of laying gravel on the new driveway, Karen did her best to remain cheerful. I, of course, bore a heavy responsibility as the organizer of this gathering. Certainly the map hadn't shown the whole park, but I'd hoped Dan could find South Boundary Road. Well, at least he didn't have to endure the squeaky beds and the abundance of rodents that Greenstone is famed for. Our plan was simple. To comb the woods as thoroughly as we could, while trying not to let it spoil our good time. We surveyed the park from Summit Peak. No sign of Dan. We scouted the Lily Pond area and found not a whisper of him from the passing hikers. One mentioned seeing boot holes in the muck approaching the Cross Trail, but we preferred not to think about the import of the words. I must bear the blame, I suppose. I invited him. I thought after last year, he'd do fine on his own. We returned exhausted from spending an Indian summer day searching, searching for Little Dan. Our hearts sank when we opened the door. The woodpile was still piled high, a sure sign that Little Dan had not found his way here. We are cooking spaghetti now for we must retain our strength. We talk of pet turtles to distract ourselves. We note alpenglow on the clouds in the east to assure ourselves that it will soon be dark. Perhaps using the flashlight to write our entry in the journal was a poor idea, one of many it seems. When darkness comes, the search will resume. I spent several hours saving John and Big Dan from the Connection Trail last year. I certainly hadn't expected them to handle the Cross Trail on their own. And what a joy it was to return to the Big Carp 6-bunk and see their smiling faces. I hope this year things turn out as well. Karen is flaming the stove now to save the flashlight. I'm pulling on my wet shoes to begin the awful task. God help us all.

I'm sorry if this has dampened your spirits, Greenstone travelers. I hope your trip is as wonderful as we wished our had been, and may still be, if only I can hear that bespeckled little guy with the grizzled beard and nasal voice open the door and say:

"Hey, you weren't worried, were you? Let me tell you what happened man. No shit, this is the honest truth..."

Head idiot and commander signing off.

NOTE: As it turned out, Dan M. found a "really great breakfast buffet in Ironwood. All you can eat for $3.99." I think we felt better when we thought he was lost.

Unknown Author

September 6, 1995
Little Carp Cabin

Just a comment to John who wrote in this log, at the end of August, how "disappointed" he was at the general look of the cabin and its associated carvings. He should remember that the park doesn't check IQ levels or give quizzes as to one's moral/ethical standing with regards to the park. Rather than let it ruin my time here, I choose to let their etchings and my imagination tell a short story of these people. For instance, on the seat of the great, wooden, homemade chair, Mike has deeply carved his name. You see, Mike (in my mind) is a rather large, lumbering behemoth. He walked in with a couple of friends, carrying a case of beer in each paw and a backpack loaded with Fritos. You must understand that Mike spends most of his time either watching wrestling on TV or working on his car. This trip was a big step for him. I'm sure it brought him closer to nature since I can envision Mike baying at the moon outside after drinking that beer! By the way, the upside of this story is that, somehow, Mike fell in love this trip. The next time you take a trip to the outhouse, please notice on the right wall that Sally has somehow gotten the attention of Mike's few brain cells, and captured the big lug's heart.

Then we have Fawn. Fawn was not Fawn when she arrived here, but Meagan was Meagan prior to being Fawn. Meagan and her family are usually more of the Minoqua type adventurers. Meagan hiked in carrying a suitcase and purse and wearing what used to be sparkling white tennis shoes. Standing in front of this cabin she dropped her purse and suitcase, and with a vertical shake of her head to emphasize each word, she said for the hundredth time, "Oh—my—God." Meagan then spent the next half hour running around the cabin looking for an electrical outlet. By this time, her spiked bangs, which most of the time appear to shoot out from her forehead, were drooping over her eyes. With a pronounced stamp of her foot she decided then and there to change and be a person of more depth and understanding. To evolve into someone with stamina and true grit. To crown this most momentous occasion, she changed her name to "Fawn" and carved it on the lower end of the west bunk! Unfortunately, there is a downside to this story. As Fawn still refused to use the outhouse, and wouldn't think of squatting in the bush, her bowels revolted and she had to be Med-A-Vac'd to the hospital. Later in life she would marry a rich lawyer, drive a Lexus, and live in Lake Forest, Illinois never to return here again. See, a happy ending anyway.

So, the long and the short of it is this; these people are unfortunately a part of our society. If their only impact is a scrawled name on wood, then I can deal with that. After all, they did manage not to burn the cabin to the ground! Hopefully, some of these people did come away with a little more soul than what they had. I hope!

Rich & Pam

July 25, 1997
Speaker's Cabin

Teresa laughed at me when I showed her that I was going to bring a sling-shot on our trip. She's not laughing now. On our first day coming into the cabin area, the weather was wet. The ground was at best spongy, and usually muddy. We walked and I carried the cooler. Teresa had the picnic table, dinner service, lawn chairs, portable generator, TV and VCR. I thought that this was a little much, but she was willing to carry it in, so OK. We reached the stream and behind us Teresa heard a "growl." I turned and there, coming down the stream, was the biggest bear I had ever seen. As the man in charge, I made the critical decisions necessary in such a crisis and took action immediately. I dropped everything and ran. Having the key, I was able to get into the cabin and close the door. Here, I made myself useful by cowering in the corner until dark. It was then that I realized that Teresa had the flashlight. I began to wonder what had happened to her. Fortunately, some nice, prior camper had left a box of wine and I soon was able to forget my fears. When I awoke next morning, I was still alone. I had to rough it by putting one mattress on top of me as a blanket. I ate jelly packets and waited for what would occur next. About 2:00 P.M. or so (I don't know exactly as I had dropped my watch), Teresa showed up. She looked a bit tattered and dirty, and when I had finished chewing her out for staying out all night "who knows where" and having all of the provisions with her, I insisted she go to the lake and clean up. She didn't seem to be in what I thought would have been the proper mood. And no amount of my forgiveness of her lack of attention to my needs would bring her into a romantic frame of mind. When she returned from the lake she told me how she had been forced to barricade herself behind the TV and VCR using the lawn chairs to hold off the bear. She had eventually had to abandon these amenities as they proved ineffective in bear defense. She had spent the night in a tree where she held the bear off using my slingshot. Having not first secured our backpacks as she might have done with a little forethought, she was now unable to account for the whereabouts of our food and other necessities. Needless to say, the trip was ruined for me. I just want to go home.

Dave & Teresa

October 1992
Speaker's Cabin

Saw the Speaker's ghost last night
And it seems he'll come again
Was an October day of mists and rain
That drew him from his den

He spoke no word but looked around
As chiefly for some thing
And knocked against the counter
Where my flashlight should have been

I raised off my bunk alert
Each move he took intent
But finding not of what he sought
His ghastly image spent

This all could last but for a second
He turned and was not there
All seemed as it had been before
Except for me in my prolonged stare

J.S.F.

July 13, 1993
Gitchee Gumee Cabin

I had been convinced that the cold and dark would last for eternity. I and the rest of the crew, except for Abrams, had been entombed below deck since...since that day. We all told Captain Abrams that the ship just didn't feel right, she seemed to have a yearning for the deep. And then to think that Abrams would leave us with her! I shall not rest 'til Abrams pays his due.

But by some force I have risen to the world of the living. A world whose presence I had given up for lost. But, alas, by some mad stroke, I find myself again in Gitchee Gumee, but a warm and dry rest.

My guests, I find for the most part, amusing. But the children, the children! I never had a mind for children. I find myself drifting to the edge of the forest when there are children, to peer through the windows just beyond their light. Perhaps I shall hence forth make the children aware of my ghostly being. A sight I am sure they will find less than enchanting.

But I will not forget Abrams. It seems my search will be limited to Gitchee Gumee. Perhaps he or his kin will be on my guest list. I shall check this journal. I am prepared to reach beyond my world and grasp the life of...of any who may be in support of my captain.

My words will again find their way to this journal as it is my intent to possess the mind and pen of another of my guests.

Nameless Being Over My Left Shoulder

October 11, 1994
Mirror Lake 2-Bunk Cabin

I wouldn't have believed it if I hadn't seen it with my own two eyes. Yesterday, on a hike to Summit Peak (actually on our way back along South Mirror Lake Trail) off in the distance, I saw a large, dark shape move off up the hill. I turned to my wife and said, "Did you see that? I think it was a bear on top of that ridge. A big bear." Well, she hadn't seen it and gave me hell for most of the hike back. Once back at the cabin she continued to kid me. That is until, that evening around dusk, when we went to the lake for water.

As we walked down to the lake we both felt a strange presence. As if something was watching or following us from along the ridge just north of the cabin. We heard a couple of twigs snap from up that direction and I told my wife (and myself) that it was nothing. "Probably just a squirrel, or chipmunk, or something."

Later that night, after dinner, as we played cards by the dim candlelight, I got that funny feeling again, as if someone was staring at me from behind a tree. That's when I saw him, it, whatever! A huge, dark, shadowy figure. He moved swiftly away from the back window of the cabin. Then there he was again, moving past the side window after stopping briefly to peer in one more time. My wife shrieked as I jumped up, wide-eyed, to check the door latch. As if it could stop such a creature.

Let me tell you this for certain. This was no bear that had come to visit for a late night snack. Nor was this any Northwoods prowler coming around to case our cabin. It was, in fact, more beast than man. He had long, shaggy hair covering his body from head to toe. I guess to measure him at close to seven feet tall, as he had to crouch considerably to stare in through our windows. Oh yes, I have heard these stories of him before, but I never truly believed in him. Until now, that is. Because now I know. He's out there.

Steve & Beth

September 24, 1979
Speaker's Cabin

The flames from the campfire blazed brightly, forcing back the thick blackness of the night. The night air was chill—my companion and I were city folks and not used to braving the elements. Still, we'd put in a hard day of hiking and exploring the wilderness around us, appreciating the views that nature had to offer.

Our bones were weary as we rested by the fire sipping Drambuie. It was a black night, no stars shone, and gradually the wind died down and the incessant roaring of the waves diminished. And an eerie stillness overtook the woods.

"This place must have been holy for the Indians," I remarked. My companion nervously poked the fire, as unfamiliar sounds from deep in the forest echoed round. The flames jumped brighter, their glow reflecting off the smooth rocks we'd set nearby, Indian artifacts from much earlier times. How odd it was to hold a rock, feeling the smooth, round grips, which had been carved there by another living soul, possibly centuries ago. It was easy to imagine the Indians living here in this mighty place, long ago.

And suddenly, the wind picked up and fed the fire, flames danced, the waves began to crash in a frenzy, the wind howled through the trees, and we realized we were intruders in a sacred spot. The flames glowed off the artifacts' surface until they appeared red hot, as though the fire was coming from them. My companion and I exchanged glances. We knew what we must do. Trancelike, we carried the artifacts down the steep hill to the lake, and gently returned them to a resting place where they would remain undisturbed, with only the water and wind to caress them.

Slowly the waves subsided, and the lake became calm once again. Now the forest sounds were gentle and contented. My companion stirred the dying embers, one last flame shot up, flickered and died, and then feeling tranquil, we went to sleep.

P.K.

October, 1990
Speaker's Cabin

This is no tale of a specter pale
Or the work of a mind-warping pill
Not a tale of a ghost or a Sam McGee roast
But a nobody people call Bill.
He was one of four who opened the door
Of Speaker's Cabin last night
After backpacking there, by a flashlight's glare
And Loren's night-light sight.

With Murriel and Beth, all four risking death
Staggered under their packs
On through the gloom as dark as a tomb
Without a thought of going back.
The cabin's chill was welcome to Bill
And the others so late at night
Yet their spirits soared as a fire roared
And they basked in its warming light.
Soon warm grub and a tot from the tub
Restored their usual state
Except for Bill, who's over the hill
He yawned, "It's getting late."
The air got stale as the odor of jail
So a window was opened a mite
And the aroma of meat along with the heat
Went rapidly into the night.
The bill of fare attracted a bear
A huge beast with claws like a rake
Which whipped over the sill and sank into Bill
Leaving three stunned pals in his wake.
Now often it's said with a sense of dread
When the three friends return to the site
That they see old Bill float in over the sill
A most peculiar sight.
His smile is still there, though he's covered with hair
From the bear which dragged him away
He just picks up his steak, gives his tail a shake
And quietly goes his way.

Luge, Beth, Ma, & Bill

May 8, 1984
Mirror Lake 8-Bunk Cabin

There is a Legend that says once you have written in the log book, you are bound to return to this spot and write in this book again. Now I have done what you have done. Once at Mirror Lake, always at Mirror Lake!

Kelly M.

Transformations

November 8, 1992
Speaker's Cabin

Tom and Helen have left, and I'm here by myself for one more night. It's more and more difficult to get people together for these little forays into the woods. We all have more commitments and less time as we get older. Surely that's not an improvement over the way we were ten years ago. It's as if we've been consumed by our jobs.

But we have money now that we didn't have ten years ago. We have benefits and insurance and some of life's rough edges have been padded. We are compensated for the time and energy we devote to work. I suppose it's up to each one of us to decide if what we've gained is an adequate replacement for what we've lost.

In the summer of 1988, I came up here about once a month. It felt necessary at the time.

But nothing is as it was, and what was necessary then is not necessary now. I am not who I was then, and neither are you.

Of my friends, I am the one who plans things like this. Is that because I am foolishly clinging to the past, trying to recreate good times when no such thing is possible, unwilling to move on? Or is that because I don't believe in disposable friendships? Why do I ask too many unanswerable questions?

I am haunted by thoughts of mortality here, brought on by the timeless lake and the sense this place has been like this for thousands of years and will be like this for thousands more years after I'm gone. It seems to bring each of our passionate dances of life into perspective. I'm trying to remember Bogart's great line near the end of Casablanca, something like, "It doesn't take a genius to understand that the problems of a few little people like you and me doesn't amount to a hill of beans in this crazy world…." But it's still hard to accept that everything you are and everything you know will be left behind, that your stay here is purely temporary, that everything in the world existed before you came into it, and will for the most part be unaffected by the fact of your existence.

And thoughts like that make me wonder what I'm doing working at a job that means nothing to me. How many people can afford the luxury of a meaningful job? Somebody has to do all the stupid little jobs. But to spend so much of my life doing that? It's not worth it.

The reason I work at my stupid, little job, and probably the reason most people work at their stupid little jobs, is for security. The pay and benefits form a safety net between you and catastrophe. It's a little scary to be out there in the world without that net. But if you believe in yourself and in doing what you want to be doing, you don't have a choice. When your life is over, saying that you could have been a contender will be small consolation.

See, I get this different perspective on everything when I come up here. The isolation and the simplicity make it easier to see and understand a lot of things.

Warren

May 25, 1975
Section 17 Cabin

It's impossible to put to words the emotions this trip to nature has brought out.

When we planned this in January, I didn't really believe it would turn out as beautiful as it did. Even the black flies and mosquitoes couldn't touch the wonder we all felt towards this place.

If this isn't what life is, it should be. I've seen life enhanced in the few days I've been here in this forest. The naturalness of it all was almost too much to take in at once. I feel drunk with the beauty around me.

When I came here, I said I wanted this place for my own, but now I realize that no money on earth could secure what I feel inside about the mountains. What I feel is mine, for the experience, and can never be taken away.

Bud

August 28, 1997
Little Carp Cabin

I am sitting on one of these enormous logs by Lake Superior. I will not be waxing eloquent on the beauty and bounty of nature. I will say that the size of these virgin hemlocks is making me want to see the giant redwoods and sequoias in California; one more thing on my list in life. My theme for this trip (for the first time into the Porkies) is to "do it now." It seems like I have spent much time in my life saying "I want to do that…someday." Now I am trying to say "Let's do that now." It probably comes from my mother. I am helping take care of her as she slowly dies. She is not that old (seventy). I am not that old (forty). I don't feel old enough to be left without my mother. She has guided me through all the hard times in my life and I feel lost, alone, wondering who will guide me through her death. She had melanoma (use your sunscreen!) and it's the brain radiation that left her how she is—no memory and fragments of a personality. It is her slow descent from the joys of life that is so painful to watch. But I have learned a lot—that it is possible to connect on totally different levels. It is the loss of connection that make diseases of the brain so unbearable.

Here come the loons swimming by. And I am determined to see that bald eagle. I lack the patience to wait; I want it all now. I see everything in terms of what I can bring back as joy for my mother. Well, maybe "everything" is a bit dramatic. I don't know why I am writing all this. It is not what I sat down to do, and it certainly is not the prevailing color of this book. It started with the "do it now" theme. And trying to balance the "do it now" with the "be in the moment." And somehow death, or even the fragrance of death, brings each of the grains of sand into clear and distinct focus. What are all the ways I can keep telling my mother that I love being her daughter, because I do not know if she can hear me. Did I tell her enough before, when I knew she could hear me? I see fish in the lake jumping up to get the bugs. Still no bald eagle. I like the cabin just fine, clean or dirty, wood or no wood, carvings or no carvings. It's all just fine. I leave here still dreaming about the circle of life, where a child becomes a parent, and the children grow and finally the parent becomes the child.

Robin

September 3, 1997
Little Carp Cabin

What I feel about this park and coming here on a "regular" basis is nearly the same as everyone else's. Nothing really changes here. Robin...talks about the circle of life. People don't care for all of life's changes along that circle. I have a feeling that most of the people in this book, including myself, prefer the inner portion of the circle. Coming to this cabin in the park brings every one of us back to the center of the circle, the part of the circle that doesn't move. The essence and make-up of the center is reflected in a lot of these people's reactions to this outdoor experience. All people talk about, as being their favorite parts of the trip, are based in the center, stable part of the circle — family, kids, spouses, love, kindness, sharing, friendship, goodness, fun, humanity, decency, and on and on. Point is, the wilderness experience helps bring life back to its essence for all of us. That is why we keep coming back here. That is what makes backpackers so unique.

Geoff S.

1971
Lily Pond Cabin

The life in eternity knows
no bondage, decay, or sorrow.
It is the everlasting and ever-renewing self-affirmation
of conscious, unlimited divinity.
My mission is to help you inherit
the hidden treasure of the self.

There is no creature which is not destined
for the supreme goal,

> As there is no river which is not winding
> its way towards the sea.

Meher B.

October 2, 1969
Mirror Lake 4-Bunk Cabin

Dad went fishing and caught two dozen splake. Saturday, dad went again with mom and caught eleven trout. Mom almost gave up cause she never caught any, when just then she hauled in a fifteen inch speckled. She was so excited she almost fell in. I guess there is such a thing as beginner's luck, cause this was her first time and she beat us all.

K.G.K

June 8, 1995
Big Carp 6-Bunk Cabin

I have to be honest. From this trip's conception, it was a "forced march" on my part. I am NOT a huge nature fanatic—the last time I went camping I slept in an automobile. This was supposed to be our family's last hurrah before I leave home for college and for some reason, the thought of "roughing it" in the woods for five days with my family did not thrill me. However, I have seen the error of my ways. This has turned out to be one of the most wonderful, hysterical and memorable weeks of my life. I have seen and experienced things I was not aware existed and the fact that I was able to share these awakenings with my loved ones makes it even more precious. I am happy to say that I think Big Carp 6-Bunk has become an annual family tradition. This makes me happy. WHOA! Where did all that come from!

Katie & Co.

June 18, 1984
Greenstone Falls Cabin

I am a deeply troubled man who has come here under the auspices of friends and their sincere efforts at protecting me have worked. Like Thoreau, in my own small way and in a short period of time, have indeed communed with nature to an extent that I haven't since my childhood. My personal level of relaxation, which by virtue of my personality, habits, and profession is basically nil, has expanded to levels which I have previously thought incomprehensible. The exhilaration of catching my first trout, the romance of hiking through forests, the camaraderie of one of my closest friends and a dear man, have given me hope that I can put many of my problems behind me, and have the energy and direction to fulfill whatever my dreams may be.

W.D.

November 18, 1996
Speaker's Cabin

    I live five hundred miles from here. I've never been here, in the park, before. I live in Lower Michigan near thousands of acres of state land that is hunted by far too many hunters. I went all out, for me, a simple factory worker. All new everything. Sleeping bag, backpack, new thirteen inch hunting boots, new gortex hunting suit, and a dozen other gadgets. The information sent me said creek crossing necessary. When I bought my thirteen inch, $130 boots, the extra liners were back-ordered until December 4. No problem I thought. Well, I have a thirty-one inch inseam and all but about three inches of it got wet crossing the stream to get to this cabin. I hope it is so deep due to recent rains and snow melting. Radio on my way up said four more days like today; very windy, highs in the twenties. I got to the cabin around 11:00 A.M. and am still trying to dry boots out at 2:00 P.M. I've never backpacked anything, anywhere before so I found out on the hill after the stream crossing that my eighty-five pound pack was very heavy. Got everything in it though— except spare boots that are in the truck. They are only eight inches tall but I'd like to have them to put on rather than some extra socks. From the park office to the parking spot for this cabin, I counted thirty-six cars and trucks parked along South Boundary Road. Looks and sounds like home hunting pressure. I did see and talk to two fellows loading a skinned and quartered deer into their truck. It looked big bodied to me, but they said small rack and wouldn't show me the horns. Huh? Checked new, high-tech boot liners, and if they continue to dry at this remarkable rate, maybe they'll be able to wear out on the 22nd. I brought a camcorder and a camera, both of which are still dry. The video will be very helpful to my fellow nimrods back home. About 3:00 P.M. I put on dry socks and semi-dry boots and walked along Speaker's Creek. Found skeleton of small, dead deer and one fresh deer track. And the fact that even Speaker's Creek is about six inches over my boot height. Used a stick to measure this time. I would like to try to walk to the river and see the falls. Ah-ha! Tomorrow I'll try the garbage sacks for waders to cross! Could cross on one of the large logs, but I'm middle aged, overweight, and very out of shape. I had a bad experience hunting coon one night several years ago by myself in December. I fell off a log crossing a swollen stream and thought I was going to freeze up before I made it back to the truck. No more logs while alone! The people before me left an excellent supply of firewood, for which I am very thankful, being wet and all. About 5:00 P.M., while waiting for the proper time to get a picture of the sunset over the lake, I decided to add to the woodpile. The saw blade was broken. Sure wish those fine folks would have taken it to the ranger when checking out. I'll do just that for the next renter. It seemed like a long day, so about 6:30 I went to bed. At 9:30 I woke up wide awake! I put a log or two into the stove, lit the candle, opened the mixed nuts and trail mix, and started writing. I've worked twenty-three years at a job to feed my family and make do. Most of those years I had a second job also. I've been married twenty-three years to the same wonderful gal. We have two great daughters. Both extremely brilliant and good-looking. They are nineteen and sixteen years old now. The younger one has been a vegetarian for two years now. They both have perfect, 4.0 grade point averages. The oldest is a sophomore in college, Dean's list and all. The wife and I told them very early on that their grades would have to get them money for college, as with both of us working, we just pay the bills. There's just not enough money for kids like mine for schooling. Even after the grants and scholarships, she'll be twenty thousand in debt. We bought them both cars and pay their insurance, and will try to continue to do so as long as they stay away from drugs and out of trouble and in school. The Lord knows you can't get anywhere today without education. It seems so unfair. My oldest daughter had a couple of friends who skipped school one day in their senior year. One was several months pregnant. They were drinking with a couple of older, wild boys, had a car accident, and got huge insurance settlements. The girl who owned the car was messing around in the backseat when the other girl wrecked the car. Their insurance companies paid each of the other girl's settlements. I'm very proud of my girls. They don't use drugs or alcohol, and have suffered the wrath of their peers for it. My company just laid me off for two months and the future there is questionable. I had just bought a farm from my cousin and was trying to sell our underground home, to get rid of a second payment a month. Couldn't sell the house so I had to sell the farm. Just four years from being a centennial farm (same family for a hundred years). My dad died of Alzheimers the year before last after two years of misery. I just about lost it seeing him that way and having to see to his affairs. We were very close. He was my only steady hunting companion. Now I have to check on mom every day. She is eighty-six years old, still living alone, but not for long I am afraid. My wife and girls are filling in for me with mom. This little trip was a whim! Having to sell the farm, work at the refrigeration plant, shaky, and having some back problems, I decided to quit my second job selling guns at Gander Mountain, take this two month layoff, and watch the grass grow. Oops, bad phrase. Snow fly. I've taken well over one hundred Michigan white tail with a gun and bow, and as of this year, hunting isn't fun anymore. The last couple of years I've had a ball helping youngsters and a couple of women get their first deer. I tried buying a new twenty-two caliber and getting back to squirrel hunting. All my wife and I ate the first two years of marriage were squirrel, rabbit, and deer. Just like deer hunting around home, the woods are overcrowded with people trying to capture the enjoyment of hunting. I have a friend who has gone to Idaho each of the last fourteen years for a five week elk and deer hunt. He meets with friends from Idaho and California for over a month of outdoor experiences. He's asked me to go along each year, but you guessed it, money and time. He's single and self-employed. Now even if I had the money and all sorts of time, I'd miss the wife and kids too much to be away half that long. My dad had a 7th grade education and mom, a two year college degree. I have a brother who is the only living of the first four jet fighter pilot instructors, who after having polio while in the Air Force, furthered his education and today is a millionaire. I have a brother who is quite high up in the civil service in the state of Michigan, and a sister that has been a registered nurse and instructor. She was over the LA county poison center in California. And she became a medical malpractice lawyer. Due to migraine headaches and arthritis and such, she now works in a hospital transferring medical files here in Michigan. The old saying, life is a mystery, is true. In another thirty-some years, I will meet my father's fate, the same as his father before him. Grandpa used to be tied in bed while his seven sons and three daughters labored in factory and farm all day. Grandma couldn't control him in their absence any other way, and there were no nursing homes or medicaid. Well, it's 11:15 P.M. now and I'm still awake and (if you are still reading) I'm still rambling on. My spelling and penmanship are really bad, I know! That's probably why I really like the spell check on the computer. To whom ever reads this: I hope that God blesses you and yours. I hope that you can find satisfaction in what you have done and what you have, as I have during this dark night. It seems to be the American way to want just a little more. My dad said I was different from my siblings because I liked the doing. Once again, the older I get, the smarter he seems. Perhaps my daily caring for mom, that seems such a burden, is a gift of endearment that I've overlooked. Tomorrow I pack all of this stuff out of here and go home to cherish my wealth.

Clarence L.

June 13, 1989
Mirror Lake 8-Bunk Cabin

I'm happy to have the last entry in this log book, because this place has always been so special to me. I feel like in some ways I was born here, eighteen years ago almost exactly, and I came with three friends from camp and we entered Mirror Lake by Government Peak Trail, which I thought was boring back then, considering there was no view back then (perhaps even now) from the top of Government Peak. When we came into Mirror Lake, we entered via the old location of the North Mirror Lake Trail, which emptied into the Lake about one hundred yards east of where it does now, smack into the huge white pine which is now a snag (not quite given up the ghost at this date, mind you). I saw a few green needles and a few branches on the northwest side. That tree, which was vibrant then, and commanding with dignity the north shore of the lake, struck me as the most magnificent living thing that

I had ever seen. And I was in awe, in wonder, no, perhaps rapture. It was the beginning of a long history of love of trees to which I am committed to this day. The four of us camped that night further east down the north shore in that cozy grove of hemlocks (with a big yellow birch now under full attack by woodpeckers) which is framed on the lake by two pair of oh-so-slightly lean-ing, white pine giants. What a great spot to camp! I see you can still camp there. I camped there again six months later, October 1971, and it was the first time I used my backpack, which is sitting next to the stove, drying out at this moment. What a trusty pack it has been! That trip there were five of us, and for some reason, the oars had been left in the old wooden boat (all four of them—four oar locks in the boat), and we rowed over to the big rock exposed at the east end of the lake. The fall colors were breathtaking. We felt as if the rock were an alter, and for years, I toyed with an imaginary scenario of myself in old age, climbing up the rock to meet my Maker. On our return trip to replace the boat and oars at the unoccupied cabin, we disturbed a Great Blue Heron in one of the small inlets on the north shore, and it flew right off the prow of the boat, like an angel ascending from the calm waters of the lake. Returning to our campsite, we had a dinner of peanut butter and honey from Gerry tubes, and it still tastes as good tonight as it did then, and all of the thousands of times in between. The next trip here, one year later in September of 1972, we actually rented the cabin, a little different cast of characters, and at the time this place cost $4.00 per night. I went swimming one afternoon on a dare, and it was so cold that I raced back to the cabin and jumped in my sleeping bag to warm up. I asked a friend to build a fire for me, and he wasn't very experienced in the woods, and he couldn't get it lit. I'm very close to this friend still, and he told me ten years later, after we had been separated by cir-cumstances, that he had been profoundly ashamed when he couldn't light the fire to help me warm up. As if he had let me down when I had asked for help. That he had recalled the incident and it meant so much to him to try and care for me touched me deeply, and resolidified our friendship. This place can do that, I think, help you see who your friends are, show one what sharing and caring is, show one what serenity and power and action are. This place is one I will always cherish. To all those who have been here, or work here, or will come: we are together in this peace.

Jim

July 1, 1992
Little Carp Cabin

    I am here with my ten year old son, Jonathan.... I hope to instill in my son a love and respect for wilderness, and a self-confidence and self-sufficiency that only the wilderness can teach. But will there be any place for wild things by the time he is a man? I don't know. It's easy to despair and lose hope. But out here I am renewed and again my will to fight for a place that man has not and will not manipulate for profit burns anew. The fight to preserve the wilderness is the fight to preserve the human spirit. It cannot be surrendered....

It's strange. This world is far more real to me than back in "civilization." No dead-end job, mortgage, car repair, etc. All that stuff that has to be endured to obtain the "good" things in life. I would trade them in a heartbeat for a cabin in the woods and a trap line. I have no regrets when it comes to my family, I only wish that when they come of age, they will choose careers that truly have meaning, and I hope they will always cherish the places where the wild things are, even as I do.

Mike & Jon G.

July 19, 1996
Buckshot Cabin

I'm leaving this morning. I've learned a few lessons during my stay: of course, I wanted my vacation to be the perfect time, but the flies were getting to me on Thursday, eating into my psyche. I was reminded of the black and white horror movies my mother used to watch where people were OK in their cabin, but if they opened the door and went out, some mysterious and unconquerable force would get them. Those flies were waiting for me.

I decided to trek the three miles to my car and drive to see the waterfalls along the Black River (actually, it looks more like root beer). Everyone in the park was waving flies away. But it rained on the way to the falls, and thank goodness, there was a let up of the infestation.

But until my experience became more pleasant, I was harboring ideas of checking into a cheap motel. I dreaded the thought of coming back here where my return was awaited....

But low and behold! Back at the Porkies a fog had blown in, it had rained, and the files were gone! The fog in the woods was beautiful. Lake Superior was restless, casting up waves which crashed over rocks where I had sat days before. I sat until it got dark, watching them and meditating on my day, my fears, and the trip.

Into my mind came the words, "There's no place like home, there's no place like home." I thought of the movie The Wizard of Oz and looked for a theme in it, which would provide me with a lesson for my trip. Dorothy had unpleasant experiences and nice ones, and all the while she wanted to go home. As the viewers watching the movie, we find out she was actually home the whole time because her trip to Oz was a part of her dream.

I realized it was only the judgement of my experiences as good or bad that kept me from seeing that I was home. Monday and Tuesday I thought were nice and liked the place. Wednesday and Thursday I loathed it. But no matter where I am, no matter what I am doing, I can look beyond the fog of my judgements and see that I am home...in this living, breathing moment...being here, now...just being....

So now it is time to pack and clean up and go on to my next moment, where I can be aware of my judgements and stay connected to the gift of Life.

Celeste Z.

August 18, 1983
Speaker's Cabin

Ah, the Porkies! There's something definitely magical about this area! I was first introduced to the interior of the park three years ago on an eight day backpacking trek. Ever since, my love for this spectacular part of the world has grown stronger with each return visit. No other place I've experienced has quite the same effect on me. Seems I'm always able to return to the rat race of civilization (telephones, time clocks, people, and TV) feeling relaxed, able to cope, and extremely at peace with myself. Every year I manage to steal away to strengthen my tie with the Porkies and to build more memories to hold me over until the next visit.

I've grown quite a lot through my experiences here. Remember coming into the park three years ago, a novice packer, thinking I knew the Porkies because as a youngster my folks had taken us to Lake of the Clouds. Was there more to the Porkies than that?

Shining Cloud Falls, a starry night on the shore of Lake Superior, comet showers from Miscowawbic Peak, Mirror Lake and the bear—all these places hold special memories that warm even the coldest winter's day.

The Porkies have opened my eyes to the beautiful world which surrounds us all, if we only take the time to look. It's taught me a lot about life and love, helping me grow into the person I am today.

Judy S.

June 23, 1978
Mirror Lake 4-Bunk Cabin

This backpacking trip (my first) is a really special experience for me—good for my body and my soul. My body may forget what it learned out here, but my soul will never forget. In thanks for my wonderful stay in these hills, I am leaving nothing behind, save my footsteps (which tried to stay on the trails). I'm glad that my first visit was obscure enough that the bears didn't even know I was here.

> Somehow I must gather my powers together
> that will take me back to my other world.
> I'll be okay when I get there, but the
> transition will be a bit awkward.

Murf

April 3, 1990
Section 17 Cabin

I'm eighteen and live a simple life with many problems. I usually just set them back but I haven't been able to since my best friend died on February 19, 1990. My best friend died of cancer at the age of seventy-four. He was my grandfather, Bill K. I came here as a hope for my spirit to connect to his by looking at the great hemlocks and referring to him, but I suppose this wasn't his home. But I feel he's still overlooking my every move.

Signed with eternal tears,
Ralph

May 9, 1996
Little Carp Cabin

Enjoying our last full day here at Little Carp River Cabin. Everything here has been fantastic. I have been coming here for seventeen years and have never seen it quite like this in the mountains. Today we gathered wood on the shoreline for tonight's fire and have just been enjoying the beauty around the cabin. Some how this park transforms itself into something different than what you expect. I guess if it remained the same as my memories then it would somehow become too predictable and lose its attraction. Each year I come with my expectations of how I think the trip will go! Each year God shows me that my expectations can be useless. I often come for the fishing and catch only the wilderness.

Dennis T.

October 13, 1985
Big Carp 6-Bunk Cabin

It was nice to have been a part of this annual family encounter. It's hard fitting in when so much around you is different in so many ways. I'm an exchange student from halfway around the globe—the Philippines, and I've been in Minnesota for quite a while. I've learned to value the explicit beauty of this place, yet, as I gather firewood, I could almost hear my sisters, brother, and folks from the hills. We always used to play with each other in the hills of Sagnio, a very scenic spot back home. In another week, I shall turn seventeen and it's gonna be my first birthday away from family and friends. I miss Raffy. I miss the warm comfort of my mom, although we didn't really have much chance to share feelings. My dad is probably the sweetest man I know. It has been tough making adjustments. Somehow, I always felt secure when I was back in the old neighborhood, always having someone to fall back on whenever something goes wrong and always having people to share in your joy and sorrow in the pains of growing up. America is socially and religiously different. Commercially, the same. I've lived sixteen years and eleven months of my life in the protective care of my folks and yet it turns out that I could not have wanted more.

Being an exchange student has helped me understand and, hopefully, cope with the variations in personalities and cultures of different parts of the world.

It takes time to feel at ease inside. Time to get to know why things happen the way they do. I had great times and I had bad times. Yet, all of these make up the person I now am. Most often, silence ebbs me through....

This place is spectacular and breathtaking. Had quite an experience!

Ivy

Autumn, 1977
Speaker's Cabin

Adding my thoughts by flashlight—moon sitting on the horizon with millions of stars to keep it company. Steady breathing from buddies Daryl and Emma keeps beat to the sound of the river. Many different feelings here, mind always a-drifting. Had a campfire tonight and sat and watched the rosy sunset.

How can you hug your environment?!

Jane

September 11, 1994
Big Carp 4-Bunk Cabin

This was the perfect place for collecting my thoughts as I needed to write a farewell letter to my daughter. She will be leaving me in a few weeks, leaving the Upper Peninsula where she was born and raised, for the Chicago area. Jen wants to become a pastry chef. Her mother is sending her to a culinary school in Evanston. Divorced seven years ago, I raised her, and the past five years she endured, I suppose, her father's second marriage. Eager for her own independence, I am just as eager to say something appropriate, meaningful, permanent, as her mother finalizes and finances Jen's ticket to her future. Without a clock and without an agenda, two days of perfect weather and plenty of stationary, I found myself writing Jen a letter of hope and promise, detailed with moments of our togetherness from her youth and reflections on the good and the bad of our past seven years together. Somehow, this very special spot on the face of this earth lended itself this weekend to dig out a lot of memories from the past. Keeping those memories in mind and finally realizing from many years past that life may not always get better, we just get better at dealing with life. I wrote Jen the letter that needed to be written...for me, and hopefully, for her.

P.B.

September 26, 1979
Mirror Lake 4-Bunk Cabin

This trip we had planned to the Porkies hadn't quite been my "honeymoon dream." I have always wanted to go camping but Joe's idea of camping is different from mine. You need a pop-up camper and loads of gear. Then you spend two weeks using your gear, swimming in the lake, making big bonfires to roast marshmallows with, and taking small hiking trips into the adjoining forest for firewood. Now that I have made the 4 mile trek from Lake of the Clouds with twenty pounds painfully sitting on my shoulders and especially my hips, I have come to a conclusion. The sight of Mirror Lake and the surrounding trees in their fall splendor was worth it. I have never in my entire life seen anything as beautiful. I will do it again.

Anita Z.

October 8, 1991
Little Carp Cabin

This is my fourth year coming to the Porkies. As I sit here this fine autumn morn' looking out my cabin window into the trees last glories of life before the certain and sure winter which brings its hold of dormancy, I can't help but truly appreciate the simple fact that we still have such places to come to replenish our souls and our need for things wild.

Only six and-a-half months ago I was involved in a head-on collision, where the other driver fell asleep, crossed the center line, and smacked me at fifty-five miles per hour; and I'm still recovering. BUT, I am here. I had a close call for an appointment with the next lifetime. To put it quite simply, this is the place I would have missed most. I sure do appreciate this place. I wonder if they have anything like this place up there in heaven?

M.R.A. & D.L.H.

November 12, 1988
Buckshot Cabin

I, Kellie, am the third member of this foursome. What Rich neglected to explain is that Naperville has also been dubbed "Yuppieville" by Chicago area people. The young, urban professionals in their BMW's and Porsches-kind of like "Buffy and Biff" take a ride to the country in their beemer—don't forget the Perrier and Grey Poupon.

With blonde hair combed as if by number, and inch long, red fingernails, donned in gortex whatevers and propylene thingers, I set off on what I thought would be a weekend of pure torture (where will I plug in my curling iron?).

Let me go back a little and explain that there are only a few things I fear in my life—cold, wet, and being more than twenty miles away from the mall and styling salon. What a nightmare!

My husband, Dennis, is an avid backpacker. I've watched him leave on his trips through teary eyes numerous times, wishing I had the courage to join him—but knowing he'd enjoy himself more without me, and knowing I'd end up on the bottom of a mountain, at his loving, but fed up hand. I can picture him standing over me totally justified with thinking, "They shoot horses."

But, alas, I'm here. I'm sore, I'm tired, I miss everything back home. But the calmness of this place has basically overpowered my spoiled-brat attitude, and right now I don't think I'd give a damn if I made it home for a while. The beauty here escapes words. The cities and every place I've been pales in comparison. The world is getting so small. There's not too many places like this left. I sat out on the big rock down by the lake, and pondered at the insignificant life I have led. How little we all have done to save these places, and how arrogant I (we) have been to destroy them. I said a special prayer sitting out on that rock, and I hope that enough others will join it to make a difference in our patterns of selfishness.

I leave here changed and sad for us. I know this because the butane curling iron I bought did not leave my backpack.

Kellie C.

This meant a lot to me, for we will now have a new found interest to share.

Dennis C.

August 20, 1991
Mirror Lake 8-Bunk Cabin

It almost seems an obligation to make an entry here, not that I'm enticed by the thought of being in a Camper's Book. It's just that I can't think of anything witty or wise. Quite the contrary, I came alone with my dog, Dusty, at a fork in my life, hoping here I'd know where to go, what to do. I have always gone back to nature to clear the thoughts. However, I'm on my way out with no solution. Perhaps even better though, I do feel at peace and a little saner (if possible) than before, and confident I will make the right choices.

Margaret F.

July 19, 1998
Speaker's Cabin

We tapped into the nature that abounds here. Swimming, hiking, and getting grimy seems to bring out the lost child within. Every day was more beautiful, more inspiring than the last. One would wonder if one were to stay, if one would not become wiser than one should be, to survive within the relentless, demanding, stressful existence one lives "day to day."

We brought our three dogs, Amy, Brahms, and Buck. Brahms has cancer and will soon die, but in his last days here at Speaker's Cabin, he was rejuvenated. He came back alive. He rambled for miles with us on our hikes and he swam a bit in the lake. But when he rested, oh, how he rested. His body lay down so low in the earth, it made the rest of us seem to hover above the surface. He lay down so low in the earth, just watching, watching. He lay down so low in the earth that I caught a glimpse of what death must be like. Like resting and watching and waiting for the next hike. May God preserve this hallowed ground. Hallowed and holy, Speakers has renewed us.

Susan S.

April 24, 1997
Little Carp Cabin

Well, this has been an experience. My boyfriend has been coming up here for twenty years and this year, he brought me. I've never backpacked three miles before, and after two, I started to get a little cranky. What a sight it was to see the cabin. But not more than ten minutes after we were here, my boyfriend sprained his ankle. I thought, "Oh boy!" This is going to be a treat. Four days with an avid fisherman and we're going to be stuck here doing nothing because of his ankle. Well, he did fish the entire time we were here. One fish even took him from the bridge all the way down to the mouth. It must have been a sight to see him running down the middle of the river (with his sprained ankle) with a fish on the line. It was worth it though because it was thirty plus inches and at least ten pounds. He also caught two more. One was twenty-one inches and the other was twenty-three inches. Me? I hooked one, but I got so excited that I lost it. I had a good time while I was here. I'll come back again.

Lee & Tammi

October 1, 1993
Speaker's Cabin

This is my fourth year at Speaker's this time of year. The first three years were with my wife. This year it is alone. There has been a death that brought me here alone. Not a death in the physical sense, but a death in an emotional sense. We must all remember we are not human "doings" but rather human "beings." Our true worth is judged not by what we accomplish, but rather by what we are. No one has said, that I know, on their death bed, "I wish I had worked more hours." The three basic priorities seem to be, faith, family, and career. Number one and two may be switched for some people, but number three must never be any higher than what it is. Last. When you have passed on the company will not miss you. The same can't be said for family. Take time for your spouse, your children, your parents, because that is what matters. Imagine sitting in this beautiful spot with all the beauty nature has to offer, and experiencing it with your job. Not quite the same. Take time to become a "soul mate" to your spouse. You won't regret it. Love, unconditionally, and all life's rewards will come to you. I hope I haven't learned that too late.

D.J.C.

August 3-5, 1994
Buckshot Cabin
The H. Brothers...arrived in time to enjoy the gentle warmth of a fine summer afternoon on the shores of Lake Superior...

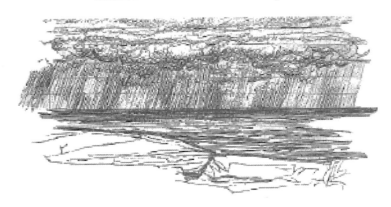

First time I can remember doing something like this with my brothers. It is, in a word, profound. There are times in all our lives when things just work. This is one. I doubt I've laughed as long, hard, and as spontaneously in a very long time—it is good medicine.

For those of us who have an affinity for nature, there are no words to describe the experience here. For those who may not be as "in tune," STOP!, slow way down...listen, it is your very past speaking and your very future staring at you. Like all "worlds"...there exists the potential for complacency; the beauty surrounding us can be so overwhelming here that you may not really even see it. So for what it's worth, don't be complacent here, slow to a grind, and cleanse your soul.

I have a real tendency to be a plugged root. Once planted, I have a difficult time with changing environments. I have a feeling, though, that a place like this could quickly ease the problem. I am enjoying the rekindling of childhood camaraderie and am able to view my brothers in a more real and mature way. Oh sure, there are still the old familial rivalries and posturings, but on the whole, we all seem to be gaining new respect and insights for and about each other. I am delighting in shedding the role of "eldest" and am finding a real sense of peace in the role of "peer."

This trip has, so far, been one of continual unfolding and shedding of layers. Maybe by the end, the bantering, the joking, the postulating, and cajoling will lose its edge of rivalry and will in turn take on a kinder and more profound tone. We have, in our separate lives, been through and shared many similar life experiences, and yet we have all kept some of our own most defining character traits.

I love this cabin and the unreal quality of the waves from the lake and the crystal clarity of the stars in the black pitch sky. I love my brothers.

Time to go. It has been a once-in-a-lifetime experience for me. We three brothers have "dipped" in the big Lake, climbed steep trails, viewed magnificent vistas, and spent time around a blazing campfire on a chilly night. We have shared the splendor of the Porkies with each other and ourselves.

David, Brian, & Michael H.

October 30, 1992
Union River Cabin

There are times when one needs to find a
place to make life simple again. To
shrug off the rush of the everyday,
real world and realize there are so
few things we need in this life to
be happy.

As I sit here writing and occasionally
looking out the window and listening
to the stream, I feel like a good
person again.

Brenda

A Final Word

March 16, 1992
Whitetail Cabin

Now, if someone comes along and sees this book full of wisdom, poetry, and wit from over the months and years, and someone takes it and publishes it, what I want to know: Do we get $$ from it? Should we take the time and copyright our "works" here?

Joseph, Susan, Melissa, & Thalia

Postscript

We pondered what to write as a fitting conclusion to this anthology, full of all the wit, wisdom, silliness, poignancy, and creativity provided by the many authors. However, words seemed unnecessary, the impact and importance of the previous text self-explanatory. We could not come up with anything appropriate to possibly do these authors justice. But we were struck by one fascinating fact that is omitted from what was written.

As stated in the introduction, we chose not to include a certain segment of entries contained within the journals. These seemed to be written by people whose actions were selfish and who demonstrated little respect for their surroundings or others. These people did not seem to share the same regard for their environment that the authors of this text displayed. So it raised a question as to why they came to this wilderness setting in the first place.

To us, after reading all the entries, editing the manuscript, and coming to know the people who loved and treated the Porkies with reverence, the answer became abundantly clear. It was so simple an answer that our overlooking it seems embarassing. They came for the same reason everyone else did. They came to be a part of the natural, untamed system. They needed to come. They just did not know how to behave.

With this insight, a simple yet powerful one, it stands to reason that this type of person came to find a part of something missing within themselves. No different than any of the other types of people. They could participate in any type of behavior they wished within the limits of their urban environment. They didn't need to travel hundreds of miles to a cabin in the woods to do so. Yet they did. And a bigger question and a much more intriguing answer surfaced from this revelation.

Most people have a desire to be a part of the natural world. It may be instinct, an innate necessity to be joined with the ecosystem surrounding us all. Maybe the coding in our DNA will not let us forget that our species was once a part of the natural order. Our ability to manufacture and modify, creating vast networks of pavement and cities of stone have not reduced our need for what is natural and wild. We have created new realms by conquering nature, yet we cannot conquer the need for nature each person has within him or herself. Why else would we design parks and landscaped yards within the locales where we live?

Wilderness really is for everyone. Everyone needs, to varying degrees, wilderness. And as such, access to the wilderness primeval is vital. The Porcupine Mountains WIlderness cabins allow that accessibility, and in this particular case and in this particular place, they imparted a wonderful experience to many, touching forgotten places within us all.

Wherever and however you find wilderness, be aware. You may find a part of yourself awakening to something special.

We shall never achieve harmony
with land, any more that we shall
achieve absolute justice or liberty
for people. In these higher
aspirations the important thing is
not to achieve, but to strive.

Aldo Leopold
A Sand County Almanac